The Homeless Imagination in the Fiction of Israel Joshua Singer

Jewish Literature and Culture
Series Editor, Alvin Rosenfeld

The Homeless Imagination in the Fiction of Israel Joshua Singer

ANITA NORICH

Indiana University Press
Bloomington and Indianapolis

The paper used in this publication meets the minimum requirements of American
National Standard for Information Sciences—Permanence of Paper for Printed
Library Materials, ANSI Z39.48-1984.
♾™

Manufactured in the United States of America

Library of Congress Cataloging-in-Publication Data

Norich, Anita, date.
    The homeless imagination in the fiction of Israel Joshua Singer /
Anita Norich.
        p.   cm. — (Jewish literature and culture)
    Includes bibliographical references (p.   ) and index.
    ISBN 0-253-34109-4 (cloth)
    1. Singer, Israel Joshua, 1893–1944—Criticism and interpretation.
I. Title.   II. Series.
PJ5129.S5Z79   1991
839'.0933—dc20   90–27480

1 2 3 4 5   95 94 93 92 91

צום אייביקן אָנדענק פון דער מאַמען
שרה וואַקסמאַן נאָריך ז״ל
וואָס אין איר זכרון האָט געלעבט אַ וועלט מיט וועלטלעך

In loving memory of my mother,
Sara Waksman Norich z'l,
in whose memory a world endured

Contents

Illustrations to follow page 12.

Preface

Near the entrance to the YIVO Institute for Jewish Research in New York, just to the right of the elevator, stands a display case that has given me pause since I first entered the building in the mid-seventies. It contains what appear to be dozens of miniature shrunken heads behind a sign indicating that they are figures from Maurice Schwartz's dramatization of Israel Joshua Singer's *Yoshe Kalb*. The faces are expressive, although too small and in their very presence too startling to be considered lifelike. I cannot imagine what inspired anyone to produce them. But, through various circuitous routes, they have led me to the play, the novel, and, in due course, I. J. Singer.

My subject is the cultural tensions that inform Singer's writing and our own reading of it. I hope to contribute both to the examination of Yiddish and Jewish literatures and to the appreciation of the broad range of linguistic and ethnic groups that have shaped literature in America. Certainly, the cultural life of American Jews can only be understood within the context of Yiddish culture, which has had and continues to have considerable influence on a large number of American writers.

In these pages, I have attempted to identify the Yiddish and Jewish cultural structures to which Singer responded, as well as their European and American contexts. Singer hoped that the broader cultural milieu might expand the more parochial one, but he came to doubt whether the two were compatible. Contemporary readers of modern fiction will no doubt be more familiar with the European and American settings of Singer's works than with their Jewish environment, perhaps more familiar with the epigraphs heading several of these chapters than with the material that follows. Establishing a dialogue between these contexts is necessary in order to grasp Singer's work; they illuminate one another and, in truth, I cannot think about one without the other. I address both contexts because I understand Singer to be addressing them in his own terms. There is a growing community of people for whom Yiddish is both memory and presence, people who write and teach in English or Hebrew and continue to read and think in Yiddish as well. In this study, I have tried to speak to them as well as to the larger community of readers who cannot read the original Yiddish texts but may be drawn to Singer as a major twentieth-century Jewish voice.

This book is neither a biography nor a strict survey of its subject's works, although it is informed by both Singer's life and the range of prose writings

he produced. Instead, each of the following chapters considers a different thematic or structural concern in an attempt to reorient familiar strategies of reading in light of the demands of modern Yiddish literature and of Singer in
particular. The first chapter considers the varying contexts within (and often
against) which Singer wrote, the cultural history to which his texts refer, and
the different ways in which he has been read. It considers the strains of
messianic-utopian thinking that surrounded Singer and his resistance to all
of them. The second chapter examines the function of place in Singer's fiction,
analyzing, in particular, his engagement with Zion and America. Singer sees
no possible geographical or psychic locus for the Jewish imagination, and his
characters remain unrooted in all of the locations they inhabit. Wandering and
dislocation, as both Jewish and modern tropes, emerge as central themes of
Singer's writing in a number of short stories and especially in his finest novel,
Yoshe Kalb. In the third chapter, I consider Singer's novels *The Brothers Ashkenazi*
and *The Family Karnovski* and what they reveal about the different dynamics
of Jewish history and of the larger world in which Jews lived. In these novels,
Jewish history repeats itself, following a cyclical pattern independent of the
linear axis along which the rest of Europe seems to progress. There exists no
period, no felicitous moment, during which the Jews are in temporal harmony
with the rest of the world. Singer's protagonists are in a constant state of tension
with a menacing universe they view as overwhelming. The fourth chapter examines Singer's view of the individual and the self. He presents the first as a
social construct and the second as a psychological one. As the novel *Comrade
Nakhmen* illustrates most clearly, character development follows unusual, often
confusing patterns marked by discontinuity, abrupt transitions, and tenuousness. Chapter 5 examines the relationship between artistic creativity and social
reality as developed in Singer's fiction and essays. Artists in his stories address
the limitations imposed by an environment they cannot hope to overcome
even in their art. The sixth chapter considers Singer's memoir, *Of a World That
Is No More*, and the autobiographical writings of his older sister, Esther Kreitman, and their younger brother, Isaac Bashevis Singer. These texts comment
on one another, contributing to the discussion of representation and referentiality implicit in the preceding chapters.

When I first entered YIVO, each new sign that my native tongue had a
cultural life beyond certain familiar walls was an exciting discovery. That innocence has inevitably abated, but not the excitement. Unlike the subject of this
book, I have found a small community of readers, scholars, and friends who
have responded in similar ways. Academics like to lament even as they revel
in their lonely fate, writing in solitude, unsure of an audience. I am surprised
and gratified that this has not been my experience. The first course in Yiddish
literature I audited at YIVO was taught by Dan Miron, and my own scholarly
path has been inspired at every turn by that most inspiring of teachers.

The present study was conceived during the two years I spent as a Lady
Davis Fellow in the Hebrew University's Yiddish Department. I am grateful

to members of that department, and especially to Professor Chone Shmeruk, for their support during and since that period. Later, the Littauer Foundation provided a generous research grant, which the University of Michigan's policy on research leaves allowed me to spend in Jerusalem.

The major repositories for Yiddish research are in Jerusalem and New York. The archives of Abraham Cahan and Maurice Schwartz housed at the YIVO Institute and Melekh Ravitch's archive at the National Library in Jerusalem were essential resources for my work. I am grateful to Yosl Birstein of the National Library and to Dina Abramowicz and Zachary M. Baker of the YIVO Institute for answering impossible questions with extraordinary grace and certainty.

This study would not have been completed in its present form without my father, Isaac Norich, who volunteered to serve as my research associate and as my most encouraging supporter. Whether undertaking the formidable task of poring over microfilm copies of the *Forverts* in pursuit of a complete bibliography of Singer's works, deciphering Singer's handwriting, or assisting in other areas, he showed a patient attention to detail and a sensitivity to context that I hope I have inherited.

It is also a great pleasure to thank a number of friends and colleagues who will recognize their influence on these pages and may recall conversations in Ann Arbor, New York, or Jerusalem. James Gindin, Benjamin Harshav, Kathryn Hellerstein, Anne Herrmann, June Howard, Deborah Dash Moore, Avrom Nowerszztern, David Roskies, Susan Slotnick, and James Young read parts of this manuscript and were both generous and helpful in their comments. Susanne A. Shavelson was an ideal research assistant, complete with the requisite skills intelligently applied and a sense of humor. I am grateful to Michael Patrick O'Connor for being that rare combination of an equally terrific editor and friend. My thanks to Yaron Ezrahi for insisting that things be called by their proper names, and then naming them. And to Arlene Agus for turning challenges into opportunities and for showing me the difference between friendships that simply last and those that flourish. Sidra DeKoven Ezrahi generously shared with me her exciting research and insights on the themes of exile and place in the Jewish imagination, including material from her work in progress, *Exiles in the Holy Land*. She also read every word of this study in all its stages, but my debt to her is not merely professional; I can only hope she will understand that my gratitude is more profound than I can express.

My extended family, many of whom are named above, has kept me working through the most difficult times. Sam Norich, Deborah Ugoretz, Gila and Nessa occupy a place in my life for which the word "relative" is terribly inadequate. I believe I am honoring them and my father in dedicating this book to Sara Norich *z'l*, my mother. In life, her memories brought me to a world that had been destroyed but that resonated in her voice with wit, resilience, and a compassion that only love can understand. The letters *z'l*, added after the name of one who has died, are an abbreviation of Hebrew words meaning "May her memory be a blessing." And that is exactly what her memory has now become—my first blessing.

The Homeless
Imagination in the
Fiction of
Israel Joshua Singer

ONE

Introduction to a World
That Is No More

Mir yungen, mir—a freylekhe tsezungene
  khaliastre
Mir geyen in an umbavustn veg,
In tife moreshkhroyredike teg
In nekht fun shrek
Per aspera ad astra!

Moshe Broderzon, "Tsu di shtern"

We youth, we—a happy songful gang
We walk an unknown path
In deeply awesome days
In nights of fear
Per aspera ad astra!

"To the Stars"

In 1933, at what was to prove the midpoint of a successful and volatile literary career, Israel Joshua Singer (1893–1944) left his native Poland in search of a more hospitable political and cultural environment in the United States. Such a significant journey and quest may have invited certain readers to see an epic design in the story of Singer's life and work. Indeed, both his contemporaries and ours have discovered such a design there. Yet in his fictions of the individual's quest for teleological certainty in an apparently disintegrating world, Singer presents us with no heroes or significant historical figures. The liminal situations of his novels and short stories about love, revolution, apocalypse, grand vision, and enterprise allow for no heroic triumphs. Singer's literary imagination resists and finally defeats the temptation to find victories and epic structures in the events that his fiction describes.

The present-day search for heroic readings of Singer's fiction and of Yiddish fiction in general can be more clearly understood as a response to twentieth-century Jewish history than to the texts themselves. It is, in large measure, a compensatory act, seeking finally to claim critical significance for the literature. The reading of Yiddish literary texts of any period is affected by the horror with which we view the destruction of Eastern European Jewry during World War II. The Stalinist purges and the Holocaust seem to invite us to view these texts through the distorting prism of their demise. They are sometimes treated like invalids who must be guarded against harsh scrutiny and made as comfortable as possible before death. Such a critical stance is never legitimate; in the case of pre-Holocaust writing it is, at the very least, premature. It is also rather perverse, shielding writers from legitimate analysis as if they were not healthy enough to withstand criticism. Yiddish still suffers from the stigma of being a rootless literature of the *folk*, a victim of history that must be protected from the further tragedy of oblivion.

Scholars have reason to view the recent surge of interest in Yiddish literature with delight and some wariness. This renewed interest is once again making available a number of writers and a cultural milieu that seemed to have been destroyed along with the communities that first sustained them. In addition to a study of Yiddish texts as representational documents, there is a growing, impressive discourse applying the methodology of contemporary literary theory to classical Jewish and Yiddish sources.[1] Yiddish has become eminently respectable in academic circles as well as in popular Jewish life. This recent interest must struggle, however, against a persistent tendency towards a skewed perception of Eastern European and American Jewish culture that either romanticizes the shtetl and the immigrant experience or seeks to document the bitterness of Jewish suffering. Neither approach is compelling from a scholarly, cultural, or historical perspective.

The connections between Eastern European and American Yiddish culture and the more subtle connections between these and the American Jewish culture that evolved in English have yet to be fully explored. Yiddish exercises a profound influence on contemporary Jewish American writers, an influence complicated by the distance between these writers and Yiddish texts. Many of them explicitly pay homage to a language few of them really know. The "anxiety of influence" for such writers may not be a function of direct knowledge of any strong poet; it is, rather, a function of displacement and absence. However, while Jewish literary antecedents are severed by ignorance of the language, Yiddish culture remains as a strong memory. It is that memory, rather than actual Yiddish authors or literary movements, that has become most significant for Jewish American culture. Renewed interest in Yiddish attests, in part, to the widespread desire for a more thorough and more intimate knowledge.[2]

The protectionist critical stance has been countered by attempts to locate Yiddish within the context of other literary traditions in order to normalize our view of its development and provide a public, scholarly vocabulary with which to consider it. The invocation of comparatist language and familiar structures and tropes is indicative of a desire to endow Yiddish literary study with an academic prestige it has rarely enjoyed. To the modernist sensibility, literary merit is often determined by the discernible complexities of a text and its position in relation to canonical literature. Modern Yiddish literature enters the polemic surrounding high and low culture in provocative ways. A significant body of Yiddish literature, including Singer's, was both popular and engaged. Writers lived and labored next to their readers, typically sharing their physical space as well as their financial and educational status; the writers published not only in literary journals with limited distribution but also in the dailies and papers of mass appeal.[3]

The comparatist urge should be tempered—even as it is informed—by the tension between present-day hermeneutics and the polemics of much of Yiddish fiction, written in response to quite a different set of historical expectations and ideological stances. The obverse of the comparatist trend is the equally problematic view of Yiddish literature as *sui generis*. Writing in a language that has no national homeland and that is dispersed to all corners of the world, Yiddish writers are sometimes seen in isolation from other writers and often from one another. Another contending view posits a cultural community triumphantly emerging against all odds. Post-Holocaust impulses toward generalizing the Yiddish cultural experience or reifying it, making it an expression of the *folk* or a heroic and defiant act of creativity, tell us more about nostalgia and myth making than they do about Yiddish authors and their texts.

The problem of canon is evident in any attempt to normalize discussions of Yiddish literature. Recent debates about canon formation and attempts to reconsider the canon by examining its political and social functions[4] assume a particular urgency in the case of Yiddish fiction where, whatever we consider the canon to be, it is already reaching closure. The act of identifying a literary tradition and the authors and texts who belong to its core assumes an interesting dynamic in Yiddish. The history of Yiddish literary criticism is comparatively recent, as is any explicit sense of literary authority or influence. A century ago, when Sholem Aleichem (1859–1916) called Mendele Moykher Sforim (Sh. Y. Abramovitsh; 1835–1917) *der zeyde* [the grandfather] of Yiddish literature, he radically altered the prevailing view of Yiddish authors as discrete individuals unconnected to one another historically or textually. In linking the two most popular writers of Yiddish prose—Abramovitsh and himself—Sholem Aleichem asserted the existence of a Yiddish literary tradition.[5] It is not surprising that poets and fiction writers (but not critics) almost immediately sought to distance themselves from the tradition. Authorial claims to rupture and innovation were more common than discussions of heirs and influences. Even in Sholem Aleichem's construction of a literary genealogy there is already a sense of rupture: the authority of the father, who is symbolically killed by being ignored, is entirely absent.

By 1927, when the Yiddish critic Y. Y. Trunk published his study *Idealizm un naturalizm in der yidisher proze* [Idealism and naturalism in Yiddish prose], several literary groups had arisen, declaring their newness and freedom from what were already termed the restraints of Yiddish literary hegemony. Trunk's study divided Yiddish writers into two schools: those who followed the satiric naturalism of Abramovitsh's *maskilic* [Enlightenment] texts, and those who followed what was perceived as the oppositional presence of Y. L. Peretz (1852–1915).[6] Peretz, who was understood to have introduced modernist themes and forms even as he introduced romanticized views of Jewish religious and social life, was at the center of pre–World War I Yiddish culture in Warsaw. The triumvirate of Mendele/Abramovitsh, Sholem Aleichem, and Peretz was quickly enshrined as *di klasikers*, the classicists of Yiddish literature. The term attests to the telescoping of Yiddish literary time: movements that in other European literatures took generations in Yiddish collapse into synchronic moments. Less than a generation separated Abramovitsh, the "grandfather," from Sholem Aleichem, the youngest of the three; the three authors died within two years of each other.

A young contemporary of *di klasikers*, I. J. Singer entered a literary culture that regularly claimed it was shedding its old skin in favor of fresh new beginnings. In the teens and twenties, literary circles such as *di yunge* [the young] in New York, *yung Vilna* [Young Vilna], and *di khaliastre* [the Gang], which Singer joined in Warsaw, were all loosely constituted but influential groups that opposed both *idealizm* and *naturalizm*. In their very names they distanced themselves from the "old" world, which was, in fact, coterminous with them. These Young Turks proclaimed their own status as modernists, renouncing the ways of their mythicized Eastern European grandfathers in favor of Western European and American literary figures with whom they shared a desire to break free of the past.

II

Singer was born in 1893 in the small town of Bilgoray, in the Lublin province. He spent most of his childhood in Leontshin, another small town in the province of Warsaw. When he was fourteen, the family moved to the hasidic court at Radzimin (also in the Warsaw province), where his father taught and Singer studied before moving to Warsaw. There he worked as an unskilled laborer and a proofreader, studied painting, and hid in an artists' atelier to avoid the military draft. By the time he traveled to Kiev in the Soviet Union in 1918, he had already written his earliest stories.[7] In 1920 he went to Moscow and fell under the influence of the preeminent Yiddish writer, Dovid Bergelson. Singer returned to Warsaw in late 1921 and, after much difficulty, published the story "Perl" [Pearls].

Singer's literary fortunes were made when Abraham Cahan, the powerful editor of the New York Yiddish daily, the *Forverts*, read "Perl" and republished it in his newspaper amidst great praise.[8] Cahan offered him a position as correspondent for the *Forverts*, and Singer traveled throughout Galicia in 1924, writing essays for the newspaper under both his own name and the pseudonym G. Kuper. In 1926, he extended his journalistic activities by traveling throughout Poland. At the end of the year, he returned to the Soviet Union as correspondent for the *Forverts*, writing essays about Jewish life in Eastern European communities and about the wider European culture to which it was increasingly exposed. He met Cahan in Berlin in 1931 and visited the United States for several months in 1932. In letters to his friend and literary colleague Melekh Ravitch, he expressed his desire to remain in New York and complained about the difficulties imposed by American immigration rules.[9]

The descendant of generations of rabbis, Singer was influenced by sharply opposing strains of Jewish religious thought. The conflict between his father's hasidic enthusiasm and his mother's rationalist beliefs and practices is often cited as his earliest literary inspiration. In his rejection of both strains of thought in favor of fiction, Singer was joined by his older sister, Esther Kreitman, and his younger and now more famous brother, the Nobel laureate, Isaac Bashevis Singer. (The youngest brother, Moshe, remained well within the family fold, following his father into the rabbinate and remaining in Poland with his mother after the departure of his siblings to the West; he perished during the Second World War.)

In many respects, Singer's life and writings are typical of the tensions experienced by his generation of Eastern European Jews and the choices made by its artists. Like most of them, he received a traditional religious education that he experienced as confining. And, like many of his young peers, he joined avant-garde art movements that proclaimed independence from the demands of social realism and relevance that they believed dominated the Yiddish literary world. His travels and his frequent contributions to the periodical press of Warsaw, Kiev, and New York were of a piece with the activities of many Yiddish writers between the two world wars and exemplified the global scope, mobility, and restlessness of Yiddish culture in this period. In addition to his journalistic activity, there was another facet to Singer's celebrity: several of his works were adapted for the Yiddish stage to considerable acclaim. He was a remarkably successful and popular literary figure who moved in both the established Yiddish literary world and the world defined by the scores of short-lived journals founded in opposition to it.

At the age of fifty, Singer died suddenly of a heart attack in his New York apartment. His popularity did not survive him. The themes of which he wrote, his depictions of the harshest aspects of contemporary Jewish life, and the despair about the future that characterized his writing did not find the kind of responsive audience in the years following World War II that they had in earlier years. His death on February 10, 1944, one year after the appearance of his last novel, *Di mishpokhe Karnovski* [The Family Karnovski], which examined the lure of Nazism, has served to link him to those who were then dying in the land he had left a decade earlier. He thus shares the fate not only of scores of writers who have become linguistically inaccessible but also of a culture that is now engulfed by the language of mourning. His unrelenting critique of Jewish life could hardly serve to memorialize those who had died or offer consolation to those who now desperately sought it.

Eclipsed for decades by his younger brother's fame, I. J. Singer has more recently benefited from the increasing interest in Yiddish culture. Irving Howe reintroduced him to an American audience in 1966 in an article entitled "The Other Singer," a clear acknowledgment of the Singer with whom his audience would more likely be familiar. Twenty years later, I. J. Singer's novels appeared again in English and Hebrew translations,[10] a sign of the renewed recognition of his central place in any attempt to formulate a Yiddish literary canon.

Singer was a central presence in the almost frenetic international Yiddish cultural activity of his period. His texts examine the political and cultural upheavals in Jewish life between the two world wars and on two continents. Placing Jewish history and culture within the broader European and, later, American contexts, they refer to a seemingly endless series of wars, shifts in borders, class conflicts, pogroms, and the secular and religious forms of messianism out of which these events grew and to which they contributed. These texts offer an extraordinary view of Jewish culture at a crossroads leading in a number of alluring directions. Traditional religious life persisted, but so, too, did secularism, Yiddish culturalism, Zionism, socialism, and more than one revolutionary vision. In his fiction, Singer follows each of these paths, but unlike many of his contemporaries he discovers no refuge in any of them. He probes all the options, finds each wanting, and dismisses them one by one. En route, his fiction compels readers to identify and confront the tensions that formed the fabric of interbellum Jewish life.

III

The connections and distinctions between modernity and literary modernism —particularly in the Jewish context—have often been obscured by critics in their considerations of Singer's fiction. Entrance into the modern world is usually understood to mean a departure from traditional Jewish life. Accompanying this are changes in identifying characteristics, in symbolic codes, and in venue: from shtetl to city, market to factory, study hall to workplace. There are radical shifts in what is eaten, worn, read, spoken. An emphasis on the individual is understood to replace an emphasis on the community just as dramatically as Western dress replaces traditional clothing and Polish, Russian, or German replaces Yiddish and Hebrew.

Modernist sensibilities among Jews parallel the general European model in its privileging of individual behavior, but the Jewish and European models diverge when they confront ideas of history and causality. We generally regard literary modernism as having de-historicized human experience. It is marked familiarly by a terrible awareness of randomness, displacement, and a lack of causal connections. Powerlessness identifies the modern condition as one in which the individual can only be the victim of political structures and the self in conflict with historical process. Even in this general view, several of these modernist tropes are akin to the prevailing Jewish sense of political powerlessness and homelessness. Nonetheless, modernism takes on a different complexion among Jews. Eastern European Yiddish writers were influenced not only by these views of the modern era or of Jewish history but also by Eastern European anti-Semitism and by the revolutionary movements in which they were engulfed and to which many of them subscribed. Such Jews were, no doubt, inclined to temper the apotheosis of the self with a skeptical view of what the self could attain, given these surroundings. At the same time, modern

Zionist ideology and socialism, and the belief shared by these heirs of the Jewish Enlightenment that the Jews could live as a normal people, as citizens undistinguished from their compatriots, also influenced their sense of history. The process of history could be embraced because there was a causal connection between secular education, socialist or nationalist activity, and progress; positive political change could, in large measure, be achieved by groups of individuals. Within the Eastern European Jewish community, then, writers could still adhere to ideas of progress and causality that had been undermined by Western modernism. Within the non-Jewish community to which they aspired, however, these ideas continued to be challenged by contemporary events—legal barriers and pogroms—and by the ideas of modernism.

The experience of modernity is different for Jews and non-Jews and different in Eastern and Western Europe, and it is encoded differently in the literature of each. While it is difficult in principle to determine what Yiddish critics meant when they referred to "modern literature" in the early decades of this century, criticism of Singer's fiction may provide a clue. In the twenties, when Yiddish literature in Eastern Europe was caught up in contemporary debates about the place of politics and especially socialist ideals in literature, recognition of Singer's status as a modernist often depended on a particular critic's avowed political stance. Thus, in 1927 Peretz Markish, writing from the Soviet Union and in full accord with its cultural and social agenda, heralded Singer as one of the few worthy prose writers in Poland, while regretting that he still lived in a time and place marred by class distinctions that limited his imagination.[11] In the same year, I. M. Fuks argued that Singer had not yet entered the ranks of modern writers because he refused to see the literary value of ideas—and especially socialist ideals.[12] Underlying such arguments is an embryonic version of the views of bourgeois critical realism and bourgeois modernism that Georg Lukacs was later to articulate. In Lukacs's terms, Singer would undoubtedly rank as a modern bourgeois realist who viewed the individual as a social animal, inseparable from a social and historical context.[13]

The defining trait of European modernism for many Yiddish critics lay elsewhere. In addition to political and social discourse, and superseding them in importance, were considerations of the psychological depth revealed in the portrayal of characters. The arguments within Yiddish criticism in the early decades of this century echo nineteenth-century Western European discourse, once again a sign of the curious telescoping of Yiddish literary time. At the core of many critical discussions about Singer as a modern novelist are questions about his examination of character and individual development. Among those who welcomed Singer into the ranks of modern writers precisely because of his subtle analysis of the individual psyche were Sh. Bikl, Sh. Niger, Melekh Ravitch, M. Taykhman, and Y. Y. Trunk—some of the most influential and prolific Yiddish critics writing in America and Europe. Their reviews of Singer were not always favorable, but they were remarkably uniform in their conceptualization of how character appears in fiction. Bikl praised Singer's "psychologically interesting figures."[14] Trunk heralded the "psychological depth" of his characters and their "psychic and spiritual rejection of every collective."[15] Taykhman, though lamenting the terrible pessimism of Singer's *The Brothers Ashkenazi*, lauded its great historical and psychological understanding.[16] Niger linked his criticism of Singer's stories in the collection *Perl* to the "nuances of psyche" developed in them.[17] Ravitch, typically, was most florid in his comments about Singer as a great "psychoanalytic writer."[18]

These comments indicate the extent to which psychological discourse had penetrated the study of Yiddish texts and provided evaluative criteria. They are most striking, however, when compared to the starkly different views expressed by critics years later when the English translations appeared. Reviewers of *The Family Karnovski* (Yiddish, 1943; English, 1969) writing in the *Nation* and *Atlantic Monthly* pointed to Singer's stereotypical characterizations and the absence of psychological analyses in his fiction.[19] The *New York Times* reviewer of Singer's posthumous memoir, *Of a World That Is No More* (Yiddish, 1946; English, 1970), informed his readers that Singer's art "is not modernist."[20] Clive Sinclair and Irving Howe agree. Both compare I. J. Singer to Isaac Bashevis Singer in order to illustrate how far the former was from the latter's modernist sensibilities. Howe's comments in his introduction to a translation of *The Brothers Ashkenazi* (1980) are particularly interesting when juxtaposed with the Yiddish criticism we have already encountered. "Of inner psychic being," Howe writes, "of the nuances of feeling and reflection that we have come to expect in the depiction of character, *The Brothers Ashkenazi* has rather little."[21]

It is hardly noteworthy to find critics who disagree about individual texts or a body of work. What is striking here is the extent to which the disagreement depends upon the specific Yiddish- and English-language contexts, underscoring the differences in the historical, social, and literary sensibilities of the audiences who read Singer in this century. For the most part, Yiddish critics eagerly embraced Singer as a modern writer with a sophisticated approach to psychological detail; for the most part, English critics rejected this view, heralding instead the mirror Singer had held up to Eastern European Jewry in the years before its destruction. This latter perception is perhaps best encapsulated by A. Brody, who, as early as 1933, in a *Nation* review of the English translation of Singer's *Yoshe Kalb* (Yiddish, 1932; English, 1933), wrote what very few Yiddish critics would have believed in interbellum Europe: "A contemporary Yiddish novel has an almost posthumous quality at birth, and apart from its value as a work of art it already has interest for us as a social document."[22] Anticipating the demise of Yiddish culture, Brody sets forth the view that would later predominate. Yiddish texts were museum pieces, archaeological finds even at their moment of creation.

The stance of most Yiddish critics, however, was quite different. Y. Rapaport offers a succinct instance of it in pointing out that Singer entered Yiddish literature when it was undergoing "its strongest illusions of normalcy," the illusion that it might be "a normal literature of a normal people," by which

Rapaport meant that it might be able to break free of the confines of Jewish thematics and explore themes that were at once more universal and more psychologically interesting. Writing in 1943 in Shanghai, while in flight from the Nazis, Rapaport was understandably disillusioned.[23] Claims for normalcy, exciting as they had been in the interbellum years, became more difficult to maintain as Yiddish writers confronted the Holocaust. Still, Rapaport could not avoid the recognition that within the previous two decades Yiddish had seemed to promise a wonderfully dynamic literature. The irreconcilable views of Yiddish and English critics of Singer's fiction underscore the different cultural orbits in which it was received, as well as our own distance from the vibrancy of pre–World War II Yiddish culture.

Isaac Bashevis Singer continues to view his brother as an exemplar of Yiddish modernism. In Yiddish, the Nobel laureate writes under the name Bashevis (a name derived from his mother, Batsheva) to distinguish himself from his elder brother, who was already a well-established writer when he introduced Bashevis into the literary circles of Warsaw and New York. Bashevis claims I. J. Singer as his only literary progenitor, joining ranks with those who have rejected the attempt to construct a Yiddish literary tradition. Claiming that earlier writers could not speak to a modernist sensibility, Bashevis locates his brother's modernism in Singer's refusal to romanticize Jewish life and in his exploration of sexuality.[24] Singer, he notes, taught him his craft and was largely responsible for introducing modern European literary concerns into Yiddish literature.

Bashevis's comments about his brother reflect the use of "modern" as a sign of praise, setting certain twentieth-century Yiddish writers apart from their folksy or didactic predecessors. Singer was influenced by both European and Yiddish modernism, but he was by no means its most daring practitioner. That role might better be assigned to Peretz in Warsaw, to Dovid Bergelson, Moyshe Kulbak, or Peretz Markish in the Soviet Union, to *di yunge* or the *inzikhistn* [introspectivists] groups in New York, or to others among the numerous innovative poets and novelists who radically changed Yiddish literature in this century. Singer sought out some of these men, no doubt drawn by their self-proclaimed independence from Yiddish literary norms. Singer was disappointed by Bergelson, who was something of a Moscow literary pundit when Singer met him in 1920. At Bergelson's invitation, Singer read his story "Perl" before a group of Moscow literati, who then proceeded to attack him for writing about bourgeois concerns during revolutionary times. Bergelson, having earlier admired the manuscript, refrained from defending the young writer. Singer took his silence as proof that one set of insidious Yiddish literary norms had simply been replaced by another.[25]

Singer fared better with Markish and a small, fluid group of writers who came together in Warsaw for a brief period in the early 1920s. Pejoratively called *di khaliastre* [the Gang] by their contemporaries, these writers transformed the name into a cultural and social battle cry. Only two issues of their journal, *Khaliastre*, appeared: one in Warsaw in 1922 and the other, following Markish's peregrinations, in Paris in 1924. The journal, largely under Markish's direction, included illustrations by Marc Chagall and poems, stories, and essays by Markish, Singer, Ravitch, Uri Zvi Greenberg, Y. Opatoshu, Oyzer Varshavski, and Dovid Hofshteyn. Opposing both social realism and romanticized depictions of Jewish life and familiar with the language of passion, alienation, and doubt, *Khaliastre* announced a new energy—but one that was quickly dissipated. The individual fates of these writers paralleled the drifts of modern Jewish history. They were a wandering group, covering much of the globe before settling in several of its corners: Singer went to New York; Markish to the Soviet Union, where he died a victim of the Stalinist purges; Ravitch to Australia, Argentina, Mexico, Israel, and Canada; Uri Zvi Greenberg to Palestine; Varshavski to France and Italy and—in the end—to Auschwitz.[26] Like his later affiliation with the better-known and longer-lived Warsaw *Literarishe bleter* (1924–1939), Singer's work with *Khaliastre* linked him with the leading figures of modern Yiddish literature at its most productive moments.

Aaron Zeitlin, Singer's friend and literary colleague, later recalled a remark that Singer often repeated before his emigration from Poland: "We are lost people, Zeitlin, lost people."[27] Neither Singer nor Zeitlin would have known that Gertrude Stein had coined a similar epigram at about the same time about her generation of expatriate writers. Stein did not include herself, however, in the lost generation to which she referred. Singer's statement may serve as a reminder of the sensibilities that Yiddish writers shared with their Western contemporaries, as well as the different resonances in their use of the same terms.

IV

Singer's significance lies somewhere between views of him as a heroic genius of Yiddish prose and as a representative model of a once vibrant culture. He was well known, widely read, an inescapable presence in popular Yiddish literary circles of the period framed by the two world wars. By the time he arrived in New York in 1934, he had been writing for almost twenty years. His first novel, *Shtol un Ayzn* (1927; English: *Blood Harvest*, 1935, and *Steel and Iron*, 1969), had generated considerable controversy about the place of politics in fiction. (Singer suffered from these reviews, and he renounced Yiddish literature for a while, turning to journalism instead.) His second novel, *Yoshe Kalb* (1932; English: *The Sinner*, 1933, and *Yoshe Kalb*, 1965), was much more successful. In addition, he had published two volumes of short stories (*Perl* [1922, *Pearls*], and *Af fremder erd* [1925, *On Foreign Ground*]), two plays (*Erdvey* [1922, *Earth Pangs*] and *Savinkov* [1933], a volume of travelogues (*Nay rusland* [1928, *New Russia*]), essays, and criticism. He had also been publishing in the *Forverts* since 1923, and his popularity in America was rivaled only by that of the prolific Sholem Asch. Under the name G. Kuper—his wife's maiden name—he earned a certain notoriety as a writer of sensational, often titillating journalistic pieces describing scenes from Eastern European and, later, American life.

In the ten years during which Singer lived in America, he was equally productive. He published three more novels (*Di brider Ashkenazi* [1936; English: *The Brothers Ashkenazi*, 1936 and 1980], *Khaver Nakhmen* [1938, *Comrade Nakhman*; English: *East of Eden*, 1939], *Di mishpokhe Karnovski* [1943; English: *The Family Carnovsky*, 1969]), a volume of stories (*Friling* [1937, *Spring*]), the material for a memoir (collected from the pages of the *Forverts* and published posthumously as *Fun a velt vos iz nishto mer* [1946; English: *Of a World That Is No More*, 1970]), as well as other essays and short stories. The latter were collected in a posthumous volume, *Dertseylungen* [1949, *Stories*]). Some of his short stories were translated into English by Maurice Samuel in 1938 in a volume entitled *The River Breaks Up*, but most remain untranslated. His novels were also adapted for the stage: *Yoshe Kalb* was performed in 1932, *Di brider Ashkenazi* in 1938, *Khaver Nakhmen* in 1939, and *Di mishpokhe Karnovski* in 1943.[28]

Singer's fiction militates against ahistorical readings and myth making. His contemporaries and subsequent critics have pointed to the fatalistic view of life and of individual potential that pervades his work. Deluding oneself about the role of history or politics creates as perverse a situation, in Singer's writing, as ongoing anti-Semitism. His narratives reject all the avenues of escape available in his culture: religion, the triumph of the individual, the brotherhood of mass movements as a solution for historical evils. They focus neither on humanity's tragic fate nor on the erosion of Jewish life. These play an important role in his fiction, but they are invoked in the name of another thematic concern: the destructive nature of any form of messianism. In Singer's stories, belief in political, social, or religious redemption arises from a misunderstanding of history and a kind of magical thinking that cannot be sustained. His fiction rejects the solace of messianic or mythic alternatives as illusory and deeply destructive. No ideological haven can be found in Singer's fiction, since all ideologies are equally suspect.

The disquieting themes at the center of Singer's fiction are echoed in the language, characterization, and structure of his novels and stories. In reading Singer, we encounter texts in which the experienced life of modern Jews is transformed into a semiotic system from which there is no escape but which no longer seems to have material reality. A religious system once considered coherent and inclusive now survives only in the symbols traditionally associated with it. Singer's Jewish protagonists typically yearn to free themselves even of these symbols, but, just as typically, the fictions in which we find them confine these individuals within the cultural boundaries that identify them as Jews. In collective fate and individual memory, no less than in clothing, speech, and their very carriage, they cannot break free. Non-Jewish and female protagonists are less common in these texts. When they do appear, however, such figures only serve to underscore a similar view of restrictive contemporary political, ideological, and cultural possibilities.

V

The semantic differences signaled by similar terms in the Jewish and wider literary contexts elucidate one another. This book is written for a diverse audience that may be unfamiliar with these texts or the milieu from which they emerged; it attempts to bridge the historical and cultural distances between Singer's contemporaries and ours. His fiction suggests the foundation for such a belated reconciliation. Refusing any belief in better days to come, Singer offers a sense of the present informed by the imperative to face the past and to make stories out of the conflict.

Above left, I. J. Singer at seventeen years old, 1910. (From *Fun a velt vos iz nishto mer*); *Right,* I. J. Singer, Genya Singer, and their sons Yasha and Yosl, 1924. (From *Fun a velt vos iz nishto mer*)

Israel Joshua, Genya, and Joseph Singer, 1936. (From *Fun a velt vos nishto mer*)

Some of the men associated with *di khaliastre* (from left to right): Mendl Elkin, Peretz Hirshbein, Uri Zvi Greenberg, Peretz Markish, Melekh Ravitch, I. J. Singer. (YIVO Institute)

Editorial board of *Literarishe bleter* (from left to right): Nahum Mayzl, Peretz Markish, Yosef Opatoshu, I. J. Singer, Melekh Ravitch. (YIVO)

I. J. Singer and Maurice Schwartz. (YIVO)

Albert Einstein with the cast of *Yoshe Kalb*, 1932. (YIVO)

From the production of *Di brider Ashkenazi*—Maurice
Schwartz and Samuel Goldenberg as the brothers, 1938.
(YIVO)

From the production of *Di brider Ashkenazi*—Maurice Schwartz as Simcha-Meyer. (YIVO)

I. J. Singer (left) and I. B. Singer. (YIVO)

TWO

The Wandering Jew
In/Fertile Ground

the essential feature of Jewish life in our time: a
perpetual restlessness, an anxiety in perpetual
motion

Saul Friedlander, *When Memory Comes*

When Singer left Poland for the United States in 1933, he was by no
means simply enacting the story of Jewish immigration that had been typical
a generation or two earlier. He had already established a significant literary
reputation on both continents. It was his second trip, his first having been
occasioned by the opening of the dramatic adaptation of his novel, *Yoshe Kalb*.
Written by Yiddish stage legend Maurice Schwartz, who also starred in it,
Yoshe Kalb had become one of the most critically acclaimed and financially successful plays ever produced in the Yiddish theaters of Warsaw and New York.[1]
Singer was a popular writer; he had friends in New York, work with the *Forverts*,
and a secure standing in the Yiddish cultural world. Like others before him,
he fled Europe, but not because of its pogroms or its poverty. Singer was
fleeing not only the religious strictures of Eastern Europe, which he believed
antithetical to personal and cultural development (and which, in any case, he
had already emphatically renounced), but also the internal political debates
and literary squabbles of Yiddish journals and writers. He sought in America
what he had failed to find in Poland and Russia: a home in which he could
be both politically and imaginatively free.

That search had already led him to live in several cities and to travel exten-
sively in Poland and the Soviet Union. Singer's peripatetic activity was by no
means unusual for Yiddish writers between the two world wars. Following
the movements of Jews within Eastern Europe, from east to west and—for
some of the significant cultural figures caught up in the short-lived excitement
of the Russian Revolution—back again, Yiddish literati both lived and debated
the question of a suitable home for Yiddish. Discussions about a geographical
center for Yiddish culture were particularly heated in the 1920s. At various
times and under the influence of different literary groups, Kiev, Moscow, Warsaw, Vilna, New York, even Berlin or Buenos Aires, were considered likely
sites for such a center. Dovid Bergelson entered the debate with the essay "Dray
tsentern" [Three centers], considering the role of Yiddish in America, Poland,

and the Soviet Union. Not surprisingly, he concluded that only in the latter could Yiddish literature flourish amidst the productive workers who would inaugurate it into the modern age. Arguing along lines reminiscent of the social-ist realists he supported, Bergelson saw a new literature emerging after the revolution, free of both American assimilation and Polish-Jewish religious or Zionist sentimentality. But it was Warsaw, Singer's home, that emerged as the most vociferous in its claims to centrality. The appearance of the *Varshaver almanakh* [Warsaw almanac] in 1923 (including Singer's story "Shpinvebs" [Spiderwebs]) prompted the critic Shmuel Niger, then living in New York, to write that though there was no real center, only Poland could conceivably serve as one, Russia having forfeited the role because of mass emigration and America not yet having established its right to Yiddish cultural leadership.[2] Singer never agreed with this position. He responded to a 1927 collection of Warsaw Yiddish poetry and prose by calling the volume an embarrassment that only proved the poverty of local Yiddish literary expression.[3] In an essay in the Warsaw *Literarishe bleter* the previous year ("Vilne"), Singer had com-pared Warsaw unfavorably to Vilna. He maintained that Warsaw had only man-aged to adopt the negative elements of European culture, while Vilna had benefited from its contact with Europe. He insisted that "Vilna was and remains our cultural center." Nakhmen Mayzl, founder and coeditor of the *Literarishe bleter*, traced the absurd practice of arguing about Yiddish literary centers to World War I, when fruitful Polish-American Yiddish cooperation had been interrupted. Mayzl's apparently conciliatory gesture appeared in a self-congratulatory volume published by the Warsaw *Haynt*; the irony of offering such a gesture within a publication lauding Warsaw's major cultural achieve-ments seems to have escaped Mayzl.[4]

Singer put his faith in none of these centers, even when he called for a unification of disparate and dispersed groups of Yiddish writers. In October 1927, having just returned from the Soviet Union, he was met by hostile re-views of his first novel, *Steel and Iron*, and he issued a proclamation entitled "Yidishe shrayber fun ale lender fareynikt aykh" [Yiddish writers of the world, unite]. In response to the fractiousness of the Yiddish cultural world, the oblivi-ousness of readers—and even writers—in one country to works written else-where, and the cultural isolation of Yiddish writers, Singer espoused the idea of a nongeographical center. The rallying cry was actually quite modest. It called for a conference more or less on the model of Czernowitz, a new journal, and a literary center like the recently formed YIVO.[5] What is significant is that Singer did not conceive of the center in physical terms. To do so would have meant entering into political debates with Zionists; their opponents, the Bundists, who argued for a secular socialist Jewish nationalism in Eastern Eu-rope; or the other fiercely competing socialist or religious groups arguing over the future of Jewry. He was rarely willing to engage in such debates. Only later, in the middle of World War II, would Singer adopt an explicit if short-lived ideological stance in favor of the Zionist alternative. In an essay entitled "A tsvey toyznt yoriker toes" [A two-thousand-year-old mistake] he would reluctantly, and quite uncharacteristically, echo the call for a Jewish national homeland, for a place where Jews could live normal lives rather than be regarded as intruders in foreign lands. In 1942 Singer believed that only such a political solution could adequately address the age-old delusion that Jews would ever be accepted within other lands. Normalcy now seemed to require an actual geographical place rather than an idea of community. Nonetheless, even during World War II, his acceptance of a nationalist ideology was an expression of both the problem of physical survival and the problem of finding a home for the Jewish imagination.

In the late 1920s, Singer's desire to find a location for his own imagination was at least as pronounced as any of the broader political questions that he could not escape. Within six months of his call for Yiddish writers to unite, Singer announced his renunciation of Yiddish literature. In an April 1928 letter to the Warsaw press, he declared in the most uncompromising language that Yiddish could no longer nurture the creative imagination. He suggested that because the Yiddish world was fractious and boorish, he would eschew belles lettres in favor of journalistic essays. He added:

> I am not doing this as a response to assaults by untalented journalists of whatever stripe who, because of competition and shopkeepers' accounts, have begun to attack me. I know the value of such attacks. I am not doing this because of any positive or negative critical judgments. I know the value of good and bad criticism.
>
> My decision to leave Yiddish literature came the moment I saw that on the Yiddish street under present conditions there is, unfortunately, no room for the Yiddish writer. It is impossible to write Yiddish now.[6]

He does not offer an explanation for his renunciation so much as a declaration of his own disgust with the state of Yiddish literature in Europe. He was even more emphatic in his correspondence with Abraham Cahan, his most powerful supporter. In a letter dated August 9, 1928, he told Cahan:

> I stood too close to the Jewish schools, literary journals, authors, parties in which I believed, and that was not good. In the Yiddish street it is no longer writers or experts who control literature, but party hacks, poetasters, swindlers. . . .
>
> I no longer believe, and how can one write without belief?

He expressed considerable pique in this letter, but he also claimed that he needed to find a more lucrative means of support for his family than Yiddish literature could provide.

In each of these explanations for his renunciation of Yiddish literature, Singer alludes to but refrains from explicitly naming the more substantive reasons for his conviction that the Yiddish world could no longer provide an ideational or imaginative base. By the time his letter appeared in the press (April 20, 1928), Singer had been engaged in a bitter struggle with hostile reviewers of *Steel and Iron*. He had also been defending himself against charges that the journalistic pieces he was writing for Cahan's *Forverts* had destroyed his artistic sensibilities and rendered him unfit for imaginative prose.[7]

Despite Singer's protestations that harsh reviews of *Steel and Iron* were politically motivated, the novel did warrant criticism as a severely flawed text inorganic in plot, construction, and characterization. Indeed, Sh. Niger, one of the most respected and temperate contemporary reviewers, criticized the novel in just such terms.[8] But the harshest attacks—and the ones to which Singer seems to be responding in his renunciation of Yiddish—criticized the novel's disillusionment with socialism and its inability to provide an ideological substitute. The novel's protagonist, Benjamin Lerner, is a Jew from Warsaw who serves in the Russian army during World War I. He deserts and wanders through the streets of Warsaw until the Germans replace the Russians as rulers of the city. Engaged in strenuous physical labor for the Germans, Lerner is converted to socialist ideas of cooperation and resistance. Hiding in Warsaw from the Germans as he had earlier hidden from the Russians, Lerner falls under the patronage of a rich, energetic Jew with a romantic attraction to the land. He goes east to establish a workers' agricultural commune, but when his benefactor deserts the enterprise in favor of involvement in the Russian Revolution, the Germans take control of the farm. Arrested on a false charge of agitation, Lerner escapes and flees further east. Finally, he finds himself in Petrograd and is willy-nilly drawn into the revolution when he is presented with a rifle and a group of men and told to lead an attack on the Winter Palace. Poles, Russians, Germans, Jews, laborers, capitalists, socialists—all are equally degenerate and corrupt in the novel, and Lerner can find no refuge among them. Singer's lack of faith in the beliefs of his day is as clearly revealed in this novel as it is in the more explicit statements he later offered Cahan as justification for his literary silence. Religious systems, the secular religions of socialism or Zionism, the romantic love of agricultural labor, and the Enlightenment belief in education and culture were already discarded in this first novel.

Like the novel, Singer's rejection of Yiddish generated considerable debate, as did his writing for the *Forverts*. Even a cursory look at the accusations surrounding his renunciation of Yiddish will convey a sense of the atmosphere he was trying to escape. When the New York Communist daily, the *Frayhayt*, claimed on October 25, 1927, that Singer was hiding behind the name Kuper in order to write *shund* [trash], Singer responded in the *Forverts* on March 23, 1928, only to evoke an even more indignant response from the *Frayhayt* five days later. (In the earlier article, the *Frayhayt* had referred to a "hot" item that Kuper had submitted about hasidim finding a rabbi's wife in bed with his assistant.) In the pages of the influential Warsaw *Bikher-velt*, Singer was similarly accused of misleading his public and demeaning his art by writing *shund* for the New York daily.[9] The Warsaw papers, *Folkstsaytung* and *Haynt*, also entered the fray when Singer attacked the former in the pages of the latter (June 22, 1928) because, claimed the *Frayhayt*, the *Folkstsaytung* was associated with *Bikher-velt*. The *Frayhayt*'s sarcasm was inescapable, although it was also more lively than accurate in its political labeling: "der korespondent, vos shraybt in tsitsilistishn 'Forverts,' falt on oyf der bundisher 'Folkstsaytung' halemay zi drukt shund. . . . Un vu tut er dos? In tsionistishn 'Haynt.'" [The correspondent who writes in the orthodox/socialist *Forverts* attacks the Bundist *Folkstsaytung* for publishing trash. . . . And where does he do so? In the Zionist *Haynt*.][10] Singer, not surprisingly, wanted to be rid of them all. He continued to write journalistic pieces for the *Forverts*, however, and there was some speculation that he might try his hand at another language—Hebrew, German, English, Polish, or even French.[11]

Singer's search for a language and a literary haven seemed at this point to overlap. Despite his success and his work with important Yiddish periodicals, echoes of the crisis of faith he expressed in 1928 were heard in each of his novels and stories. He continued to lament his inability to find a home, seeing it as a microcosm of the plight of the Jews in Eastern Europe: always subject to the vagaries of changing national allegiances and political powers, and never fully integrated into any of the cultures whose physical territory they shared.

Few of Singer's characters are ever truly at home either. They are out of place everywhere, wandering from town to town, forced by historical or personal exigencies to leave their homes, confined to shrinking spaces within their own walls, or, more frighteningly, condemned to roam and yet unable to reach any destination. Wandering serves as the physical correlative of their existential conditions.

As if to contain this perpetual restlessness, Singer peoples several short stories with characters who have a strong relationship to the soil. But even these men cannot remain rooted in the land they want to cultivate. They are farmers, disgusted with city life, lovers of nature, physically strong, happy when engaged in agricultural labor. Vili in the story bearing his name, Sholem and Ben Melnik in "In di berg" [In the mountains], Rafel in "A fremder" [A stranger], and Reb Uri Levy of "Dorfsyidn" [Village Jews], are such characters. Their love of the land differentiates them from much more typical Jews who yearn for communal social life. These farmers are lone but not lonely men, quite deliberately severed from other Jews until wars, pogroms, or less catastrophic forms of anti-Semitism jolt them back into the community they have rejected. Nature and the land are romanticized; descriptions of nature are interpolated into the texts with no apparent order or necessity. In the midst of their crops and horses, these men are naive, innocent of both political and social knowledge. They have broken with their communal, economic, and religious past. Yet their attachment to a place is tenuous, since it remains entirely portable. The Polish countryside and the Catskills are equally likely sites for their longing, and they are essentially indistinguishable from one another in climate, soil, or environment. Only the foreign sounds of the local language differentiate these places from one another. We know where we are through the medium of speech as conveyed through accents, dialects, and the occasional use of Polish or English words.

The lack of a material sense of place in precisely the stories in which the soil plays such a central role reveals how attenuated the connections are between these Jews and their land. There exists a crucial distinction between the physical reality of the earth in which these men sow and reap and the transitory political status of the land in which they are never truly rooted. In part, this is a reflection of the problem of national identity that Jewish writers from Eastern Europe could not escape. National boundaries change with dizzying rapidity; conquering armies bring new languages and laws and an ever-changing relationship to minority or ethnic cultures. In Singer's fiction, attachment to the soil is an objectification of an elusive quest for normalcy, home, and permanent associations independent of those political upheavals that make the concept of a home-land something of an oxymoron. But all this appears as no more than wishful thinking, and the narratives collapse as these hopes are disappointed by the physical world. No land can become a secure, permanent home for these or any other Jews.

II

Singer's most intriguing depiction of a homeless wanderer appears in *Yoshe Kalb* (1932), where his personal, political, and imaginative turmoil over home and exile are clearly revealed.[12] The meaning of place is a central question in the novel, as it was for Singer during the years of its composition. *Yoshe Kalb* is a transitional work pointing away from European myths and toward American ones without focusing on the physical reality of either continent. Wandering is central to the novel, and it is linked to questions about the nature of free will and causality. The wandering is also a countertext to Singer's own itinerancy and to the movements of Jews in the period between the years depicted in the novel and the date of its composition. The narrative ends just before the major period of migration from Eastern Europe to America (beginning in the 1880s); it is also written just before Singer's own migration to America, following his journalistic travels through Poland and Russia. The novel's central concern with Yoshe as a wanderer whose identity cannot be clearly discerned can be understood in light of these other journeys. The severed connections between the individual, his community, and any ideological or imaginative locus are inescapable.

The appearance of *Yoshe Kalb* after Singer's 1928 crisis of literary faith could be heralded as a victory for Yiddish literature and as an affirmation that the writer could never separate himself from his linguistic and cultural origins. However, only five years had elapsed between the publication of *Steel and Iron* and *Yoshe Kalb*, certainly not an unusual length of time between major works. Had he not pointedly renounced Yiddish literature, Singer's "silence" might easily have gone unnoticed. Abraham Cahan is often credited with having finally convinced Singer to return to Yiddish literature when the two met in Berlin in 1931 and Cahan advised him to ignore his critics and assured him of the

Forverts's support.[13] Serialization of *Yoshe Kalb* was preceded by numerous laud-atory announcements highlighting Singer's popularity and controversial his-tory. The novel appeared in daily installments in the *Forverts* between June 4 and July 19, 1932. The Warsaw *Haynt* heralded its own serialization of the novel (July 8 through October 26, 1932) with equally expansive announce-ments. In the same year, *Yoshe Kalb* appeared in book form in Warsaw. The novel and its successful New York dramatic premiere (in the fall 1932 theatrical season) were widely and generally favorably reviewed.

Because of Singer's own public declarations and the ensuing popular specula-tions about his return to Yiddish, *Yoshe Kalb* was greeted as a kind of homecom-ing, and debates about it invariably reflected on the kind of home Singer had chosen to depict. According to some detractors, Singer had joined the disrepu-table ranks of those who presented Eastern European Jewry and particularly hasidic life as bleak, hypocritical, and unremittingly ugly. Niger saw the novel's greatest flaw in Singer's inability to understand and evaluate the role of hasidism or to capture its "great soul".[14] Criticisms by Dov Sadan[15] in Palestine and A. Mukdoyni[16] (among others) in New York castigated Maurice Schwartz's dramatic adaptation of the novel for its unsympathetic portrayal of Polish Jewry. Y. Y. Trunk interpreted the novel as a great satire—in the tradition of Mendele Moykher Sforim's *naturalizm*—on Peretz's romanticization of hasidism.[17] Mayzl offered a particularly telling comment when Schwartz brought the Yid-dish play to Warsaw. Mayzl reminded his readers that in New York the play might appear as an exotic piece describing some aspect of the audience's own past; in Warsaw, however, its ethnographic details could still be seen as reflec-tions of a present reality.[18] In the Polish environment in which it was writ-ten, the novel addressed such current concerns as the ongoing oppressive-ness of religious institutions and hasidic control. In the American context to which Singer was already looking, the novel could be seen as both a period piece and an affirmation of its readers' own choices in leaving Eastern Europe.

In these responses to the text, we may perceive the different cultural orbits of Yiddish literature at this pivotal moment in Jewish history. Poised between Eastern Europe and America, the novel, like many contemporary Yiddish works, is also poised between pressing realities and the burgeoning nostalgia created by geographical and temporal distance. His critics were acutely aware that Singer himself was not at all nostalgic in his depiction of hasidic life or the shtetl. But an American Jewish audience in the thirties might well look back with a tolerance afforded by distance.[19] In Poland, the Enlightenment battle against the fervor and antirational, anti-intellectual stance of hasidic sects was still being waged, even as an equally prominent revisionist view of their religious life was developing. This continuing source of social tension is one of the realities to which Trunk refers. Trunk might have added that Yoshe Kalb, whose silence may recall that of Peretz's famous Bontshe Shvayg [Bontshe the Silent], in the story of that name, did not encourage the kinds of romanticized readings to which Peretz's story has been subject. Singer's contemporaries could add biographical details to the cultural and historical explanations for his harsh treatment of the hasidim in the novel. He had never sympathized with his own father's adherence to hasidism, viewing it as one of the primary indications of his father's inability to act in the practical, mundane world. Still, the belief shared by many Yiddish readers that *Yoshe Kalb* is largely an attack on a certain premodern way of Jewish life does not do justice to the much broader and more profound disillusionment expressed in the novel.

Singer's unwillingness to claim any ideational, spiritual, or physical haven may have contributed to the tentative, precarious tone of his novel. Aaron Zeitlin suggests that Singer, very much like his hero Yoshe, had separated himself from his society, only to return with a profound sense of uncertainty.[20] "Ikh veys nisht" [I don't know] is Yoshe Kalb's refrain in the second half of the novel in response to questions about his identity and his travels. It might well have been Singer's at this period, too, observes Zeitlin. It is tempting to follow this reading and view the novel as a kind of allegorical spiritual autobiography, but Yoshe emerges as an infinitely more complex and intriguing character when considered in terms of the narrative in which he appears rather than in any comparison between the author and the figure he created.

Yoshe Kalb is a deliberately enigmatic character, closely related to the figure of the doppelgänger and to nascent but largely unexamined psychoanalytic models. He emerges as two apparently mutually exclusive characters. One is Nahum, the learned scholar and husband of Serele. The other is Yoshe, an ignorant, silent beggar who seems capable only of reciting Psalms (a sign of having very little Jewish education). He cannot even beg properly. In Book One, Nahum (or Nahumtshe, the diminutive by which he is often called) enters the novel as a fourteen-year-old-boy, pampered and protected by his mother, betrothed too early only because his father is not strong enough to withstand the demands for an early marriage made by Reb Melekh, Serele's father. Reb Melekh's unseemly haste is actually occasioned by his own desire to marry —for the fourth time. Malkele, the bride he has chosen, is a young woman, barely older than his own Serele. Nahum is an alien in his new home, unhappy with the hasidic court and its lack of gentility. Since we never see him in his parents' home, he seems to enter the novel as a foreigner, even the betrothal having been arranged in the (Bohemian-Czechoslovakian) resort of Carlsbad. Nahum comes to Reb Melekh's town, Nyesheve, from his father's rabbinic home in Rakhmanivke. Nyesheve, under Austrian rule, is the center of Reb Melekh's hasidic court; its influence extends to thousands of followers in Galicia and Russia. Rakhmanivke, the Russian town from which Nahum comes, is hundreds of miles away. Nahum's family cannot tolerate the hasidic excesses of Reb Melekh's followers. Even before entering Nyesheve, Nahum is already a strange figure, drawn to mystical texts and acts of penitence. He is at odds with his father, "a man of the world, one who liked to enjoy the good things in life" (p. 16),[21] and who disapproved of his son's actions.

This literal and symbolic strangeness has its analogue in the sexual imagery that pervades the novel. Too young and spoiled to be ready for marriage,

Nahum is indifferent to his wife and terrified by the duties of a husband. He is able to consummate his marriage only after everyone has given up hope that he can. The transformation from the frightened, impotent boy to the strong, powerful man is as complete as it is unexpected:

> [S]uddenly . . . there awakened in him a strong feeling of ripeness, a feeling which engulfed him with such unexpected power, such a yearning, sweet strength that he felt the process of growth, felt his breast enlarging, his arms filling with power, the veins in his feet expanding, and his blood running hotter, quicker. (pp. 42–43)

But only when he meets Malkele, his new mother-in-law, does he understand what true desire and passion can mean. Immediately, the two fall desperately, silently in love and finally consummate that love in a bathetic scene of literal and metaphoric flames and confusion. Malkele, having set the scene by starting a fire in the barn containing, among other soiled items, the Cossack uniforms used to celebrate weddings, finds Nahum and leads him away from the burning town. When Malkele later dies in childbirth, attempts are made to remove the unborn child from its mother's body for separate burial (in accordance with Jewish practice). Malkele, willful and stubborn even in death, refuses to relinquish the child, and it must finally be buried with her. On the same day, Nahum disappears.[22]

Book Two of the novel introduces Yoshe, a stranger in the Russian-Polish town of Bialogura, near the Galician border. Yoshe enters this town at its lowest economic and social level, among the beggars, gravediggers, and ignorant of the community, the opposite pole of Nahum's status in Rakhmanivke and Nye-sheve. He identifies himself as a *navenadnik*, a wanderer (p. 122). In the course of this book, Yoshe is accused of having impregnated the dimwitted Zivvye and, refusing to defend himself, is married to her in an attempt to arrest the progress of a plague in the town. Contrasts in the novel's two wedding scenes point to the different social strata presented. Nahum's wedding is accompanied by extraordinary pageantry, with hasidim dressing in Cossack costume, riding out to meet the bridegroom, drinking and eating in great quantity. Reb Melekh's wedding is also a colorful and extravagant affair. Yoshe's wedding is a parody of these festivities. The townspeople do not know whether or not he already has a wife, and they compel him to marry a woman who is both dimwitted and a whore. But, according to the town elders, communal needs take precedence over all else. Following the well-known practice of performing *kholera khasenes* [epidemic weddings], they conclude:

> [O]ne remedy for misfortune was for the community to wed, on the very grounds of the cemetery, a poor bride and groom, the most unfortunate and lowly of the community. For this purpose, a pitiful fool would be sought, a madman, a cripple, an old maid, even a sinful one, who no longer had any chance of getting married. Because of such good deeds . . . the wrath of Heaven would be averted. (p. 167)

No one actually hears the silent Yoshe utter the words that make Zivvye his wife, but he is considered married to her nonetheless, and he flees Bialogura on the night of the wedding.

In Book Three, the last and shortest of the novel's divisions, Nahum returns to Nyeshave fifteen years after his departure. He is revealed to be Yoshe and is regarded alternately as a bigamist, a holy man, or, finally a *gilgl* [a transmigrated soul]. This final judgment of him is an attempt to explain on the metaphysical plane what cannot be understood on the mundane. Nahum/Yoshe neither accepts nor denies any accusations, claiming "men veyst gornisht vegn zikh aleyn" [one knows nothing about oneself] and thus implying that all attempts at self-definition are futile. We have no more than a few glimpses of Nahum as an introspective character and even fewer of Yoshe. Repeatedly, the character is described as mysterious, aloof from other people, given to inexplicable silences and gestures. He is thus severed not only from the familiar world of social and religious contexts, but also from the psychological exploration that might have replaced it. Singer allows for no clear structures of meaning.

The plot leaves several questions unanswered. We cannot know for certain that the father of the child buried with Malkele is Nahum and not her husband, Reb Melekh.[23] Reb Melekh cannot remember all his offspring, or even how many there are, and the narrative sustains this indifference, introducing us almost haphazardly to yet another heir. We never know where Nahum/Yoshe has been in his wanderings; we hear that he has traveled "everywhere," but we actually see him only in Nyesheve and Bialogura, and even there we do not see the entire town. More problematic is the fate of the child Zivvye is carrying in Book II, all mention of which is dropped in Book III. These apparent inconsistencies—particularly the last one—may be seen as flaws in Singer's text; they suggest that in some cases, or in the course of serialization, he loses sight of certain details. But they emerge more significantly as quite deliberate obfuscations, underscoring a number of major themes in the novel. Primary among these is the theme of inconsistency, or the lack of causality in the social world. Yoshe is punished for a sin he did not commit; he is irrationally forced into a union with an idiot who has conceived a child by an unknown criminal. The sin Nahum did commit with Malkele remains undetected and therefore unpunished by the social world he inhabits. But the novel denies the hegemony of that world, replacing it with an individual sense of sin and morality. That individual sense bears a complex relationship to the religious system, but ultimately no clear, externally identified context can claim authority in this novel, even if the individual were capable of identifying or comprehending such an authority. The individual may determine his own guilt and punishment, but his psychological motivations remain unexplored and cannot be articulated.

There is, then, no source of meaning on the social or individual level. The remnants of what may once have been an ideologically coherent world are rendered in this novel as a symbolic system from which the individual must struggle to break free. Only the signs of religious authority and meaning are left, transfigured into corruptions and superstitions. The hasidic world appears, for the most part, as uninformed, hypocritical, absurd. Reb Melekh is greedy and lecherous. He relies on an assistant who responds to the religious questions he is too ignorant to answer. He lives in splendor set apart from the ugly, dirty surroundings of his hasidim. When the synagogue burns, Reb Melekh is most concerned about the loss of one book in whose pages he has hidden money. Even during Nahum/Yoshe's trial, competing hasidic dynasties seem less interested in justice than in destroying Nyesheve. The nonhasidic religious world is no better. As the entire Jewish world becomes interested in the identity of Nahum/Yoshe, all social and intellectual strata reveal their limitations. The opponents of the hasidim exchange letters more remarkable for their hyperbolic salutations than for their content. Their letters underscore the extent to which religious authority is an empty semiotic system and not a moral system. One who signs himself "the lowly worm, the less than human, the unlearned, the lowliest of the lowly, the small and young smoky candle who is extinguished by the light of your great torch" addresses his letter thus:

> Great light, . . . powerful hammer who takes millstones and rubs them into powder, Mount Sinai, unique amongst your generation, in whose light we are privileged, light of the world, the greatest of the great, case full of books, rabbi of all the children of the dispersion, uprooter of mountains and fields, may his light shine forever. (p. 211)

The battle of fatuous words extends from these rabbis to hasidic rabbis poor in linguistic skills but rich in equally ornate titles, and on to the maskilim, the impious, the secularists, and even the Austrian government. And, without exception, each of these groups is entirely ineffectual.

The barrenness of this society, its inability to produce proper judicial decisions or anything else, is allegorized through sexual analogues: the physical impotence of Nahum and Reb Melekh in the early days of their marriages and the fruitless female protagonists. Serele never conceives; Malkele will not deliver her child; Zivvye's pregnancy is symbolically aborted when the writer ignores it. Whatever sympathy we develop for Reb Melekh, as for Serele or Zivvye, results only from their increasingly pathetic condition.

Finally, the rabbis convened to judge Nahum/Yoshe conclude not that he is one person who embodies two different characters, but rather that he is a *gilgl*. Their final pronouncement is symbolically correct: he is a soul condemned to wander. The desire of some hasidim, even after this pronouncement, to name Nahum as the successor to Reb Melekh is absurd not because Nahum is too saintly for the machinations of a hasidic court, but because social constructs can have no meaning for him and because they have been shown to be devoid of meaning in themselves.

He breaks free of these social constraints in two very different contexts. The first is in his passionate relationship with Malkele; the second, his ironic assumption of the role of the *navenad* [wanderer]. The passion of Nahum and Malkele stands in marked contrast to the enervation that characterizes the novel. This rare moment of energy and action is nonetheless an immoral act. It is finally Nahum's own sense of sin that condemns him. His community can neither enforce the moral code nor even recognize that he has transgressed it. The most unsettling vision of the novel lies in this affirmation of a passion that is vital and yet untenable. The individual cannot adhere to the laws of his community, but neither can he create his own laws. Yoshe's silence is a dramatic statement of this impossible condition. The language of his world is useless because its assumptions and precepts can no longer govern him. But the individual cannot speak in any other language—cannot articulate other social or psychological terms—and is therefore mute. This is perhaps the fictive analogue to Singer's own search for another literary language and his silence preceding this novel. Emerging from a rejection of corrupted codes, Yoshe can offer no clearer ideological or personal alternatives than were available to Singer.

Yet neither Singer nor his character remains entirely silent. Nahum/Yoshe speaks cryptically, with hidden, inscrutable words. In this, he recalls, perhaps surprisingly, another figure. The derogatory name "Yoshe" invokes the name Yoshke, a perversion of Yeshu, the standard Jewish form of Yehoshua, Jesus. Singer's Yoshe, too, cries out with Jesus' echo of Psalm 22: Got, farvos hostu mikh farlozt (God, why hast thou foresaken me?). Yoshe completes his lament in another echo of the Psalm: Ikh ruf tsu dir bay tog un du entferst mir nisht, ikh shray baynakht un du shvaygst. [I cry in the daytime and you do not answer; and in the night, and you are silent] (p. 129). The resonance of these names and words highlights the themes of suffering and innocence associated with the image of Jesus. In this invocation of Jesus, Singer dramatically exploits a broader symbolic vocabulary that was becoming increasingly accessible to . Yiddish fiction.[24] Unlike his namesake, Yoshe Kalb is neither innocent nor a messianic figure promising salvation. He is, rather, connected to yet another figure of Christian legend, the Jew condemned by Jesus to eternal wandering. The confusion of roles here is perfectly in keeping with the conflicting terms in which the novel is cast. The title character is both Nahum and Yoshe; he is both learned and ignorant, holy and sinful, reminiscent of the Jewish *navenad* myth and of the Christian myth of the Wandering Jew. Although he may be Jesus-like in his symbolic purging of sin and hypocrisy and in his silent suffering, he cannot embody the role of messiah. He remains a solitary, wandering figure, phylacteries and stone in his sack, preaching to no one. He is full of the mysterious knowledge associated with ubiquity and immortality, but there is no omniscience in Yoshe or in the narrative voice. A state of epistemological bankruptcy permeates the novel. In his *navenad* state, Yoshe signals the modern understanding of *goles* [exile], which now entails separation from his community and even from himself. From *this* exile there is no redemption in political, religious, or individual terms. Yoshe's connections to Jesus are thus painfully ironic, underscoring the illusion of messianic goals and the permanence of psychological and social exile. As the Wandering Jew or the *navenad*, Yoshe is associated with an archetypal figure, but that archetype has been severed from the cultural systems in which it had been rooted and could achieve significance. Yoshe is thus the personification of a rootlessness that is existential but to which he can give no name.

The concepts of exile and wandering resonate differently for a Yiddish and English audience. An authentic Jewish rhetoric of place is located in the language of *goles* and *navenad* rather than in an epic or modern search for a home to which one can return. Adam and Eve banished forever from Eden, Cain banished and able to settle only in the land of *Nod* (i.e., the land of wandering), and the Jews who must die in the desert before future generations can reach the Promised Land are all archetypal figures.[25] There are significant differences between this wandering and, for example, the exile of an Odysseus or the self-imposed exile of a Stephen Dedalus. The latter paradigms focus on the individual who is their subject; the possibility of redemption is here conceived in personal terms that depend in large measure on the individual's own actions. And there is an active, motivating, immediate memory of a homeland to which one may return, albeit with difficulty or only in the imagination. *Goles*, invoking a radically different sense of history and place, is not exile in this Western literary sense, despite the compelling desire for homecoming and return that has shaped Jewish thought. The individual, who is more clearly object than subject in *goles*, does not seek exile, does not have the power to alter it, and must regard it as a collective fate. Home, then, is a concept rather than a presence, a communal concept transcending one's personal experience.

The *navenad* embodies a radical appropriation of this sense of communal homelessness by severing himself from all social ties. Focusing on the restless, solitary individual whose place of origin is unknown and who lacks destination, the figure of the wanderer achieves a mystery born of his self-removal from the mundane world, divesting himself of earthly possessions and human relations. Folklorists see in this numinous figure the background to the Christian legend of the Wandering Jew, who is also cursed with immortality.[26] The addition of a temporal dimension to the spatial one has an important analogue in the Jewish sense of exile: the end of *goles* is tied to *geula* [messianic redemption]. *Goles* and *geula*—exile and redemption—thus frame the Jewish understanding of history.[27]

Much of the tension in Singer's fiction lies in the enormous gap between the traditional and epic concepts of sin, holiness, *goles*, and *geula* on the one hand and, on the other, the narrow sphere in which contemporary Jews may act. Wandering and homelessness are the physical signs of a gap that is also imaginative and that neither memory nor any philosophical stance can fill. If, as Michael Seidel has persuasively argued, "exile is a symptomatic metaphor for the state of the narrative imagination,"[28] then that metaphor is complicated in Singer's case by his understanding of the distinctive nature of Jewish *goles*. In the fiction Seidel considers (by Defoe, Joyce, Sterne, James, Nabokov), imagination itself serves as a homecoming, evoking the native ground that it strives to recapture. The emphasis here is not on mimetic representations of remembered territory, but rather on the allegories, metaphoric equivalents, and stories through which the imagination transforms them.[29] This offers a useful model for Singer's fictions partly because it suggests a way to undermine the prevalent mimetic readings of Yiddish texts and to insist, instead, on the imaginative function of exile and home. Still, the particular Jewish sense of *goles* presented in Singer's narratives differentiates them from these other European narratives of exile. Here, again, the major difference is that Singer's texts contain no remembered or desired terrain as Seidel presents it; homecoming remains devoid of any models, transformed as they may be. Instead of the desire for a return to familiar ground or the symbolic appropriation, transformation, perhaps internalization of that ground, there is endless wandering without the possibility of homecoming, a restlessness that even the narrative imagination cannot counter.

Singer was unquestionably influenced by the cultural elements that had penetrated the internal Jewish discourse and broadened the vocabulary of symbols available to writers. Even more dramatically, however, the confusion of Christian and Jewish myths of wandering, exile, and sin in *Yoshe Kalb* underscores Singer's sense of just how impoverished a Jewish mythical or symbolic system had become, how insufficient it was to sustain the individual in the contemporary world. Given the earlier uses of these myths, we expect banishment to evoke, by opposition, Eden; exile to evoke the redemption that will end it. Instead the novel denies—or ignores—the possibility of an Edenic past or redemptive future. The lack of causality at the novel's core implies not a pre-Enlightenment sense of *geula*, but only randomness and powerlessness. Recasting the traditional typology of *goles* and *geula* into modern terms means individuating them, which, in this novel, can only mean that the idea of a community is replaced by a fragmented vision of society, character, and expression. Yoshe's silence and exile (and perhaps Singer's as well) are allegories of the plight of the imagination faced with such a vision.

Yoshe's wanderings are said to have taken him everywhere. He cannot or will not name the ground he has covered. Pointedly, however, he does not seem to be moving at all. We never see him en route; his travels seem to lack direction and volition. It is impossible to conceive of Yoshe arriving at any destination because destination implies goal and will, which are alien to this novel. When Serele is left an *agunah* [deserted wife], she is compared to the women whose husbands went off to America. Such a comparison is ironic in this context because the historical directions of Jewish wandering—toward Western Europe and America, or toward the Holy Land—are necessarily absent from *Yoshe Kalb* because they would suggest a degree of teleological certainty that does not have credence in the novel.

The novel's time sequence underscores these themes, separating the individual even further from the community. The novel spans a little more than fifteen years (beginning approximately in 1870). The passing of time in each of its three books is carefully marked. But in overall structure, the novel begins and ends in precisely the same temporal frame. We begin with Nahum's betrothal and marriage in the spring, between Passover and Shavuouth [Festival of Weeks], a period traditionally regarded as a time of mourning by religious

Jews; we end with the trial and his final disappearance in the same season. In time and place the novel insists on the illusion of movement, but returns to its point of origin, anchoring its social and religious world firmly. There is no such anchor for Nahum/Yoshe, despite his pious repetition of Psalms or prayers. Severed from both time and place, his fate is perhaps rendered more tragic by this contrast between his individual plight and a communal sanctification of time. But there is a more heartening, though no less poignant, interpretation of this contrast: the repetition on the social level, the sameness of beginning and end, may also be a sign of the stagnation to which Yoshe is no longer subject, now being subject, rather, to more inscrutable forces.

In the face of such deliberately unsettling themes and tensions, some readers have responded with attempts to ground the novel by locating its historical sources. No less an authority than Singer's brother has traced the supposed factual roots of Yoshe's story. In the pages of the *Forverts* and in his introduction to the second English edition, Bashevis recalls that *Yoshe Kalb* is based on a true story their father had told.[30] Earlier, Mordkhe Shtrigler had recorded the story of a wandering figure with two distinct personalities who had become a Galician folk legend. Shtrigler went to considerable pains to record the factual story behind the legend, tracing one Reb Moshe Chaim with two wives in two towns and two distinct personalities who was finally condemned by a rabbinic court and came to be regarded by some as a saint, by others as an evil spirit.[31] In the pages of *Haynt*, M. A. Ger had recorded his meetings with the true Yoshe Kalb.[32] Such stories are interesting only in that they may reveal what Henry James might have called the donnée of Singer's tale. They complement the tendency we have already seen in autobiographical interpretations or in criticisms of the novel as an unsympathetic portrayal of Eastern European hasidic life. Such views confine the scope of the novel by privileging various representational readings. Singer's novel may use details of a folktale concerning an actual figure who inspired it just as it may be examining its author's own existential questions; it is certainly presenting a very harsh view of a way of life that still prevailed. But Singer is ultimately concerned with much more than a historical tale or an analysis of schizophrenia. Explanations of its sources counter the novel's speculative and inconclusive design. Historicity may be seen as an attempt to fill in the gap left by Yoshe's statements about knowing nothing at all.

While portraying an individual severed from a community whose laws, sanctions, and conventions no longer bind him, Singer refuses to offer us a man who is a hero, madman, or sinner. He individualizes the terms of moral discourse even as he laments the necessity to do so. Singer challenges received ethical categories and recognizable typologies in his novel. Homelessness and wandering, like sin, retribution, and innocence, emerge as moral tropes here as connectedness becomes increasingly impossible and the soul is left solitary and speechless. Yoshe's actions generate cosmic upheavals that appear incommensurate with his behavior and that raise unutterable questions. Yet in this novel the individual can, at least, break free of hypocrisy and corrupt social conventions while remaining subject to some moral order. Even that option would disappear from Singer's novels after *Yoshe Kalb*. In 1932, looking to a new location and a new context for his fiction, Singer still clung to a vision of individual integrity that might exist if uprooted from what he saw as infertile ground. Jewish and personal history would soon foreclose even that course.

III

At the end of 1933, within several months of his first trip to America, Singer left Poland for the last time. A number of events that occurred within those months overshadowed his relatively modest faith in a different cultural and political environment. The first trip was a successful, celebratory one occasioned by Maurice Schwartz's theatrical production of *Yoshe Kalb*. Soon after Singer's return to Poland, Hitler took power in Germany and anti-Semitism in Poland increased. The increasing tone of despair that marks Singer's subsequent work can be understood in light of these frightening political developments. To these were added the sudden illness and death of his twelve-year-old son on the eve of the family's planned departure for America. The Singers postponed their emigration and finally arrived in New York (after a brief stay in Paris) in March 1934. Communal and private tragedies made the fame he had won in America seem irrelevant; there was no longer any opportunity for the kind of triumphant arrival Singer might once have anticipated.

Nonetheless, midway through his literary career, Singer seemed to have found his own solution to the problem of a literary home for Yiddish posed in his 1927 essay "Yiddish writers of the world, unite." Certainly, by 1933, when Singer left Warsaw, the debates that had raged only a few years earlier concerning the proper center for Yiddish culture must have seemed painfully ironic in light of developing political concerns. America became, almost inevitably, Singer's literary home because Eastern Europe had become more radically hostile than even he would have imagined and because in America he found an appreciative audience. The focus on America should not be understood as an ideological choice, but rather as a pragmatic realization: the unity and continuity of Yiddish culture could only be achieved in the pages of those papers and journals that were most vibrant. Singer had consistently maintained the belief that Yiddish letters had no natural geographical boundary or home. It had therefore been perfectly natural to live in Warsaw and to write and publish for an American audience. The converse was equally true, with Singer living in New York, publishing in the *Forverts* and more or less simultaneously publishing in Warsaw. America proved to be no freer of petty literary squabbles than Poland had been. It was not cultural unity that Singer found in New York, but rather an audience and a secure forum for his writing. He no longer sought a place in which to root his imagination, only a less oppressive environment in which to express it.

In essays, stories, or his last novel, *The Family Karnovski*, Singer did not engage American myths even when he brought his characters into an American landscape. In his fiction, he remained as aloof as ever to the idea of connection to a place. Even when he attempted to shift his focus to Zion, he could not construct a sense of Jewish rootedness. By 1942, as we have already seen, he acknowledged the need for an actual physical Jewish center that necessarily entailed a government, power, and cultural hegemony. Yet neither in the essay "A Two-Thousand-Year-Old Mistake" nor the story "Baym shvartsn yam" [Near the Black Sea]—both published in 1942—is he sanguine about even the theoretical foundation for such a national entity. It is possible, but ultimately deceptive, to see the 1927 essay pointing tentatively toward America and the 1942 essay pointing more emphatically toward Zion as addressing and resolving the same problem of homelessness and powerlessness. Yiddish or Jewish cultural unity may well have demanded a physical center, but Singer can hardly be said to have been enthusiastic in embracing such an ideology. Rather, he seems resigned to it, tired of the centuries of antagonism and bloodshed, almost wistfully turning to this one solution, which has not yet had a chance to fail. He writes, "We want a land for those who can no longer tolerate being slaves, who can no longer tolerate being in *goles*."[33]

In fiction written before and after the 1942 essay, he reaches a similar conclusion about the Zionist alternative: separation, assimilation, conversion, friendship, and all else having failed for the Jews, only the possibility of a Jewish state is left. It is important to remember, too, the historical and personal circumstances under which this essay was written. Ideological confusion may be an understandable stance in the face of World War II, but Yiddish writers were more likely to assume a different stance, one that called for Jewish unity, that sought desperately for clarity and for some view of a comprehensible future. Even for a Jew living safely in New York, a belief in the hospitality of any nation must have seemed remote indeed. Citing rising anti-Semitism in America, Singer explicitly rejected the coexistence promised by democratic principles. Curiously, Singer did not specify a location for his nationalist ideal. *Eretz Yisroel* [the Land of Israel] is unquestionably implied in the 1942 declaration, but Singer's connection to place is so shadowy as to leave the locus of his hopes unnamed even at this moment.

Singer's own vision of the normalcy offered by nationhood never brought him to Palestine, where, in any case, the early antagonism to Yiddish was so great as to have discouraged an even more ardent Zionist than he. Occasionally, characters in his fiction fulfill what they perceive as the religious and political imperative to go to *Eretz Yisroel*. In *The Brothers Ashkenazi*, Max Ashkenazi broods about his brother's death and the unmistakable new wave of Polish anti-Semitism that causes it. In response, he considers becoming a farmer or an industrialist in Palestine, but chooses instead to rebuild his empire in Lodz. When the economic life of Lodz is destroyed at the end of the novel, many go to Palestine. They go to rebuild Lodz in their own land, but they also go knowing very little about its soil, climate, or language. In the wake of World War I, the Russian Revolution, and renewed pogroms, *Eretz Yisroel* gains in attractiveness as a link to a Jewish past and as a new terrain untainted by a history of anti-Semitism.

In a story that appeared several months before "A Two-Thousand-Year-Old Mistake," Singer presented his most explicit Zionist hero. Pinchas Fradkin, the protagonist of "Baym shvartsn yam," longs for the Holy Land. Repeating Yehuda HaLevi's famous poetic cry, "My heart is in the East and I am at the end of the West," Fradkin leaves his small town to travel to Odessa in the hopes of finding a ship to take him towards his heart's desire. Civil unrest, the constant sieges, military actions, and boycotts of World War I keep him poor and hopeless in Odessa. Wartime is worse for the Jews than for anyone else in this story since pogroms follow both victories and defeat. Only the Red Army seems willing to defend them, and Fradkin becomes a military leader at the head of a regiment consisting of men from various lands, each with different languages, customs, clothes, and weapons. At the end of the story, having proven that Jews can both lead and fight, Fradkin surprisingly reaffirms his desire to go "east" and work the land rather than assume the prominent political position he may now claim among the Reds. But does "east" still mean Palestine? On the surface, this appears to be what Fradkin tells his comrade, thus affirming the need for the Jews to establish their own army and structures of power. Yet the context of the Russian Revolution in which Fradkin assumes so prominent a role may invite another reading: his renunciation of a political position may not be a renunciation of the Soviet Union in favor of Palestine, but simply an affirmation of labor and land. Singer's reluctance to embrace the ideology to which he ultimately resorts in 1942 is evoked by this reluctance to name the implied object. The enigmatic ending of "Near the Black Sea" is reflected, as well, in the story's structure, where the Zionist ideal frames the tale but is missing from much of its core and is unexpectedly reintroduced by Fradkin's proclamation at the end.

Singer was always wary of political solutions and of the apparatus of statehood that would result from fulfilling the Zionist ideal. His hesitant ideological commitment is expressed differently, but no less significantly, in his correspondence with Ravitch. In August 1942, thanking Ravitch for his kind words about the story ("Near the Black Sea" is not named but the letter can refer only to this story), Singer wrote:

> The story has a Zionist tone and I do not want to hide that. Others have become orthodox. Not me. But I am certain that Yiddish secular culture and radicalism are one hundred percent bankrupt. Jews must live in their own land, without gentiles who hate us and will always hate us for no reason at all. If *Eretz Yisroel* is possible, that would be the best thing in our lives.[34]

Here, Singer is not sanguine about the practical possibilities, but expresses an unusual conviction about the ideals. Neither religion, Yiddishist secularism, nor socialist politics will save the Jews, he argues. In little more than a year, distant from the immediacy of composing and publishing the essay and story, Singer expressed a more fatalistic view:

> Never in my life have I been as deeply convinced of the senselessness of *goles* and its life and culture as I have been in recent years. Unfortunately, I don't believe that there is a cure for us. I have the diagnosis but not the cure.[35]

Interspersed with such historiosophical searching throughout these letters are Singer's fears for his mother and brother lost in the war's upheavals[36] and a growing (although not yet complete) recognition of the plight of the Jews trapped in Europe. The metaphor of Jewish life as a disease for which there may be no cure (a metaphor by no means unique to Singer) can certainly be understood in the context of these horrors.

Imagining an end to this tortured exile—even if it could be articulated in pragmatic political terms—inevitably evokes messianic images to which Singer's fiction never gives credence. The appeal of messianic beliefs may be particularly strong in times that seem apocalyptic, where causality is brought into question and nothing that is already present offers succor. For Singer, the practical realization of Zionism is a messianic dream, attractive for a while, but ultimately as suspect as a belief in the Son of David or the workers' revolution. He is left with no physical ground for his imagination to populate. Poland, America, and the idea of Zion emerge as tropes assuming varied symbolic meanings, but no place is distinguishable as a secure home.

Place, to which the Jew cannot be connected, is the correlative of an existential state rendered through certain landscapes and topography. Dirty, overcrowded slums abound in Singer's stories and novels. Whether we find them in a shtetl or in a large city, such landscapes attest to terrible poverty and to a chaotic, unenviable, tumultuous life aggravated by the social disadvantages of being Jewish and poor. Like the characters who inhabit them, these places are not all homogeneous, but they do share a similar fate.

Through Mary Rabinovitch, the twenty-four-year-old unemployed bookkeeper of "Elnt" [Alone], Singer develops the possibilities contained within the city. In the many kilometers Mary traverses each day, we learn that constant movement can be a kind of paralysis. At first she walks because there is an excitement in being free in a city full of people and always changing sights; then she walks to find a job or to peddle soap; later she walks because in contrast to her own home the streets provide comfort and a quieter refuge; finally, she *must* walk to avoid being accosted by the seedier elements of Warsaw night life. She is mistaken for a prostitute or harrassed by thugs or policemen whenever she stops. By allowing movement, the city allows the illusion of progress, but all movement here is construed as desperate, enervating, without direction or the possibility of change.

Such a view of the city finds a parallel in the threatening topography of sands, rivers, and stony ground that may exist anywhere and that encapsulate the barrenness we witness on the individual and social levels. The sands on which Lodz is built in *The Brothers Ashkenazi* indicate the tenuousness of Jewish life there.[37] The Black Sea, promising Fradkin transport to a new life, remains still and unaccommodating. Similarly, the sea and ships Bela Katz sees through the dirty windows of her New York office tease her with the promise of another world, but it emerges as a world possible only in fantasy ("Bela Saradatshi"). The river in which Fabian Reytses of "Altshtot" [Old city] drowns his cat does not point to the ebb and flow of life, but rather to the meaninglessness of existence. The Vistula—the body of water we encounter most often in the stories—is unpredictable and dangerous; it keeps hard-working Jews from reaching a Jewish community in time for the holidays ("A basherte zakh" [Something destined]). In the story "Friling" [Spring] it kills a man whose desire to reach home before Passover outweighs the obvious dangers of crossing a river that is too frozen to flow freely but too thawed to be crossed on foot. Nature seems to conspire against these Jews. Perhaps this is what Maurice Samuel had in mind in calling his translation of several Singer stories *The River Breaks Up*. The river of this book's title is, no doubt, the river of "Friling," its opening story, which allegorizes the dangers inherent in change and movement.

Even the weather of Singer's imagination is antagonistic, moving from harsh winters to equally unbearable summers without the benefit of transitional seasons. "Perl," the story that may be said to have established Singer's literary reputation, offers a rare harbinger of spring in the character of Moritz Shpilrayn. But (as in "Friling") we encounter only the antithesis of springtime imagery. Shpilrayn repeatedly gloats over his ability to survive yet another winter. Emerging from bed after a six-month hibernation, Shpilrayn dons his winter coat, takes the spittoon into which he constantly gazes for signs of blood, and by his appearance announces to his tenants that spring has come. He emerges to conduct his business affairs, but his primary activity is attending the funerals of less careful friends and giving the undertaker false alarms about his own demise. The months he spends in fear of setting foot outside his bed and the months he spends beyond this self-imposed confinement are equally marked by an inability to breathe freely the air around him. The tension in "Perl" lies in its use of illness as a central metaphor and the almost perverse health of its protagonist. Shpilrayn identifies himself as an invalid and thus sees mere existence as a triumph; in the process, he is unable to live in the world to which he clings.

The story offers a psychological view of a dilemma that Singer more typically examines in political and sociological terms. Sphilrayn internalizes the condition of paralysis that can emerge from habitual fear. He seems to anticipate the Jewish-life-as-disease metaphor that would become increasingly important to Singer during the Second World War. In this case, however, there is no external power or oppression that justifies his fear other than the inescapable threat of death. Elsewhere in Singer's writing, paralysis and aimless wandering are understood both as political necessities and as existential or psychological ones. Singer's understanding of time and history will also lead, like his construction of place and wandering, in increasingly confining directions. There is, Singer reminds us, nowhere to go from here.

THREE

The Past As Present

There is no private life that has not been
determined by a wider public life.

George Eliot, *Felix Holt, The Radical*

The relationship between historical events or movements and their literary representation is a central concern shared by critics of mainstream European and Yiddish fiction. When a strong sense of communal identity and continuity threatens to overwhelm private destiny, how do novelists claim a unique place for the individuals who people their work? How do they differentiate among various historical moments and the people who experience them? How, in more general terms, do we talk about historical consciousness as an independent and often problematic literary concern in modern novels? For Singer, the sweep of history is not merely the background against which the drama of individual lives is measured, but rather an active, dynamic literary presence as significant as character development, language, and form. History is understood as an independent, inexorable agent that—at least for the Jews—remains strikingly constant.

The temporal dimension is no more welcoming for the Jews of Singer's fiction than the spatial one that we have examined. Among his longer works, *The Brothers Ashkenazi* (1934–35) and *The Family Karnovski* (1940–41) are particularly revealing of Singer's struggle to probe the dynamics of Jewish history, individual fate, and the world history that subsumes and can overwhelm both.[1] In these novels, Singer explores the position of the Jews by trying to place them within the framework of European history. Jewish and world history are enacted in different, occasionally overlapping, but most typically conflicting symbolic universes. The Jews inhabit history-as-time and not history-as-process. Their history is marked by the passage of years and eras, but these periods are, if not quite interchangeable, certainly remarkably similar. Two structures separately order Jewish and non-Jewish history with surprisingly little mutual effect. World history proceeds more or less linearly, marked by the movement of people, ideas, and sociological forces. Events such as wars, mass migrations, or economic upheavals may repeat themselves in every generation, but change is inescapable; something new—however tenuous, or even degenerate —is always evolving. Jewish history, in Singer's representation, follows a different dynamic. It is inexorably cyclical, subject to erratic bouts of growth, progress, persecution, and decay, regardless of the externally different conditions under which Jews may live. It is, then, inherently unchanging in its repetition of these cycles.

World history is like a movie that one is seeing for the first time: there is no point at which we are meant to stop the film or return it to an earlier frame, and no two frames are exactly alike. The film is perceived as an ongoing process, and freezing it for closer scrutiny is clearly unnatural even if it proves useful in understanding its dynamics. Jewish history, on the other hand, can be encompassed in a continuously rewinding reel, always looping back upon itself; it may be juxtaposed against any moment of the ongoing film of world history without affecting either scene. In trying to understand the condition of the Jews by seeing them against the background of larger historical processes, Singer sees them as subject to different historical rules and structures, and he thereby removes them from that very process. Jewish characters can never fully enter world history and are indeed destroyed when they attempt to do so. Jewish historical consciousness is important because it may reveal this essential truth and thus prevent useless struggles.

In Singer's novels, cyclical time is not merely an inherited perception but, more profoundly, a result of the powerlessness of Jews in the modern world. For Singer, cyclicity is stagnation. As *Yoshe Kalb* has already made evident, the Jewish calendar and its attendant rituals underscore the inexorable and unrelenting nature of Jewish chronology. Beyond this lies the more disturbing circularity of Jewish experience. Singer rejects all linear views of Jewish history that might imply a movement toward a messianic age that will end the human need to act in history. Similarly, he rejects the secular version of messianic thinking implicit in the socialist or Zionist promise of redemption.

II

The Brothers Ashkenazi reveals the complexities of the dynamics governing Jewish and world history, highlighting the similarity of Jewish experience in every age. The title is somewhat misleading, implying a comparison between the twins whose name it bears but who are not, in fact, the novel's primary subject. Rather, the novel's focus is on the city of Lodz, beginning with the migration of German weavers to Poland after the Napoleonic wars and their settlement in what would become the center of a vast textile industry and a rapidly expanding Jewish population.[2] Lodz came to be called the Manchester of Poland. Central to its history in this novel is the history of capitalist development in a newly industrialized area. In the first pages of the novel, Singer traces the early settlement of Lodz by German craftsmen who are offered work and protection from taxes and conscription as an encouragement to come to Poland. Jewish settlement near, and finally in, Lodz is always precarious, even though it progresses steadily from an early stage of only a handful of tailors through the establishment of a substantial community with its own communal and religious institutions.

At the beginning, the growth of both the Jewish and non-Jewish communities seems to be intertwined: at some stages in the development of Lodz, the communities depend upon one another as models of progress; at others, the advancement of one is at the expense of the other. Jews learn the weaving trade from their exploitative German employers, imitate them, and eventually become employers in their own right, blurring distinctions between themselves and their non-Jewish counterparts. Jews force their way into economic and social positions despite attempts to keep them out. "Like a river in spring that overflows its banks and washes away all the dams and walls that would stop it, so did the Jews of Lodz and the surrounding towns and villages break through all the barriers placed in their way" (pp. 24–25).[3] Later in the novel, Jewish workers follow a similar path, adopting the ways of non-Jews from whom they learn about labor agitation and revolution. Capitalism and revolution seem to blur the distinctions between Jews and non-Jews, subsuming both under the same economic and historical forces. The communities are mutually exploitative, but while the evolution of employee into employer or worker into agitator is similar, Singer's literary focus suggests that Jews and non-Jews may not be following the same paths. The novel quickly loses sight of the non-Jewish characters, subsuming them under the broader view of Lodz and the disturbing effects of industrialization. The fate of individual Jewish characters, on the other hand, assumes symbolic significance, indicative of Jewish fate in general and particularly of the position of Jews who live according to the dynamics of the gentile world.

Singer presents a methodical if sketchy view of the growth of Lodz and its residents from its founding through the years following World War I. He traces the slow steps taken by individual manufacturers who begin by working their own handlooms and end up managing steam-operated factories. The growth of the city follows the same pattern of slow, inexorable steps from ramshackle neighborhoods built on the side of sandy roads to a crowded, booming metropolis. Singer has a similarly mechanical view of Jewish assimilation into the larger world that cannot be stemmed or even addressed by the Jewish community. A plague in the town is seen as resulting from God's anger over the neglect of Jewish ways, but where this might once have led to a ritualized attempt to ward off the punishment (as in *Yoshe Kalb*), it becomes only the source of lament. Jewish employers build factories similar to those built by their gentile neighbors. They keep their factories open six days a week, importing Christian managers who will not work on Sunday, and refusing to hire Jewish workers who cannot work on Saturday. They devise elaborate legal fictions to circumvent the religious injunction that should compel them to close their businesses on the Sabbath, but even those Jews willing to work on Saturday are rejected. Inevitably, this radicalizes many of the Jewish laborers, who are incapable of effecting any change. Singer uses often unnamed and insignificant individuals as paradigms for complex historical movements. One young Jew becomes an apprentice to a gentile master, and others follow suit;

another anonymous Jew slowly learns the ways of the gentiles, and again others follow him.

This reductive view of historical processes suggests that the developments we see in Lodz are inevitable and organic. Georg Lukacs identifies precisely such an organic view as reactionary because its determinism discourages individual attempts to initiate any kind of change. The course of history may change according to largely incomprehensible and inarticulated rules of its own, but the individual is a fixed entity, subject "merely [to] a change of costume."[4] Religious ecstasy, rationalist exegesis, capitalist enterprise, and socialist ideals are ultimately indistinguishable from one another in the effect they have on their adherents' lives. In *The Brothers Ashkenazi*, Jewish and world history run a parallel course only in this limited sense: the individual cannot affect history, regardless of the dynamic it follows.

Singer presents Simcha Meyer Ashkenazi, the elder twin, as a major challenge to this organic view of development. But in using him to offer such a challenge, Singer reveals that any other dynamic is unnatural. In transforming himself into Max Ashkenazi, Simcha Meyer is following the path toward acculturation taken by many, but the transformation is never successful. He cuts his hair and changes his clothes, his name, and even the language he speaks, but he cannot lose the signs of his youth as a hasid. They appear "on his face, in his every movement, in the crease of his German clothes. . . . As he used to do, he would talk to himself when deep in thought, tug at his beard, speak German in a singsong, answer (in the Jewish way) a question with a question, speak with half words and innuendos" (p. 260). Simcha Meyer/Max lives at odds with both the Jewish and secular worlds because he is perpetually fighting the natural course of events. Even as an infant, he did not take to his mother's breast as easily as his brother did, hurting her and prefiguring conflicts to come. Subsequent actions serve as examples of his greed and ambition, and manifest themselves in his inability to be content with any position he holds.

Max's misguided actions as a child and an adult are invariably attributed to his desire to advance too quickly. Recognizing the mechanics of individual and social progress, he wants to enter the process but skip some of the intervening stages. When others still prefer hand weaving, he adopts the new way of the machine and begins to prosper. Yet his understanding of modern technology and even his intuitive ability to anticipate the future of industrial advancement have little value in this novel because both are overshadowed by his personal greed and a dangerous indifference to Jewish and secular history. Rather than beginning with a few employees and working his way up, Max plots to take over an entire factory. He defies the law of organic growth not because he has a revolutionary ideal (as others in the novel do), but rather because his acquisitiveness leads him to disdain the path of evolutionary development in favor of self-aggrandizing acts of piracy. He displaces his father-in-law, his father, and eventually the German barons whose business he manages, taking over their factories and power. The order of these business takeovers points to Max's increasing degeneracy and to the disorder he embodies. The downfall of the German barons prefigures Max's own doom because here he enters a foreign world in which he seeks to function according to the same methods he has always followed. In the futile attempt to rule Lodz by advancing at a faster pace and on a larger scale than anyone else, Max shows that despite his many talents he is subject to dangerous self-delusion.

As an apparent contrast to Max, the younger twin, Yakov Bunem, follows a different arc of development that in the end serves only to underscore the basic, historically determined similarity between the brothers' fates. Yakov Bunem, or Yakub as he becomes, is all that his brother is not: healthy, generous, good-natured, basically happy. He is unambitious, almost haphazardly achieving positions that rival Max's. At different points each brother controls the city's largest factories and is dubbed "the King of Lodz." Yakub also enters the non-Jewish world by wearing its clothes and manners much more comfortably than Max does and by establishing his position through friendships with gentiles and relationships with wealthy women rather than through the more devious machinations used by his brother. Yakub moves congenially among Jewish converts to Christianity, as well as among Poles, Russians, and Germans. In ways that only become clear with his death near the end of the novel, his departure from Jewish norms is complete—and fatal.

Yakub dies at the hands of a sadistic Polish officer before whom he refuses to demean himself. Ignoring his brother's objections, Max grovels before this same officer, yelling "death to Leibush Trotsky" and then "death to all Jewish Leibushes," as he is commanded to do; he is told to dance and shout until he collapses (pp. 624–25). Yakub responds to the same orders with a dignified refusal, then lashes back at the officer when he is struck. The Yiddish critic B. Rivkin viewed this as a sign of heroism in which Yakub achieves a stature denied more cowardly souls.[5] Max has engaged in a pathetic, distasteful display. When his brother is killed, Max falls on the body of "his twin brother who had triumphed over him again, for the last time" (p. 626).[6] But within the context of this novel, it is impossible to attach heroic stature to Yakub in this scene. Heroism implies a plane of action and meaning that is antithetical to the terms in which Singer casts *The Brothers Ashkenazi*. Yakub's journey to Russia to rescue his long-estranged brother from a Soviet prison is successful and meaningful; his attempt at the Polish border to uphold his honor may not be. Max lives and has the final word on Yakub's actions:

> [Yakov-Bunem] followed the paths of the gentiles, upholding an idea of foolish, empty pride, and was destroyed by it. But it was senseless. A Jew should not adhere to empty gentile ways, to lose his life for foolish honor. When dogs attack a man there is no sense in the man's feeling degraded because of it. . . . Our forefathers did better by ignoring the gentile, paying as little attention to his insults and attacks as one does to a dog in the street. No, it was not worth it to lose one's life over such things. The strength of Israel does not lie in heroic acts, but in the mind and

reason. . . . For hundreds of years Jews sang and danced for the gentiles because they had to, because the murderers demanded it of them. When bitter times come to the Jews they should not destroy themselves, but placate the wild beasts for a while in order to survive and recover. (p. 632)

The third-person narration collapses into Max's internal monologue here as the novel moves toward its end and the plight of its Jews continues to defy resolution. Max's philosophical speculations are rarely as long and articulate as they are here, and in devoting pages to them, Singer seems to distance the narrative voice from this position, perhaps seeking to protect it as well from the pessimism and inexorability of this historical perspective on Jewish behavior. No other voice counters this perspective—to which, indeed, the entire novel has led—and it remains the only possible conclusion that Jews of any period can draw. Yakub and the Jewish revolutionaries in Lodz with whom he shares nothing else become different versions of a type that reappears in the novel and that epitomizes the situation of Jews who ignore their own past in favor of a wider perspective and other values, yet cannot shield themselves or come to terms with their fates. Yakub is, as Max recognizes, a most pitiful example of inescapable Jewish destiny. What Max does not go on to say, but the narrative implies, is that neither the submissive ways of his forefathers nor Yakub's active resistance makes much of a difference; both are subject to similar external forces. Yakub's way is more foolhardy and self-deluding, but Max's is no less precarious. It is not the inescapability of death that unites them, but the illusion that one can step out of one's assigned role.

Other Jewish characters and situations are contrasted in this way only to underscore their ultimate similarity. Several Yiddish critics have noted that, in *The Brothers Ashkenazi*, Singer constructs figures through opposition. M. Taykhman illustrates the impossibility of reconciliation between the dualistic worlds into which Singer places his characters.[7] Shmuel Niger describes a system of polarities in which each end is brought into sharper relief by its opposite.[8] The contrasts established in the novel seem to comment implicitly on one another, but the thrust of the novel is to reduce them to mere versions of one another and thus delimit even further the circumscribed world in which the Jews can act. Max and Yakub, the German manufacturer Huntze and his Jewish counterpart Flederboim, the Jewish revolutionary Nissan and his pious father, Max reading *Job* after Jakub's death just as his father had read it after Max's rejection of Judaism, the scenes of migration and movement that begin each of the novel's three parts—all point to a similar interpretation of the novel's parallel patterns. Nothing changes for the characters in the novel regardless of historical movements and ideological differences.

Singer's presentation of Nissan and his father is especially striking since the young rebel becomes a peculiar duplicate of his father, the *misnaged*, Reb Noske, with whom he is often explicitly compared. Nissan resembles his father physically and, like him, he is a true believer, reading voraciously, teaching, exhorting, and living with a messianic vision of the workers' revolution. "As his father had done with his holy books, so did he delve into his books, swallowing them, and, just like his father, he made notes in the margins of the books with small Russian letters, adding comments and questions" (p. 257). And when the Russian Revolution frees him from his prison in Petersburg, his faith is vindicated. "Like his father, the rabbi, who was always prepared for the moment of redemption, for the shofar blasts announcing the Messiah, so was Nissan prepared for the revolution, for the demise of the old capitalist order and the beginning of the new socialist one" (p. 511).

Nissan is also linked to his opponent, Max, because both the revolutionary and the capitalist understand the potential in the steam engine and seek to harness it to their own very different ends. The two are further linked in their opposition to their more conservative fathers, who refuse to adapt to the new industrial order. But neither the differences between Max and Nissan nor between Nissan and Reb Noske result in any sense of the different possibilities embodied in these opposing positions. Like Yakub and others, Nissan lives according to beliefs that are alien to the Jewish situation. In trying to enter Polish and Russian history and shape the future of class relations, he may have an admirable ideal, but he is no less fanatical than his father, no less ambitious in his own way than Max, and no more able to affect the future. Repeatedly, such active characters are subject to the same disappointments as their more passive brothers. Whether Russians, Germans, or Poles control Lodz, anti-Semitism is an active presence—worse under Polish rule, but always apparent to some degree. Workers' strikes, Polish emancipation, Russian military defeats and victories—all lead to pogroms, and no distinction is drawn among converted, assimilated, revolutionary, or traditionally religious and identifiable Jews as targets of persecution. Near the end of the novel, we see that for Jews the end of World War I, the Russian Revolution, and the establishment of an independent Poland do not lead to a new era, but rather conclude familiarly with the famous 1918 pogrom in Lemberg. The promises of religion as espoused by Reb Noske and the promises of Marxism as espoused by Nissan are equally illusory. Changes in the world do not lead to changes in the Jewish world.

The focal juxtaposition of the novel—between Max and the city of Lodz —is the most complex indicator of the different historical paradigms established in the novel. It is a peculiar kind of pairing, since it is not based on the apposition of characters, behavior, or ideas—as is typical of Singer's writing—but rather on the apposition of a person and a place. It is a lopsided juxtaposition in which the individual—Max—fares badly because as a nonheroic protagonist he cannot sustain the weight of comparison with Lodz. The city is not personified in this comparison, but Max is objectified by being rendered as a symbol of Jewish fate and history. The city becomes the paradigm for an analysis of historical development, while Max becomes a paradigm for a perspective on individual development. But that perspective is secondary to the novel's focus on history, and the narrative moves away from the individual to the broader view offered by the remarkable development of Lodz. Max's successes and failures naturally depend to some extent upon those of the city in which he lives. He reaps the benefits of growth, sees the collapse of his own empire when Lodz collapses, attempts to rebuild the industrial center in another location during World War I (Petersburg, now renamed Petrograd), and dies when all the tumult of Lodz is stilled. He, in turn, often serves as the prism through which we are exposed to what happens in Lodz. Workers' strikes are viewed through his reactions to them; new manufacturing techniques and styles are clarified through his perspective on them; characters may be hired, destroyed, exiled because of his political connections. He is thus the reader's mediator of the social and economic life of the city.

The novel is divided into three parts whose titles invoke the fate of Lodz and of Max. Part I, "Birth," opens with the birth of Lodz as a major industrial center and also describes the birth and development of the Ashkenazi twins. Part II, "Chimneys in the Sky," opens with the movement from Russia to Lodz during the period of Jewish migration following the assassination of Alexander II; Max, building his own empire, travels to Germany and Russia in pursuit of new technologies and workers. Part III, "Spiderwebs,"9 opens with the movement of German soldiers into conquered Russian territory; Max's empire is as flimsy as that of Lodz and as easily destroyed. The three parts articulate an increasing recognition of tenuousness as we move from birth to the smoke-stacks of the factories and of entrepreneurial dreams to the greater insubstantiality and sense of entrapment implied by spiderwebs. There is, typically, movement on a grand scale, which finally leads the characters nowhere at all. Max's death at the end of the novel signals the end of an era. "In Max Ashkenazi's end," says the narrative voice, "one saw the end of the city. In his funeral —the funeral of Lodz" (p. 667).

This final joining of the novel's two major presences invokes the opposing paradigms we have seen, even as it belies the thrust of the novel's historical sense. Singer's reliance on parallel structures appears here at the expense of his own underlying themes.10 Max's defeat, after all, is final not merely because he dies without leaving a significant legacy, but because he was unaware of the futility of his own attempts to control the city. Despite what the narrator says at this moment, the reader knows that Lodz has not died with Max; it has only entered another and most severe depression. The old men who follow Max to his grave bring us full circle to the novel's beginning scenes. "Dust to dust," they murmur, recalling the dust from which Lodz arose and the dust to which Max returns. The old Jews lament, "All that we built here was built on sand" (p. 668). Yet we recall that the novel began not with Max or with other Jews building on Jewish sands, but with German emigrés. It is not all that Lodz symbolizes which is dismissed as tenuous, but rather what the Jews built there. Lodz will never return to a preindustrial state; it will continue to undergo economic changes and upheaval so that even its apparent setbacks appear as part of the larger process of forward movement. The individual Jew, on the other hand, can only endlessly repeat Max's story, unaffected by the changes Lodz may encounter.

The stagnation implied by the circularity of Jewish experience is reflected throughout the narrative of *The Brothers Ashkenazi* as the development of a character's perspective within a scene yields to the omniscient narrator's comments and back again and as the separation of past from present becomes increasingly blurred. Past events and background information are narrated in the historical present tense. Yiddish prose readily lends itself to such a device, but it is especially pronounced in this novel, where its major effect is to imbue the present with a sense of ongoing time. Singer uses a comparable device in offering information about his characters and related events. He regularly opens chapters by placing us, in the historical present, within a specific scene; he then moves from within the scene back to a description of its personal and social past (still told in the present tense), and finally returns us to the scene itself. We see, for example, Tuvye in the synagogue organizing workers in a strike against Max's factory; we then learn the history of Tuvye's family, their poverty, the poverty around them, the people Tuvye attracts, and Nissan's support of his strike call before we return to the synagogue itself. Similarly, we are presented with the scene of Yakub en route to save his brother, then we move back to all the events, emotions, and character interrelations leading to this journey, and then forward to the journey itself. The past constantly intrudes upon the present, and it is often difficult to identify the moment at which the narrative enters a flashback or returns to the present. Covering an expanse of time and distance, the narrative, in effect, remains perfectly still.

On the semantic and structural level, Singer thus enacts the understanding of Jewish history that is at the novel's core. Serving as a countercurrent to this deliberate stasis is the non-Jewish world of revolution and politics. Here, the introduction of recognizable historical figures offers a strong contrast to the limited spheres in which Jewish revolutionaries or capitalists may act. As the revolution begins, the novel introduces us to the historical czar and czarina, the love letters they exchange while she engages in a romance with Rasputin, and the czar's dislike of political work in favor of leisure and his wife's company. Later, the leader of the Bolsheviks returns from exile and delivers fiery speeches calling for an end to World War I and devotion to the spread of communist ideals throughout the world; he is unnamed in the text, but in the two chapters in which he appears, the short, bald, charismatic orator is clearly understood to be Lenin.[11] The introduction of these world-historical individuals serves a number of functions. They are, as Lukacs identified such figures in *The Historical Novel*, the embodiment of various historical forces of the period who are able to voice the spirit of the age. Within this novel, they invoke the plane of real politics in all its severe limitations, but also in its breadth. Most pointedly, they reveal the contrast between significant action and the impotence of such figures as Max, Yakub, Nissan, Tuvye, and others. The czar and czarina are not heroic presences, but they do have real power. Similarly, even Lenin, despite his ruthless actions—and although he may be distanced and contained by remaining unnamed—enters the text as a sign cf those individuals whose presence makes a historical difference. As we have seen to be true with other non-Jewish characters, the narrative quickly loses sight of these figures. They have pointed to the broader world-historical plane of action in which none of the Jewish characters at the center of the novel can hope to function. The latter are never the objects of change or the signs of historical movement.

The historical novel, as Avrom Fleishman has indicated, tells the story of "how individual lives were shaped at specific moments of history, and how this shaping reveals the character of those historical periods." The individual, in this context, is "snatched up, without will or intention, into a great historical moment."[12] Marxist critics such as Lukács and Terry Eagleton view the author's ideological clarity and vitality as being a central determinant of the genre. The dynamics of social change must be at least comprehensible (if not subject to individual control) if there is to be an integrated fictional presentation of the tension between individual and social life.[13] In the case of *The Brothers Ashkenazi*, as in other fiction by Singer, this classic tension is recast into an opposition of Jewish and world history. Singer tries to come to terms not only with the tension between Jewish society and the Jew but also between Jewish society and its broader environment; similarly, it is not only world history and the individual that may be at odds but also the gentile and the Jew who are subject to a different historical dynamic. The "moments of history" that shape Singer's characters are moments of war, revolution, the creation of new economic and political systems. In synchronic terms, all the characters must encounter the same historical processes, but Singer interprets these processes in diachronic terms that differentiate the Jews from their non-Jewish compatriots. Viewed diachronically, the two communities cannot perceive their common temporality in similar ways and are compelled to write a different narrative about history. Jews cannot write the story of grand enterprise or change because they cannot be "snatched up . . . into a great historical moment" in the same way, all their moments being merely versions of the past. Yiddish critics such as M. Taykhman, who viewed *The Brothers Ashkenazi* as the "epopee" of Lodz or as the grand story of capitalism and revolution,[14] overlook the novel's primary concern with Jewish history. The focus of Singer's narrative shifts between the extraordinary changes of the period he is depicting and the equally extraordinary sameness of Jewish fate in all periods. No resolution of these multiple levels of tension is realized within this novel.

III

Invoking European family chronicles and the novels of Dickens, Zola, Flaubert, and Tolstoy, Irving Howe argues convincingly that it is not important to determine whether Singer modeled himself on these authors or developed parallel strategies because of parallel situations. Rather, what clearly emerges is that Singer "submitted himself to the *idea* of history," which may sweep individuals up into "vast, often incomprehensible historical forces which shape and break them."[15]

In significant ways, *The Family Karnovski* carries further the themes and structures of *The Brothers Ashkenazi*. The two titles hint at Singer's continued preoccupations: family connections suggest some element of continuity as he turns from an implied focus on two brothers to a supposedly more expansive view of three generations even as he contracts the span of time. The juxtaposition of these two novels also shows the extent to which Singer submitted himself to the ideas of history, to the conflicting dynamics of Jewish and world historical events.

The contrast between what A. A. Mendilow calls chronological and fictional time[16] points to a major difference in the conceptual framework of the novels. The distance between chronological time (the time of writing) and fictional time (the time described in the novel) decreases as fictional time itself decreases. In addition, *The Brothers Ashkenazi* begins with a historical account of the founding of Lodz, a period preceding the Ashkenazis. The focus on the twins, as we have seen, is overshadowed by the focus on Max and the city of Lodz, the latter viewed through more than a century of its history. The three Karnovski generations, on the other hand, are concentrated into half that fictional time, overlapping with one another and not framed by any view of time preceding their appearance on the scene. The brothers are traced from birth to death, a period of time approximating the number of years through which we are presented with all three Karnovski generations. In the family chronicle, then, Singer subverts expectations of a more expansive time frame, allowing its three generations no more time than he had allowed to one generation in the earlier novel. The action of *The Brothers Ashkenazi* ends some decade and a half before its publication in 1933–35; the action of *The Family Karnovski* ends almost at the moment of publication in 1940–41. Time in the later novel thus appears more cramped and even frenetic. Toward the novel's end, all sense of historical distance ends and, given the events it depicts, the present becomes disturbingly immediate. With no possibility of knowing exactly where current horror would lead, but with an almost paralyzing hopelessness, Singer tried to come to terms with the early moments of what we now call *khurbn*, or Holocaust.[17] His inability to do so may well be to his credit, since it points to his unwillingness to either romanticize or condemn Jewish life in response to its incomprehensible fate.

The three generations in *The Family Karnovski* trace the situation of Jews who live in the larger world. Foreshadowing a familiar Jewish response to the Holocaust, the novel dismisses the promise of the Enlightenment and, with it, all hopes for Jewish integration into the modern world, returning Jews instead to the situation of their ancestors. The novel is highly schematic in its presentation of place and character, following the Karnovskis from the Polish shtetl of Melnitz to Berlin and on to New York as its three parts trace the interactions between each of its three major characters and these three locations. Following a well-established convention of Yiddish fiction, the city embodies the possibilities of enlightenment, assimilation, anonymity, and radical alienation. The shtetl, here, is not a place of innocence and communal support but rather the locus of ignorance and superstition.[18] The eldest Karnovski, Dovid, flees the shtetl, and the narrative devotes very little space to the old world left behind. Dovid is a disciple of Moses Mendelssohn, a firm adherent of the Enlightenment battle cry insisting that one must be "a Jew at home and a man in the street." He becomes the model for an ideological position that his son will enact and whose viability will be repeatedly challenged until it is finally undermined in the novel. His son receives two names—a Jewish and a German one—to signal his membership in the two worlds, but the latter is given precedence. The name by which the child will be called to the Torah is Moshe, after Mendelssohn, but he will be known as Georg, a German adaptation of Dovid's father's name, Gershon. Raised to be a man in the street, Georg learns in childhood that he is considered a Jew there, too, and that the kind of equilibrium he has been trained to seek cannot be found. Georg's rejection of his father's "golden mean" (p. 12),[19] his marriage to a gentile, and the escalating anti-Semitism in Germany destroy Dovid's faith in Mendelssohn's ideals. The Jew he most admires, Reb Ephraim, cannot traverse the middle road either. Reb Ephraim's life's work involves two impossible projects: one, a Hebrew compendium to the Jerusalem and Babylonian Talmuds, and the other, a German book explaining Jewry to the world. Reb Ephraim is more firmly rooted in the traditional Jewish world than is Dovid, but he cannot successfully transmit his ideals and is not allowed to live by them.

Georg is thrust back into the Jewish world by the Germans among whom he has lived intimately. Having served as a doctor during World War I and then as a respected obstetrician in Berlin, Georg discovers that he is no different from his father, Reb Ephraim, or his forefathers. When the Nazis forbid him to practice medicine, he seeks out his father, with whom he has had no direct contact since his apostasy, and says: "There is no longer any reason for us to quarrel. . . . Now we are all equally Jews" (p. 273). Even more poignant is the job he finally takes after he arrives in New York. Like the peddlers who were his ancestors, Georg becomes a traveling salesman, once again explicitly and bitterly (the adverb is used in both statements by Georg) commenting on Jewish destiny: "This is our national profession through the generations," Georg says, "this our fate. . . . And one's fate cannot be avoided" (p. 463). The fate he laments is no longer Nazi persecution or even more benign American modes of discrimination, but the inexorability of Jewish destiny.

His own son, Yegor, embodies these tensions in more radical ways, moving further from Georg than Georg did from Dovid, or Dovid from his own father. Yegor is the most extreme expression of the failure of the golden mean. Spiritually, he is far removed from Enlightenment attempts to be both a Jew and a citizen of the world, but he bears the marks of the combination on his body. A physical mixture of his Jewish father and German mother, circumcised by his father without any attending ceremony, Yegor cannot erase the marks of Judaism he despises in himself. This unhappy physical presence propels the novel to its conclusion. Yegor responds to an insult on the body he has himself despised by killing the Nazi who has made homosexual advances to him and

then fleeing home to shoot himself at his father's doorstep. Exceedingly melodramatic, the novel ends with Georg performing emergency surgery on his
now calm and loving son.

Dovid, Georg, and Yegor traverse a similar but increasingly disastrous course
of alienation from other Jews, the surrounding community, and even themselves. The danger they face is imposed primarily from without—by overt,
brutal Nazi anti-Semitism—but it is also the result of their own desire to enter
the non-Jewish world. Ironically, the farther they move into that world, the
more difficult is their adjustment to New York, the only truly open society
depicted in the novel. Given the conventional wisdom about assimilation, it
is perhaps surprising that the younger generation in this novel has a much
harder time adjusting to America than the older. Dovid becomes a *shames* [syna-
gogue warden] in New York, perfectly content to return to the lifestyle he
had vehemently rejected in Melnitz; Georg, as we have seen, becomes a peddler,
bitterly reconciled to his fate and able to function within it; Yegor's loathing
for his own Jewishness leads him first to work for a Nazi group in New York
and, finally, to return to his father severely wounded and with an uncertain
future. Each generation surpasses its predecessor in trying to accept the life
of the larger world, and thus each finds the inevitable return to Jewish fate
increasingly difficult. Only a minor character like Solomon Burak can live without unbearable tension and only because he embodies Jewish historical consciousness by adjusting to historical exigencies without allowing them to affect
him. He effectively manipulates his way in the business and social world while
keeping Melnitz alive in his home and in every aspect of his life. He adjusts
to the changes in the world with indomitable good nature because in his inner
being he remains independent of them. The Karnovskis, on the other hand,
are subject to the tension born of their desire to enter the world of change
that is the non-Jewish world.

These tensions find their symbolic expression in two areas that are curiously
linked in the novel: language and sexuality. The question of language is sub-
sumed and eventually rendered subordinate to that of sexuality, but the two
are united by the potential of great power and degeneracy associated with each
of them. Sexuality is the sign of both modern, enlightened ideals and the perversion to which modernity, with its perceived lack of order and decorum, may
lead. Just as the city signifies the possibility of freedom and alienation, so,
too, do sexuality and the use of various languages—Yiddish, Hebrew, German,
English—reflect a similar tension about Enlightenment ideals and the entrance
into the modern world that they encourage. Yiddish is a symbol of the antithesis
of these ideals, associated with the Old World and its ways and viewed in
Enlightenment literature as a retarding force. Dovid Karnovski follows his mentor, Mendelssohn, in eradicating Yiddish. He learns a stilted German and chas-
tises his wife, Leah, for her poor mastery of the language. Leah speaks Yiddish
to her son, tries to teach him Hebrew prayers, and is mocked by Georg for
her efforts. In making love to his wife, Dovid loses himself in passion, momen-

tarily forgetting his stature in the community and the pose he assumes there. But he does not forget to speak German, and the terms of endearment he utters are alien and even insulting to Leah, who feels no love in them (p. 21). In the very act of love, the foreign language intrudes to separate and alienate. Yiddish, relegated to being the language of home and the feminine, is subdued and fully overpowered by German.

The tension among languages on this level has already been resolved for Georg. In New York, Georg struggles to learn English in order to obtain work; that struggle, however, is rendered not in symbolic, but in quite pragmatic, terms. With Georg, sexuality has replaced language as the sign of a mature acceptance of the modern world. Disgusted by what he inchoately perceives as the homosexual advances of a young Christian friend, the adolescent Georg seeks the embraces of the family maid, who becomes the first of many lovers. She signals his necessary separation from the world of his parents into a healthy sexuality and, at the same time, initiates his gradual movement into the world of beer halls, student clubs, and sexual license. He becomes an obstetrician, rejecting the decadence he has witnessed but not his desire to be surrounded by women. His profession is overloaded with painful symbolic ironies. What is a Jewish doctor to do in the 1930s? For Jews, birth is no longer a hopeful sign pointing toward the future and continuity; we know the fate awaiting these mothers and babies. The Nazis force Georg, who administers to non-Jews, to leave his practice. Labor is denied to him—both his own labor and his ability to assist in the labor of childbirth. There is an ongoing struggle in Georg between an inclination toward a stable world of study, medicine, and devotion to a beloved woman and the family and an opposing attraction for many nameless women and their adulation. This struggle is not so much re-solved in favor of the former as it is dissipated by the pressure of historical events as they begin to engulf German Jews. Within the novel, it is also dissipated structurally by the shift in focus from Georg to his son, Yegor.

The shift to Yegor signals an unequivocal rejection of the goals toward which Dovid's espousal of Mendelssohn have led. Enlightenment, which has secula-rized the idea of the Messiah and seen deliverance in education and accultura-tion, is reduced to yet another ideational delusion. In his German school— the locus of Enlightenment hopes—Yegor becomes the subject of a biology lesson in which he is forced to strip and is then measured from head to toe in order to show the "scientific" bases of racial inferiority. The principal who subjects Yegor to such treatment is a precursor of the American Nazi who makes homosexual advances to him: both are weak, unpopular, effeminate. The promise of Enlightenment is thus belied by the power of the Nazis, which, in turn, is symbolically contained in the novel by sexual images of impotence and shamefulness. Singer constructs homosexuality as the sign of political and social degeneration, and locates it within German culture as if to counter the myth of manly strength that his characters associate with Germany. In *The Brothers Ashkenazi*, a blustering, ruthless, inept German officer who rules Lodz signals his powerlessness by fondling a young lieutenant (p. 474). Similar scenes appear in *The Family Karnovski* as first Georg and then Yegor are repelled by this hidden side of German culture.

Yegor, assuming the role of the faithful German, hates his own body and clings to his non-Jewish mother, Theresa; he cannot adjust to English in New York and continues to speak it in a highly stilted manner that sets him apart from his schoolmates. His racial theories are dismissed in New York as being simply "nuts," and the principal of this school advises masturbation as an anti-dote to these perverse ideas (pp. 411–12). Yegor seeks instead the company of other young Germans in New York, fleeing his home and all reminders of his father's Jewish past. Before he returns home, he is deserted by these friends, reduced to pawning all his possessions, and forced to suffer insults at the hands of his former Nazi employer. At the end, wounded and in a dependent, childlike state, he finally returns to his father, recognizing the love that has always awaited him.

The terror of contemporary history and politics in *The Family Karnovski* is displaced onto the more comprehensible and symbolically accessible view of the constraints of language and the body. Horror is controlled in the novel when it is figured in the person of Yegor, a disturbed adolescent who confronts public tragedy in the form of personal trauma. The public and private are linked in the symbolic system of illness as the hysteria of the historical moment is rendered through the psychic disorder of a boy confronted by the allure of belonging and the inescapable marks of otherness. Yegor functions met-onymically as a sign of Jewish history, but our focus on him deflects the more desperate view of a wider social illness over which there can be no control and which Jewish history has proven to be incurable. In other words, since history is too overwhelming in this novel, there is a shift to the individual whose progress and fate may, at least theoretically, be encompassed by the novel. That shift is also a disturbing indication of the ideological despair we have already seen in Singer's fiction because (as in *Yoshe Kalb*) psychology of-fers no clearer epistemology than politics, sociology, or history.

IV

The novel's bathetic conclusion supports the views of theorists such as Lukács and Eagleton who, as we have seen, suggest that an integrated fictional presen-tation of public and private tensions cannot be achieved without a certain de-gree of ideological vitality. The difficulties Singer faced are revealed in an ex-change with Abraham Cahan about the novel's ending. Singer could not find a way out of this novel, could not decide what to do with the family whose generations he had brought to this awful moment in history. When he sent the manuscript to Cahan (September 26, 1940) for serialization in the *Forverts*, only the first two parts were complete. In a telegram sent to Cahan three weeks later (October 15, 1940), Singer outlined the ending he had in mind. Singer was in California at the time, and this is one of the rare exchanges he was forced to conduct in English. The telegram format serves to punctuate the sensational conclusion Singer proposed.

YEGOR POISONED MORALLY AND PHYSICALLY BECOMES ENTANGLED IN NAZI CIRCLES PLAYING THE ARIANS [sic] STOP BEING DISCOVERED AND HUMILIATED KILLS HIS TORMENTOR STOP IN DESPAIR COMES TO FATHER FOR HELP BUT IT IS TOO LATE STOP DOCTOR KARNOFSKY LULLES [sic] TO DEATH WITH CHLORIFORM [sic] YEGOR THERESA AND HIMSELF STOP COMPRESSED IS PICTURED THE RISE OF SOLOMON BURACK FAMILY THE SYMBOL OF ETERNAL VITALITY AND OPTIMISM STOP

Cahan was not impressed. He remarked that "the poisoning business sounds like a cheap trick" and advised Singer to drop that ending and substitute one in which Yegor becomes "an ardent Jew, a Nazi hater" (October 16, 1940). Offended by Cahan's letter, Singer responded (October 16) by saying that Cahan had "misunderstood the word poisoned" which he claimed to be using in a metaphoric sense. "My reputation is a guarantee against cheap stuff," he wrote. "I have my ideas based on psychology, not on murder effects. I am responsible for my writing. Please leave it to me." On December 24, he wrote to Ravitch, complaining of his seemingly endless revisions leading nowhere. One month later (January 25, 1941) Cahan wrote again, asking for the continuation of the novel, since he had only one hundred pages of the manuscript left to print. The ending that finally appeared in the *Forverts* is vaguer and less melodramatic than the ending he had outlined a few months earlier. The narrative does not reveal whether Yegor will die, or what his return to his father's doorstep signifies, or whether his killing of the Nazi may be seen as a symbolic reassertion of Jewish identity. Its uncertainties are not the sign of open-endedness, but of the difficulty in conceiving of a coherent conclusion to the conflicting terms of the novel.

In part, Singer's energies were directed elsewhere. Letters written during these months are full of increasing concern about his family's fate and the obvious Nazi menace. Finding a literary resolution to the conflicts within the Karnovski family paled beside the onslaught of historical events that, in quite personal and immediate ways, were proving the powerlessness of the individual.[20] But the problem of closure in *The Family Karnovski* is not simply a result of compositional circumstances. It reflects a more general problem of meaning that can be discerned in Singer's fiction. The sense of his endings points to this more disturbing problem. Death and the repetition of Jewish history are the only conclusions toward which Singer's fictions move; in neither can we discern a future consonant with a meaningful past because every conceivable structure of meaning has been negated in the fiction. The cyclical nature of Jewish history offers no solace in its familiarity or predictability, despite Paul Ricoeur's reminder that "repetition is a kind of resurrection of the dead."[21]

In Singer's fiction, repetition is accompanied by the rejection of both familiar and bold new systems that might provide a teleological framework in which any kind of resurrection makes sense. Anomie, uncertainty, and despair accompany both the repetition and rejection, and that is how the novels end.

Singer's beginnings offer another curious view of a similar problem. Often he begins with a prepositional phrase that serves to delay the introduction of the main character or action. This is especially pronounced in novels and stories written in New York in the second half of his career. *Steel and Iron* opens with the name of its protagonist and a description of him; the next four novels open with prepositions. Of the eleven stories in *Perl* (1922 [Pearls]), four begin with prepositions, as do three of the stories in *Af fremder erd* (1925 [On Foreign Ground]); *Friling* (1937 [Spring]), the first collection of stories composed in America, contains five stories, each of which has a prepositional opening; the same is true of six of the eight stories appearing in the posthumous volume, *Dertseylungen* (1949 [Stories]).

The prepositions vary, but their symbolic weight is striking, pointing to an increasing hesitation about introducing a character and plot. The opening sentences of Singer's last four novels indicate the extent to which this stylistic choice encourages the passive voice and delays the action:

> *Yoshe Kalb*: In groysn Galitsishn gut-yidishn hoyf, baym rebn R' Melekh fun Nyeshave, hot men zikh gegreyt gor shtark tsu der khasene fun rebns tokhter Serele. [In the large Galician hasidic court of Rabbi Melekh of Nyesheve, they were energetically preparing for the wedding of the Rabbi's daughter, Serele.]
>
> *The Brothers Ashkenazi*: Af di zamdike vegn fun Zaksn un Shlezye keyn Poyln, durkh velder, derfer un shtetlekh, khoreve un opgebrente nokh der Napoleonisher milkhome, hobn zikh getsoygn eyns nokh s'andere furn mit mener, vayber, kinder un zakhn. [On the sandy roads from Saxony and Silesia to Poland, through forests, towns and villages, ravaged and burned after the Napoleonic wars, stretched, one after the other, carriages with men, women, children, and goods.]
>
> *Comrade Nakhmen*: Khotsh es iz nokh fri un fun di lange shotns fun di beymer ken men zen, az es iz nokh hipsh vayt tsu mitog-sho, sreyfet shoyn di zun mit a helish fayer di flakhe Poylishe erd. [Although it is still early and from the long shadows of the trees one can see that it is still a long time before noon, the sun already burns the flat Polish earth with a bright fire.]
>
> *The Family Karnovski*: Vegn di Karnovskis fun Groys-Poyln hot men gevust, az zey zaynen akshonim un tsulakhesnikes, ober derfar lomdim un keners, mamesh ayzerne kep. [About the Karnovskis of Greater Poland it was known that they were stubborn and contrary, but therefore scholars and knowledgeable men, with heads as strong as iron.]

These prepositional beginnings are the semantic correlatives of the pervasive stagnation we have already encountered. Grammatically, they delay the verb and the use of any tense. They are inactive joiners hinting at uncertainty, at a reluctance to enter a story that cannot be concluded or even to name its subject and verb. Although it is perhaps tempting to view these beginnings, *in medias res*, as invoking an epic element in the stories, in tone and scope they are as remote as possible from the prepositional phrase that introduces mythic time—"In the beginning." In Singer's fiction, starting in the middle suggests hesitation, the undifferentiated nature of time, and the sameness of every moment. In highlighting a broader social, temporal, or natural scene as they typically do, these prepositional beginnings—like the scenes of migration, revolution, war, or seasonal and historical transitions that they often introduce—hint at the epic which is *not* their subject. Measured against the background of such purposefully unrealized epic possibilities, the characters we encounter and the situations in which they find themselves seem limited indeed. History may have an epic dimension, but individuals and, more pointedly, the Jews in Singer's fiction cannot inhabit or comprehend that dimension even when it frames their stories.

Singer's Jews always seem to live in the middle of a historical tale that is not really theirs to tell. Individuals can, at best, hope to recognize their situation but not to alter it. That very recognition implies a degree of self-awareness that is highly valued in Singer's narratives. Subject to a different constellation of historical patterns than the rest of the world, Jews cannot expect to move in tandem with worldwide movements. Singer's most painful lament is not that the Jews are doomed to destruction, but rather that they are doomed to endless repetition.

FOUR

Fictions of the Self

> . . . the world, which seems
> To lie before us like a land of dreams,
> So various, so beautiful, so new,
> Hath really neither joy, nor love, nor light,
> Nor certitude, nor peace, nor help for pain;
> And we are here as on a darkling plain
> Swept with confused alarms of struggle and flight,
> Where ignorant armies clash by night.
>
> Matthew Arnold, "Dover Beach"

Discontinuity marks the presentation of the individual and the self in Singer's fiction. Character development, like the exposition of place, time, and history, follows a narrative pattern that undermines the heroism, causality, and significance it invokes. How are we to construe the individual who is faced with both the expansive promises of modernity and the repetitions of Jewish historical tragedies? What can individual development mean in an inexorably circular world? How can a Jew, in particular, progress toward any goal or position independent of collective fate? How can the private self be differentiated from its public surroundings?

In his narratives, Singer evinces a desire to shield the inner life from the unbearable pressures of communal life and history. Interest in the inner life is tempered by a suspicion that its dynamics do not explain or even adequately confront basic existential questions. In effect, Singer separates the idea of the individual from that of the self. The two terms operate in different spheres and along intersecting but distinct axes. The "individual" functions in the social world, affected—usually adversely—by it, the product of a particular political and historical moment, subject to a set of established customs and norms. The "self" is a psychological entity that seeks independence from the individual's condition, is weakened by that condition, and yearns for uniqueness. One way to protect the individual from the pressures of the external, material world is to confuse or, more radically, destroy all sense of the self that may be subject to them. If the self is presented as indeterminate, severed from a comprehensible sense of order and development, then, Singer's narratives suggest, one may hope for independence from an environment that can be neither controlled nor affected by individual behavior. "Severance" and "independence" are not used as psychological terms in the fiction, but they are commonly figured by the characters' movements between the traditional Jewish world and the modern secular world and their inability to be fully anchored in either.

Discontinuity of character and plot are structural signs of the tension between individual and self in Singer's texts. Singer can, in fact, construct characters only by losing sight of, or obscuring, certain textual unities in ways that are usually considered unacceptable in realistic fiction. Yoshe Kalb, the most remarkably discontinuous of his protagonists, has already shown us that integrity is only imaginable for the self when it is independent of the social and religious world that would contain it. But such independence is not possible. The focus of Singer's narratives lies more in the public world, in the arenas of politics and economics—Jewish and non-Jewish—than in the self. An interest in character development is overtaken by the concern with historical situations.

Individual existence—particularly Jewish existence—in Singer's fictional universe is tenuous because it is utterly powerless. The confrontation with modernity underscores this despite the desirable alternative it provides to traditional Judaism. "Tshuve" [Repentance], a story appearing in Singer's first collection, presents his starkest, most uncompromising view of religious Jews. The story illustrates why Singer never considered traditional Judaism as an antidote to modern secularism. "Tshuve" tells of a *misnaged* [antihasidic Orthodox Jew] who practices abstinence from all sensual things and yet is beset by sinful thoughts about the temptations of the physical world. Reb Naphtali travels to the court of a hasidic leader who teaches him that true repentance is only possible if one partakes of the joys of the world, surrounding oneself with food, luxuries, and sensual pleasures. The hasid, Reb Ezekiel, feeds the stern *misnaged*, encouraging him to drink, sing, and rest. When Yom Kippur, the Day of Atonement, ends, Reb Ezekiel joyously extends his hand to Reb Naphtali as if to lead him in dance. At that moment Reb Naphtali falls dead at his feet. Reb Ezekiel continues the interrupted celebration, concluding that his visitor was too steeped in gloomy habits to be saved even by his religious fervor.

What may at first appear to be an affirmation of the popular, celebratory hasidic style is, on closer reading, a story that denigrates both sides in the dispute. Reb Ezekiel is a glutton, a huge man with little learning who leads his followers into the kinds of excesses Singer always disdained. He is overpowering in his teachings, and the power he wields is deadly. Reb Naphtali, unable to enjoy either an ascetic existence or an indulgent one, fares no better. Obsessed with the idea of sin, Reb Naphtali cannot live in the real world. Reb Ezekiel is only considered a worthy leader by a limited number of misguided enthusiasts. Neither misnagdim nor hasidim ultimately have anything to teach us. As he said about the problem of a place for Jews in the modern world, Singer describes a diagnosis here, but not a cure.

Singer's major protagonists do not pursue a traditional religious life in the enclosed communities that make such a life possible. Repeatedly, he presents us with Jewish men who function in the secular, modern world of business, politics, or culture, far removed from the communal structures in which they have been raised. This movement from religious to secular life is not presented as a matter of personal choice or tension. It may be desirable; what is more important is that it is inevitable. The psychic upheaval such movement entails is rarely the subject of Singer's narratives. As we have already seen in *The Brothers Ashkenazi* and *The Family Karnovski*, the inverse direction—back to Jewish identity—is more often an important source of conflict and reconciliation. But any movement back to traditional Jewish identity is highly problematic in Singer's fiction. It cannot fully be achieved, since it would imply a rejection of modernity that Singer could not imagine. The individual cannot resist the power of modernity, but, as we have seen, the Jew cannot be fully integrated into it.

II

In Singer's fiction, individual fate is portrayed as being overdetermined by social and political constraints. His 1938 novel, *Khaver Nakhmen* [Comrade Nakhmen], depicts these external forces as they destroy its protagonist's belief in personal and communal enlightenment. The long-awaited son of an impoverished family with many daughters, Nakhmen grows into class consciousness and revolutionary activity. But there is no place for him in either the Jewish world of learning that his father wants him to enter or the workers' causes he tries to promote. *Comrade Nakhmen* is a particularly appropriate novel to consider in exploring the tensions in Singer's development of character. Even in its title, the novel proclaims its focus on one man's development. It also proclaims a political dimension: Nakhmen's adherence to Communist ideology. A bildungsroman that ends with a desperate vision of its protagonist's failure to overcome the fallacies of collective and messianic thinking, *Comrade Nakhmen* rejects not only the social and political choices of its day but also the private retreats of the individual. Home, family, love, learning, and work are stripped of meaning in this relentlessly bleak novel.

Comrade Nakhmen is an uncompromising rejection of Soviet communism, exposing the hypocrisy and corruption of its leaders. The novel asserts that differences of class and status are only exacerbated under a political system that, in effect, isolates individuals from the sources of political power and from one another. Y. Y. Trunk may have gone too far in calling the novel a "revised epilogue to *Steel and Iron*";[1] it carries further the earlier novel's critique of socialism and the hypocrisy with which it is promulgated, but Singer's novels are consistent in maintaining this political stance. Written under the influence of the first wave of Stalinist purges, *Comrade Nakhmen* might also be seen as a radical continuation of *Yoshe Kalb*'s depiction of corrupt external powers from which the individual can never be free.

In theme and structure, the novel appears to pit traditional Judaism against modern social activism, moving inexorably to Marxism and then to the failure of that—and, by implication, all—ideology. *Comrade Nakhmen* follows the three-part structure favored by Singer in each of his novels. The structure is suggestive, inviting several modes of reading, all of which the narrative subverts in its conclusion. In its tripartite division, the plot seems to exhibit a dialectical structure that parallels the political and historical reasoning of its characters as they accept Marxist ideology. This division also parallels the structure of logical arguments, particularly of syllogistic or deductive reasoning. By such formal devices, the novel announces that its conclusions are inevitable, based on familiar, dispassionate philosophical procedures. As the novel unfolds, readers are invited to anticipate some resolution between the traditional, impoverished Jewish life witnessed in the first part and Nakhmen's dawning political consciousness. By the novel's end, however, all hope of resolution has been destroyed, undermining even further the dialectical thinking that has encouraged it.

The geographical and thematic focus of each of the novel's parts follows this structural dynamic. The novel begins shortly after the turn of the century and ends in the 1930s. The first part, introducing Nakhmen's traditional home and education in the shtetl of Piask, ends with the family's move to Warsaw in flight from the public embarrassment caused when his sister gives birth to an illegitimate child. The second part begins with the mobilization of Mattes, Nakhmen's father, into the czar's army and ends when Nakhmen is imprisoned for revolutionary activities in Poland. In the third part, Nakhmen smuggles himself into the Soviet Union, only to suffer under the Communist rule he has long sought. The movement from the shtetl governed by Jewish law, to Warsaw and the rule of labor and politics, and finally to Soviet communism parallels the historical path followed by many Jews. It is not a movement from the particular to the general or even from bad to worse. Rather, the novel traces a trajectory along equally untenable positions. Each is marked by the anonymity of the individual in all aspects of life—familial, sexual, political, economic—and by the absence of meaningful change in place or time. *Comrade Nakhmen* carries these themes further than Singer's earlier novels, at once individuating them and expanding them beyond the Jewish world in which his imagination had once firmly rooted them. The situation of the Jews is now offered as paradigmatic, representative of what individuals encounter in both traditional and modern spheres. Jews must still face the additional burdens of internal strictures and external prejudice, but rather than making them an exception in world history, this only serves to make the Jews a more fitting vehicle for Singer's broader concerns in this novel.

There can be no successful hero of a story in which there are no reasonable choices to be made. Nakhmen is virtually a caricature of misfortune in the novel, unfortunate in birth and training, disappointed in love and politics, always poor, an active man who attempts to take his fate and that of his class into his own hands, but who becomes the dupe of various powerful individuals and social forces. Even Nakhmen's name proves ironic. He is born after Tisha b' Av, the fast day commemorating the destruction of the First and Second

Temples, and on the eve of Shabbos Nakhamu, the Sabbath of Consolation, so called because of the first words of Isaiah 40 read on that day: "Comfort [*Nakhamu*], comfort ye My people." He is not named after his deceased grandfather, as custom would dictate, but for the day, as a sign of the consolation he may (but does not) bring his father.

Nakhmen, who enters the novel in the second chapter, is a sickly child, his physical weakness a correlative of the tone and setting established in the novel's opening. In the first chapter, his father Mattes, a ragpicker who barters whatever he can through neighboring villages, is introduced in the motionless, burning Polish sun, looking for a place to turn off the road where he can quietly say his morning prayers and eat his meager breakfast. Surrounded by filth and taunted by hostile shepherds, Mattes believes that "because of the sins of our fathers, who left the ways of Israel to serve foreign gods, Jews were driven into exile among people who mocked and shamed them" (p. 11).[2] The irony of the exilic theme only becomes clear later in the novel when Nakhmen leaves Poland and is exiled from the Soviet Union through no sin of his own, his father's, or the Jews. Mattes is faithful to Jewish ritual and law, but his suffering is not eased within his own community, where poverty makes him nearly anonymous, literally and symbolically unrecognized in his own synagogue, where he is mocked as a man who can only sire girls and then barely feed them. In Piask for the Sabbath, he stands near the door of the synagogue (the least prestigious spot), dressed in ill-fitting, patched clothes, and then goes home to a haggard wife and to a bed shared with their children.

In various ways, the subsequent narrative echoes the theme of the individual's inconsequential nature introduced with Mattes. Characters are brutally reduced, symbolically or, in several cases, literally stripped of the social and personal trappings that might identify them. Sartorial metonymys most often convey this process. Mattes appears in synagogue in clothes that would be comic if not for the misery they bespeak:

> With boots polished with pitch to hide their patches and holes, with his blackish, patched shirt, buttoned with its colored button, with a greenish, tight Sabbath coat he had outgrown since his wedding, with buttons of every size and color, with patches sewn onto his elbows, he went to the synagogue. (p. 15)

He goes off to war in a comparable outfit of "old, wrinkled, soiled, and oversized" clothes (p. 118). And when Mattes dies in his first battle, the Jewish ritual garments he has taken care to wear do not save him from burial in a mass grave topped with a makeshift cross.

Nakhmen's clothes are also the sign of his lowly status. As a child, he must wear his mother's shoes while she works to buy him his own pair. As a young student, he is literally a misfit, wearing beggared clothes: "a coat that is too large, a pair of pants that are too short, a pair of run-down shoes, a ritual undergarment whose fringes are knotted from too much washing, and a worn, once-silken hat" (p. 77). Apprenticed to a baker in Warsaw, he is told to shed his traditional garb, and after three years, he is able to buy his first set of cheap new clothes. Like his father before him, Nakhmen enters the military in an outfit which suggests that national—in this case, Polish—identity is as vague and amalgamated a construct as personal identity; he wears French shoes and a Polish hat, and he carries an Austrian rifle (p. 165). He has lived under Russian, German, and Polish rule in Warsaw, each regime marked only by a change of costume, language, and symbols. The sartorial code, which is central to the semiotics of Jewish mobility from traditional Jewish into modern European culture, is stripped of its significance. Returning from the army, Nakhmen is arrested for revolutionary activities and is tortured in prison. He fears being left naked more than anything else because "as long as he is dressed, he believes, he is protected" (p. 212). But while clothes may identify the Jew or the poor man, they are entirely without power in conferring protection or dignity.

Sexuality, too, signals a degrading powerlessness. The portrayal of Nakhmen's parents introduces this theme in the novel's first chapter. Mattes sleeps in a bed surrounded by some of his children while his wife lies with the rest of the children in her bed. Having waited for the children to fall asleep, Mattes quietly disentangles himself from the arms and legs around him, and crosses the room to his wife's bed. "Restraining her breath so as not to awaken the children lying near her, Sara greeted him and surrendered to him her over-worked, prematurely withered and haggard body" (p. 17). Sara bears a child every year and dies in childbirth before she is thirty, leaving Nakhmen and an unspecified number of daughters. Their number is only hinted at after Mattes remarries and his new wife brings three bagels home so that each child can be given half of one. This shrewish wife is a fairy-tale version of the bad step-mother, tormenting Nakhmen, his sisters, and father before deserting them all. Mattes, having only agreed to the wedding because he was drunk, consum-mates this marriage in a rare moment of energy: "Mattes suddenly forgot all the sorrows of his life in the softness and warmth that engulfed him. His bride laughed wantonly and wildly" (p. 41). The scene ends not with the couple but with the smells and sounds of the bride's father, asleep in the same room. Singer establishes an economy of sexuality in these scenes where poverty pre-cludes privacy, enforcing restraint and silence. Passion may be a relief from excessive, unrewarding labor, yet it cannot be fully or freely spent, and it pro-duces equivocal results. The labor of childbirth and the burden of large families that almost invariably ensue from passion are constructed as equally excessive and unrewarding.

Only two of Nakhmen's sisters are named in the novel. As they enter the economic and social life of Warsaw, they become typical female victims of the sexual economy that Singer introduces through their parents. The eldest, Sheyndl, leaves Piask and her role as surrogate mother to her younger siblings in order to earn money in the city. She is confused by the sexual advances of the coachman who drives her to Warsaw, the baker in whose house she works, and his apprentices. She is surrounded by signs of physicality and ripe-ness—in her own body, in the appetites of the men in the house, in the very bread they bake. Illiteracy does not protect her from the kind of escapism that, in another place and time, is associated with romantic fiction: she decorates the corner in which she sleeps with magazine pictures of loving couples engaged in the kinds of romances for which she yearns. She is wooed by a lively, charm-ing Jewish soldier from Russia just before he leaves Warsaw, succumbing to him "in shame, pain, and the greatest pleasure in the world" (p. 96). Pregnant, she returns to Piask. She hopes to induce an abortion but instead hides in the courtyard toilet to give birth to her son, whom she thinks of killing before his cry awakens her maternal instincts.

This is the stuff of melodrama, but Sheyndl's plight is clearly the result of the harsh social realities and ignorance that are Singer's real subject in *Comrade Nakhmen*. Moving to Warsaw after her child is born, Sheyndl eventually marries Menashe, a boorish baker who drinks, plays cards, and is stricken with chroni-cally diseased eyes, the physical sign of his unappealing nature. It is an economic arrangement for Sheyndl: "Closing her eyes so as not to see his sick red eyes looking at her with dreary lust, she let him do with her whatever he wanted —he who fed her and the household in the hungry years of the war" (p. 135). Menashe's lust is never satisfied and is tamed only after he becomes completely blind, a development he understands as the price paid for a dissolute life. There can be no compromise between his former loutishness and his humility in blind-ness. When he can no longer work and support the family, he loses all other signs of power, too. "Although he loved Sheyndl more strongly than ever, felt her womanliness in the house with all his senses, he would no longer pre-sume to approach her or touch her" (p. 227).

Sheyndl's sister Reyzl appears in the novel only to make inescapably clear another facet of the economy of sexuality, now extended to contacts with Jews and non-Jews alike. Unable to find work during the German occupation of Warsaw, she is found instead by a German soldier who gives her bread and jam before seducing her. German military police, who stop her and the soldier and learn that he has no pass, assume Reyzl is a prostitute. When the soldier does not come to her defense, Reyzl is compelled to accept the yellow identifica-tion card that marks her as a prostitute. She disappears from the novel with this card, but Nakhmen's own first sexual encounter has shown what is likely to await her. When Nakhmen completes his apprenticeship, he signals his new status as a worker by a number of ritual changes. In addition to acquiring his first money and suit of clothes, he gets his first haircut at a barbershop, smokes his first cigarette, and, for the first time, enters a brothel complete with a mezuzah on the door and all the appearances of a respectable Jewish home. He is sent to a tired middle-aged woman who is loudly chewing the bread and jam that connotes the displacement of one gratification onto another, the grossness of sensual desires, and the impossibility of satisfying any appetite.

Politics enters the novel as a corollary to these other passions. For Nakhmen, unemployed and lonely, socialist politics has as much to do with his longing for community and companionship as with economics. Taken to his first Party meeting by a pretty girl, he succumbs to her and her idol, Comrade Daniel. The narrative evinces equal degrees of sympathy and disdain for Nakhmen and the masses whom he represents. Easily duped by the handsome, charismatic Daniel, they allow themselves to be manipulated by a charlatan. Daniel believes that "workers and women . . . are emotional people" who will be swayed by "a nice word, the right gesture, an appropriate emphasis" (p. 152), and the open-collared black shirt that he dons to address them, replacing the white silken one he favors at home. An effeminate man who reads French novels and remembers his own affairs modeled on them, Daniel is the stock political figure preaching self-sacrifice in the name of socialist principles while living in luxury and protecting his wife from exposure to the Jewish workers whom she loathes. In order to organize the Jewish workers of Warsaw, he even learns to speak Yiddish, despite his assimilated family's disdain for the language. First in Poland and then in the Soviet Union, he betrays Nakhmen and the ideas Nakhmen learned from his speeches. Daniel will not help Nakhmen enter the Soviet Union, nor will he acknowledge that poverty and class differences continue there, and he finally rejects him totally when Nakhmen is (absurdly) accused of sabotage after defending another worker. Daniel embodies a number of characteristics that are also emblematic of Soviet communism: he represents only the outward appearance of change; he is attractive but assumes deceptive poses; he seems to encourage outspoken commitment to personal freedom but enforces restraint, silence, and conformity. Singer collapses politics and sexuality into similar concerns in which a great deal is promised but never realized; political activity mirrors sexual activity in the way it seduces, finally spending its energies and betraying the desires it has aroused.

The penetration of Jewish identity into this view of politics and sexuality is a constant motif in the novel. Rarely, but dramatically, Singer highlights the fate of the Jews by recognizing them as victims of other people's wars. Just before his death, Mattes sees the Russian officers under whose command he is to fight enter a shtetl, call for the rabbi and leaders of the community, and hang them as traitors. Years later Nakhmen witnesses an identical scene, this time perpetrated by Polish officers. The only difference is that "unlike his father, [Nakhmen] did not ask God for an explanation; he only gnashed his teeth in pain" (p. 166). The first scene takes place during World War I, when the Poles are under Russian rule; the second occurs five or six years later, during the Polish-Soviet war that followed the reestablishment of Polish independence after World War I. Polish national identity is insignificant to the Jews, subject as they are to the same cruelty from all sides. This second scene seems to offer Nakhmen a graphic warning that Jews are scapegoats, no matter which uniforms surround them. But the warning is ignored in the socialist struggle and class consciousness to which Nakhmen returns after this battle.

Nakhmen is again reminded of the particularity of Jewish experience, even in the midst of the workers' fight. When Comrade Daniel orders his Jewish supporters to strike, Nakhmen initially opposes the strike because it will only affect already impoverished Jews. Jews, he reminds an indifferent Daniel, are at a unique disadvantage, since they alone lack access to the machinery of an industrialized economy. As Nakhmen predicts before giving in to Daniel, Catholics working in mechanized bakeries do not follow the Jews out on strike, and they continue to provide Warsaw with bread. Only the Jewish workers go hungry, and their strike is broken. Nakhmen condemns the most blatant forms of anti-Semitism among both common folk and officials, but remains unshaken in his devotion to the socialist cause.

The narrative shifts between the recognition of the special problems of the Jews and the more common view that Jewish characters are implicated in the corruptions of the wider world because they take an active and willing part in it. In order to emphasize that he is examining universal principles, Singer is at some pains to expand the scope of the novel beyond the familiar tensions between Jews and gentiles or even between traditional and modern Jews. The soldier who seduces and deserts Sheyndl is a Jew; the brothel Nakhmen enters is run by a Jew and employs Jewish prostitutes; Comrade Daniel and his wife are assimilated Jews. Distinctions between these Jews and other unsavory characters are blurred.

The young woman who becomes Nakhmen's wife reveals the difficulties Singer faces in attempting to expand his scope in this way. He cannot quite give up the Jewish themes he sought to transcend. When Nakhmen's future wife introduces him to the workers' movement, she is described as blonde, blue-eyed, red-cheeked. She is transformed in each subsequent appearance in the novel until she emerges as a simple, traditional Jewish girl named Khanke. She becomes literally unrecognizable. Singer replaces her blonde hair and blue eyes, appropriate to her role as temptress, with the traditional accoutrements of a pious Jewish housewife. Khanke's concerns turn quickly from politics to the household and the need to marry Nakhmen once their child is conceived. Nakhmen is troubled when he realizes that "her earlier fervor was no more than the fantasy of a young girl, a respectable daughter, who agitated a bit while she was young and forgot it all as soon as she had her own pots" (p. 187). Khanke's metamorphosis underscores Singer's suspicion of political action and particularly the motivations and commitment of revolutionaries. Caught up in the fervor of revolution, Nakhmen cannot understand what has caused the obvious changes taking place in his own home. But Khanke's metamorphosis represents a troubling narrative shift. The changes in Khanke are too rapid, relying on inconsistencies or unexplained revisions in the presentation of character. Such gaps are not unusual in Singer's writing, but they are especially acute in his portrayal of women who, in each of the novels, appear as little more than symbols of a thematic concern that the male protagonist must confront. Khanke's return to traditional Jewish ways runs counter to her earlier political beliefs, counter to the unwed life she leads with Nakhmen and the child she bears. It even runs counter to the lack of sympathy that the narrative has established for Jewish tradition.

Unable to resolve the real crises faced by his characters, Singer retreats to a past that the novel has already uncompromisingly rejected. Women like Sheyndl and Khanke are the economic providers for the family. They raise their children and support the men whose moral or political weaknesses make them unfit for the social world. The stability and comfort they may offer are entirely at odds with the more prevalent vision that the novel presents of squalid sexual, political, and economic arrangements in the Jewish and non-Jewish world. All their limitations notwithstanding, Sheyndl and Khanke are the final signs of an idealized Jewish life that is nowhere else given credence in the novel.

Comrade Nakhmen proceeds through a series of focal shifts. Singer presents various political and social theses, which he proceeds to refute or to weaken by allowing them to stand only in an underdeveloped state. There is a continuing tension between discursive and narrative modes evident here as in each of Singer's novels. Such tension leads to stasis. In addition to the central story of Nakhmen's birth and development, there are several other stories told in the novel. Centered on a variety of characters, character is not their real focus; they appear less as subplots or plots related to Nakhmen's own than as vehicles for social and political analyses. Most evidently in Part III, when Nakhmen is in the Soviet Union, descriptions and arguments about the causes of social conditions and ways to address them are interjected into the narrative. Singer analyzes the high ideals and disappointing realities of the Soviet Union. He comments on the condition of women, arguing that equal access to the labor force only makes their workload more onerous than it was under the old, corrupt regime. He examines the disastrous effects of the five-year plan and its slogan—"two plus two equals five"—urging rapid industrial advances. There are criticisms of communal living, of the assembly-line methods imported from America, of the attempted erasure of ethnic differences, which, in theory, might have protected Jews but which becomes only another hardship to overcome. Such discussions are familiar from *Nay Rusland: bilder fun a rayze* [New Russia: scenes from a journey], the travelogue Singer had written on his trip to the Soviet Union as a correspondent for the *Forverts* in 1926–1927. In *Steel and Iron*, and again in *Comrade Nakhmen*, he repeated many of his earlier observations. In the novels, they appear as a parallel text, a running commentary on the unfolding plot. Singer has, in part, adopted the methods of the socialist realists he disdained.

At the end of the novel, Singer turns to the plot from the political and social analyses that have interrupted it. Nakhmen is finally disillusioned with the reality of Soviet life, but there is no other place for him to go. The assault on independence and individuality assumes its most graphic forms as workers are dehumanized and transformed by the imagination of a perverse bureaucracy into various animals, symbolic systems rendered grotesquely literal. Afanasiev, the only man to befriend Nakhmen in his new land, drinks excessively. At the entrance to the factory where he and Nakhmen work, his name appears next to a picture of a turtle. Confronted by Party officials, he refuses to respond to his name and crawls on the floor, bobbing his head, saying: "For forty-seven years I was a person . . . and now I have been made into a turtle" (p. 299). When Nakhmen speaks up for his friend, Comrade Daniel retorts: "You're a Communist and not supposed to think, but to follow orders" (p. 314). Nakhmen's name soon appears on the list of inefficient workers, and he witnesses a reenactment of the scenes of his arrest in Warsaw. Then as now, police enter his home and destroy it. Accused of counterrevolutionary activities, he is again tortured in prison; this time the pain is not physical but psychological as he is interrogated by a man called "the mouse" because of the way in which he gnaws away at his victims' resistance.

The novel ends with the most haunting image of homelessness that Singer ever created, one that dramatizes the fate of the individual to which each of his novels leads. Nakhmen, having fled to the Soviet Union, is now exiled back to Poland. He is caught in the neutral zone between the borders and threatened with death if he enters either land. Finding an emaciated, nearly dead horse abandoned in the woods, Nakhmen sees himself in the animal. Recalling one of the most familiar images of Yiddish fiction, Sh. Y. Abramovitsh's *Di klyatshe* [the nag] and its allegory of the Jewish people as beasts of burden subject to powers they cannot affect, the narrative voice comments on the two beings stranded between borders:

> At the last moment, when it could no longer carry on, someone must have driven out his horse, which had carried the yoke for him all its life. Nakhmen felt an extraordinary affinity for the dying being and patted its hide with pity. In the dying, abandoned, overworked, and beaten horse he saw himself and his own life. (pp. 335–36)

In recalling Abramovitsh's *klyatshe*, Singer acknowledges the plight of the Jews and the burdens they have always carried. But his emphasis does not lie here. It lies rather in the individual's literal inability to move in any direction, inhabit any space, or separate from corrupt structures.

For Singer's characters, the Soviet Union only proves how fatuous the idea of political messianism is. Maurice Samuel's English translation of the novel indicates the prominence of this reading. Samuel called the novel *East of Eden* (1939) and added as an epigraph the verse from Genesis 3:24, which says that God "drove out the man; and he placed at the east of the garden of Eden Cherubims, and a flaming sword which turned every way, to keep the way of the tree of life" (Authorized Version). Samuel's title points to the Edenic language associated with the Soviet Union. But such imagery is quite inappropriate for Singer. As we have seen, the banishment from Eden initiates the idea of history in Jewish thought and invokes the Messiah, whose appearance will make Eden once more accessible. A mythic system that includes Eden, messianic beliefs, or the individual's ability to act in meaningful ways is antithetical to Singer's fiction. Characters are not banished from Eden; they learn that it is one more illusion.

III

By the time Singer came to write his next novel, *The Family Karnovski*, developments in Jewish and world history had brought him back to the more pronounced Jewish emphasis of his earlier novels. His fiction is always firmly and self-consciously grounded in a particular historical and cultural context. In Singer's fictional construction, such contexts often seem to suffer from a narrative hypertrophy that is linked to an opposing atrophy of individual will and power. The individual is overwhelmed by inescapable political and social exigencies. Readers of Singer's stories and novels, as well as other modern Yiddish literary texts, may seek to contain such conflicts by succumbing to a belief in the power of a sentimentalized community or an individual struggling against hegemonic structures. Clearly, however, a close reading of Singer's stories and novels encourages no such sentimental perspectives.

Singer presents a harsh material world and characters who reproduce structural and thematic versions of Nakhmen's inability to break free of his surroundings. The English reader may find Singer's characterizations more reminiscent of the Victorians than of the modernists who were his contemporaries. Avrom Fleishman, referring to the late Victorian historical novel, points to the genre's combination of "a display of great events with the drama of the individual's response to those events." In later texts, Fleishman concludes, "the inner life assumes an autonomy that turns historical circumstance into a background or frame."[3] For Singer, the great events are as much the subject of his stories as are the characters who exist within them and who serve to explicate them. The inner life can never assume autonomy from the historical moment or from the past. But the comparison between Singer and the Victorians, or Singer and the modernists who followed them, is limited. Terms and constructs such as continuity, explicable motivations, or the integration of character do not assume a significant role in Singer's fictional imagination. Nakhmen's devotion to socialism, Yoshe Kalb's transformations, the differences between the Ashkenazi twins, or the varying responses to the Enlightenment, nazism, and America in *The Family Karnovski* cannot be explained by any view of character development but rather by some view of the environment that they serve to illustrate. Individuals in Singer's fiction can no more free themselves or be indifferent to that environment than can the Jews as a whole.

The abundance of minor characters who often wrest the narrative focus away from the novels' protagonists (as Sheyndl does in *Comrade Nakhmen*) underscore this perception of the difficulties that the portrayal of individual characters caused Singer and the extent to which his characters are overwhelmed by their contexts. His four volumes of short stories offer another perspective. In the stories, he resorts to two apparently competing but ultimately quite similar strategies for exploring the fate of the individual. Characters are generally marked either by anonymity—which makes them all alike, not typical but rather merely undifferentiated—or eccentricity—which makes them stand out as objects of curiosity, often in sinister ways. Like caricature, to which they are linked in their use of exaggeration, both strategies work against what may be considered an essentialist notion of the complete self. Only discrete fragments of character can be known or depicted. These strategies are clear in the novels, too, but there they may be overshadowed by the more expansive form. In the relatively concentrated scope of Singer's shorter works, anonymity and eccentricity become more pronounced.

Anonymity is signaled by the recurrent invocation of coercive institutions in which characters are confined or incarcerated. Armies, prisons, and hospitals abound in Singer's fiction. Individual differences are ignored in them, and nothing good ever comes of them: military victories yield to pogroms or defeats; prisons are full of torture; hospitals fail to heal the sick. Soldiers are buried in mass graves or clothed in an odd assortment of uniforms; most commonly, national and personal identities are confused. Like the armies we encounter in *Steel and Iron*, *The Brothers Ashkenazi*, or *Comrade Nakhmen*, those in "Blay" [Lead], "Af der fremd" [Estranged], "Baym shvartsn yam" [Near the Black Sea], and "Dorfsyidn" [Village Jews] suggest that individuals are indistinguishable, dispensable, and transformed by the powerful institutions and forces that control them. The patients in the hospitals of "Af der fray" [At Liberty] and "Klepik" [Contagious] cannot return to a healthy life and will only continue to spread disease. In the former, a young woman cured of what seems to be venereal disease leaves the hospital (named, pointedly, Holy Magdalene) only to stand shivering under a streetlamp until she is propositioned by a man. This story makes the associations among various institutions explicit, describing the reactions of newcomers to the smells of the patients who reek of "vinegar, gruel, bedding, and something else that always emanates from prisoners, soldiers, and hospital patients" (p. 94). Depersonalization marks the characters in other ways, too, as individuals are repeatedly referred to by adjectives or pronouns, rather than by names. The woman's lover is simply called "he"; the patients are called "the new ones" or "the girls." In "Klepik," a tubercular patient who has been warned that he is contagious makes love to a prostitute and, at the story's end, cannot resist his desire to be comforted by the woman who has always cared for him. The only doctor who is as successful and caring as Georg Karnovski is another George, in the story "Doktor Georgie." The similarity in names is ironic since Dr. Georgie treats cars rather than people in his "hospital"/garage, having rejected medicine and engineering. As a Jew, Dr. Karnovski could not practice medicine in Germany; Dr. Georgie leaves college because he believes that a Jew will never find work as an engineer. Patients and doctors, like soldiers and prisoners, are forced by social conditions or their own foolishness into situations they have not sought. Social determinism and personal weaknesses conspire against the individual, and no one emerges with any meaningful autonomy.

Singer's earliest stories contain, as Sh. Niger was the first to note, "lines toward the depiction of character, rather than character itself." Excepting only

"Perl" [Pearls] from Singer's first collection of stories and "Altshtot" [Old City] from the second, Niger observed that characters are seen as if in profile, thoroughly revealed from one side rather than faced directly and fully.[4] Niger's apt comments apply as well to the two stories in which he found a more complete presentation of character. As we have seen, in "Perl," Moritz Shpilrayn embodies an exaggerated fear and paralysis that make mobility or energy impossible. His responses to winter, illness, age, even the fear of death, are inappropriate by rational standards, and their motivations remain unexplained in the story.

In "Altshtot,"[5] Singer presents a world where appearances are deceptive and where all objects and personalities are deliberately distorted. Fabian Reitses is an antique dealer who specializes in art forgeries; he raises his activities to a philosophical stance, arguing against the uniqueness or integrity of the individual and arguing in favor of imitation as the identifying principle of human behavior. He perceives humans as bestial, and trains his poodle, cat, and canaries to have the human manners (politeness, neatness, orderliness) he finds lacking in his society. Called by his assistant "the devilish Jew," Fabian's connections to religion are rare and perverse: he reads the Bible to his animals, and he cheats and is in turn robbed by a priest who frequents his shop. Fabian's response to the priest's attempts to engage him in discussions about religion is to show him pornographic pictures. "Altshtot" moves through a series of exchanges in which Fabian's actions are as curious as they are inexplicable. When a rich young man finds a rare antique in Fabian's shop and pays him a huge sum for it, Fabian gives him an imitation instead and then presents the original to the priest as a gift, passing it off as a copy. The story invites us to speculate about why Fabian does this. Perhaps he resents the young man's smug certainty that he can dupe Fabian out of a treasure; Fabian may be proud of his own ability to create forgeries and dupe others; or the deed may be a sign of the cynical worldview that identifies Fabian. But although all of these explanations are plausible, the psychological structures that give them meaning make them inappropriate. Fabian must remain an enigmatic character, in this regard a precursor to the considerably more sympathetic Yoshe Kalb whom Singer created a decade later. In "Altshtot," Singer suggests that identity itself is forged: it is not merely fashioned out of certain materials, but is also a fraudulent invention.

The last section of "Altshtot" offers a haunting image of a Darwinian struggle for survival. Fabian leads his cat, Baltazar, to the Vistula in order to drown him. The cat is presumably to be punished for killing one of Fabian's canaries.[6] Tortured by Fabian and his dog, Baltazar breaks free, leaps at Fabian, and rips out his eye. The story ends with Fabian clutching his dripping eye, the dog and cat struggling fiercely on the banks of the river, and the mighty river itself lapping at its banks "as if it wanted to catch something, swallow it, and carry it off in its depths" (p. 65). The threatening personification of nature parallels the grotesqueness of Fabian's actions and fate. More significantly (and familiarly), however, it shifts attention away from the main character and his personality to forces over which he has no control. This by no means makes

Fabian into a victim or an innocent or one who gets his just deserts; such categorizations are irrelevant not merely because Fabian remains enigmatic but rather because Singer rejects causality and agency in reference to the self as emphatically as he does in reference to the community.

Like *Comrade Nakhmen* and "Altshtot," several of Singer's stories culminate in tropes linking humans and animals. In "Magda," the protagonist is a silent, unhappy young woman who cares for her father and his farm and loves only their horse. The horse's virility is the symbolic analogue to her own repressed sexuality. The same displaced passion appears in "Davnen" [Praying], where the female protagonist who cannot express her love for her cousin hugs and kisses her dog instead. Similarly, the sounds of a bull straining to reach a cow is the metonymic sign of a young boy's awakening desires in "Leymgrubn" [Clay Pits]. In the story that bears his name, Sender Prager is also a lonely man. A misogynist who seduces every woman he meets, he suffers a stroke, loses his business, and ends his life beloved only by his dog. Hersh Leyb of "Friling" [Spring] tries to cross the Vistula, but drowns as he and the bull he is bringing home fight one another for a firm footing on the melting ice. In "Liuk," the dog of the story's title is described in human terms, showing the fate of a privileged being who is stripped of status by the Russian Revolution. He belongs to a once-powerful czarist general who can now train and discipline only him. About to be castrated, Liuk breaks free, copulates fiercely with an ugly bitch, and flees back to his old home where he finds new soldiers of the revolution, who name him after Czar Nicholas and acquire a ration card for him.

The animal imagery functions on several levels. Most simply, it reifies such dead metaphors as (in English and Yiddish) "a dog's life." More emphatically, the imagery announces unreasoned passions and inarticulateness as the signs of the human. The most articulate characters in Singer's fiction express various political, religious, and philosophical stances that are discredited almost as soon as they are voiced. Dialogue that does not simply pit opposing social theses against one another is rare in his writing, interior monologue even rarer; other forms of communication among individuals is also rare. Like Singer's own 1928 declaration of silence, these absences suggest that language is severely limited: it renders the speaker vulnerable to seemingly inevitable misunderstandings, and it deceives by formulating positions that imply a consistency or wholeness that human experience contradicts. These other forms of silence are closely linked to the discontinuities and abrupt shifts in plot, characterization, and narrative perspective that distinguish Singer's fiction. They point to a sense of the individual as alone, severed from any understanding or meaning that can be expressed by the self or to others. Even the inertia that identifies so many of Singer's characters is less a sign of passivity than of powers that the individual cannot address. It is not a psychological state but an ontological one.

Context repeatedly overwhelms character in Singer's fiction. Even if the individual is capable of resisting initially, he quickly learns that he cannot succeed.

Nor does Singer allow his characters to withdraw from the struggle. He severely limits the extent to which the self's inner resources or psychology can be understood to explain individual behavior and fate. All elements of the material world —the only one in which Singer is interested—conspire against the very idea of independence or coherence.

FIVE

Creativity and the Artist

I said, "A line will take us hours maybe;
Yet if it does not seem a moment's thought,
Our stitching and unstitching has been naught.
Better go down upon your marrow-bones
And scrub a kitchen pavement, or break stones
Like an old pauper, in all kinds of weather;
For to articulate sweet sounds together
Is to work harder than all these, and yet
Be thought an idler by the noisy set
Of bankers, schoolmasters, and clergymen
The martyrs call the world."

William Butler Yeats, "Adam's Curse"

Singer never repeated his 1928 renunciation of Yiddish literature, but the sense of hopelessness with which he regarded the literary enterprise was a recurrent theme in his stories, essays, and correspondence. The inefficacy of the written and spoken word and of art itself appears in Singer's texts as a corollary to his view of the individual as thwarted by external forces. All forms of self-expression are necessarily limited, since they allow individuals to do little more than rail against the historical and social structures they would seek to change. The artistic character is distinguished only by his or her heightened awareness of this limitation.

Nonetheless, in creating the artist, Singer suggests a way to challenge his own presentation of a stagnant and unyielding environment. Without romanticizing the self, familial and communal structures, or the past, he examines the relationship between artistic creativity and social reality. Only in writing and art, in human constructions of the world, can individual control hope to be made manifest in Singer's fiction. Art is not a Promethean act or an attempt to reproduce divine attributes on the human plane. His artists affect nothing, often producing forgeries, copies, or work that no one will ever see. Yet these figures suggest a tension between the despair with which Singer regarded the social world and the form and substance he continued to give that world by writing about it.

Never sanguine about the role of his own texts, Singer poses questions about the nature of the artist and the function of art throughout his writing. Within the diverse group of his writings that touch explicitly on art, there is a distinct thematic difference between stories containing an artist figure, on the one hand,

and essays and letters in which the writer is the explicating voice, on the other. The latter most commonly examine the role of the Yiddish writer and of writing in the Jewish world; the stories—with the one significant exception of "Stantsye Bakhmatsh" [Bakhmatsh Station]—appear further removed from the specifically Jewish questions that concerned him elsewhere; rather, they examine the more general question of the function of art, its representational powers, as well as its ability to distort both reality and its practitioners.

Singer's first artist figure, Yolek in the story "Leymgrubn" [Clay pits], makes animate figures out of clay and water. In his art, the adolescent Yolek recalls a number of Jewish tropes of sacred and profane creative powers. He replicates both the creation of man and of the *golem*, the being created by ambitious men misusing the magical power of speech and letters. At the same time, Yolek invokes the Aggadic tale about Terah, who made idols which his son, the patriarch Abraham, destroyed. Yolek wants to emulate his father in fashioning beautiful, lifelike statues, but he cannot understand how his father can bear to sell them. Yolek loves the beauty molded by human hands and hates the grossly mercantile use to which it is put. But these sentiments have no place amidst the terrible poverty in which he lives. Drawn to church figures as models for his own art, Yolek is presumably saved from both apostasy and unproductive labor when he is apprenticed to a hatmaker who insists that the boy will have to stop fashioning "idols." "Leymgrubn" is one of Singer's earliest stories; he was only twenty-three and beginning a writing career in 1916, the date appearing at the end of the story. Read allegorically as a story about the extraordinary obstacles faced by art in the contemporary world, "Leymgrubn" anticipates the views Singer would express a decade later in essays and letters renouncing Yiddish literature. There is no place for the artist in Yolek's world, no appreciative audience for his art; its only function is economic, and even then it cannot support him. It is also a dangerous act, assuming divine powers of creation that are sinful, leading to idolatry.

Singer's view of creativity rarely deviated from this early construction of it. The romantic myth of the artist as a powerful but suffering and misunderstood genius shares the fate of other mythic systems in his writing: it is invoked only to be repudiated. The archetypal Western images of the artist are thus both present and denied by Singer, rendered impotent by the enormous gap between art and life. Singer's artists belong to neither of the traditions that Maurice Beebe associates with the "ivory tower" and the "sacred fount." In one tradition, art is regarded as the re-creation of experience and the artist as one who lives more fully and intensely than others. In the other, art is equated with religion, and the artist is viewed as a being who must stand aloof from experience.[1] Singer's artists can follow neither path. The apotheosis of art runs entirely counter to the demystification on which Singer insists in all realms and to his unequivocal rejection of religious thinking. The artist can no more redeem the world or remain independent of it than can anyone else. The perception of the artist as one who re-creates intensely felt experience is, to Singer, perhaps the more threatening of the two views, given his presentation of experience as a reality that can only overwhelm the individual, yielding silence and despair. To be creative, such an artist must be protected from experience, and since that remains impossible in Singer's fiction, he repeatedly resorts to a kind of structural sleight-of-hand deflecting attention away from the art with which he begins. As we see so often in the novels and stories, a disembodied sexuality and a harsh presentation of society replace all other foci. "Leymgrubn" ends with Yolek seeking comfort in the arms of the poor girl who has befriended him and who now tells him the meaning of the sounds made by the bull and cow in the barn.

In addition to "Leymgrubn," *Perl* contains another story of a failed artist: "In der fintster" [In the dark], the story Singer first published in *Khaliastre*. There is an enormous difference between the defiant tone of *Khaliastre* and the enervation of this story's protagonist. Even at a moment marked by the apparent literary vitality and community of *di khaliastre*, Singer did not mute his characteristically pessimistic tone. Hershl, the protagonist of "In der fintster," once aspired to become a painter and is now employed as a photographer. Near his darkroom are an artist's atelier and a female model. Hershl seems equally attracted to the woman and the painting. As the model, who seduces and then leaves him, remarks, he is always in the dark. And, indeed, the story will not shed light on his psychological state or motivations. At the end, Hershl stays in the lab, refusing to go home at his employer's urging, saying simply, "I'd rather stay here."

Hershl's final line reminds an American reader (though it would not have reminded Singer's primary audience) of Melville's Bartleby. The comparison is appropriate up to a point. Like Bartleby, Hershl is a kind of copier, reproducing images of lives in which he has no interest. Both characters are known only obliquely, Bartleby through the first-person narrator who explicitly comments on the difficulty of knowing any more about Bartleby than he has personally witnessed and Hershl through a third-person narration that claims no omniscience. But the narrator of "Bartleby" cannot bear the hopelessness contained in his employee's refrain, "I would prefer not to," and tries—even after Bartleby's death—to find some rationale for it. Although he questions its validity, the narrator seizes upon the rumor that Bartleby once worked in the Dead Letter Office. The rumor offers a psychological explanation for his extreme passivity and peculiarity. Unlike most of Singer's fiction, "In der fintster" also suggests a psychological explanation for Hershl's final words. He has seen too much through a particular lens, seen it all in shadow and darkness, and finds himself betrayed by both art and love. Singer also shares Melville's critique of the world of business in which eccentricities such as Bartleby's or the artist's cannot be tolerated.

There is, however, a significant difference between the two stories that overshadows these similarities. "In der fintster" is univocal. There is no other center of consciousness, no voice other than the narrator's, and that voice is never far from Hershl's. Although "Bartleby" presents itself as a first-person narrative in which one speaker tells a necessarily incomplete story from one perspective, other interpretations repeatedly interrupt the narrator's. Turkey, Nippers, and Ginger Nut, the narrator's business associates and others who enter his building, the men in the prison, even the coda about the Dead Letter Office vie with the narrator's voice, challenging and affecting his (and the readers') perceptions of Bartleby.

Such multiplicity of views is entirely absent from Singer's story. The narrative strategies that Bakhtin calls polyphonic[2] are alien to Singer's short stories. The observation that Singer's narratives are univalent may appear to challenge earlier perspectives on Singer's shifts in narrative focus, but, in fact, it complements them. The shifts we have encountered first suggest a range of voices and experiences that prevent the author from focusing too narrowly on one character or privileging any one perspective.[3] That range serves rather to underscore the same authorial perspective, to overwhelm the reader with evidence and examples that make this perspective irrefutable. The narrative presented resembles a courtroom proceeding in which various views compete, yielding in the end to a single verdict.

Singer's narrative center is not a character or a voice, but an idea of society and the forces at work on the individual. These remain constant whether his narratives move from one character and plot line to another (as in *The Family Karnovski*, for example) or focus unswervingly on one (as in *Yoshe Kalb*). The shifts in focus in the novels present different angles from which to regard a similar set of social exigencies. In those stories where Singer maintains one angle of vision throughout, the narrator and protagonist confirm the same social perspective.

The artist figure cannot be sustained in such narratives. The artist is not merely an eccentric character but one who is allowed, perhaps even created, to challenge prevailing norms. In the artist's ability to live beyond the normal restraints of social life, he or she seems to embody an exaggerated independence from, and unique perspective on, the world. This special liberty cannot exist in Singer's narratives, and the artist is weakened in a number of structural and thematic ways. As we have seen in "Leymgrubn," artistic urges may be overpowered by harsh social realities or by the technologies of modern culture that stifle the creative impulse by rewarding other activities. Similarly, the artist may be encouraged to turn from creativity to copying, as Hershl does in "In der fintster," or to forgery, as Fabian Reytses and his assistant do in "Altshtot." In some cases (such as "Profesor Arkadi Gritshendler" and "Bela Saradatshi"), art is part of a story's setting rather than its subject or foreground. Or, as in "Stantsye Bakhmatsh," the narrative may simply lose sight of the protagonist's artistic desires as they are replaced by other characters and scenes. The peculiar status of the artist is undermined by each of these devices, and the univocal perspective is thus allowed to remain unchallenged.

In his stories, Singer is particularly drawn to the most representational forms of the visual arts. Portrait painting (which Singer himself had attempted before he began to write) and sculpting are more common as artistic media than is writing. And the failure of such visual artists is inescapable in the stories.

Only once, in "Profesor Arkadi Gritshendler," did Singer portray a musician, the least representational of all artists. Singer seems not to have known what to do with such a figure and to have had trouble locating a protagonist, plot, and theme. The story is excessively symbolic, revealing the financial and professional insecurities of the professor, who was once a Jew with a wife and son and, having rejected his own past, is now lonely and unsuccessful. The affectations of the artistic temperament never mask the personal limitations of the man.

Romantic portraits of the artist have led readers to anticipate the kinds of connections between creative energies and the artist himself[*] that we encounter in several of Singer's works. Indeed, the closer Singer came to the artist as writer—that is, the more the artistic role encroached on his own role—the more he disrupted the narratives, apparently reluctant to condemn the writer to the fate of other artists and, at the same time, unable to claim his independence from it. In "Bela Saradatshi," "Stantsye Bakhmatsh," and his own memoirs, Singer constructs a view of the writer as fantasist, as one who would escape from reality into the imagination, but cannot.

The life of fantasy in which the artist and particularly the writer may live assumes its most disturbing expression in "Bela Saradatshi." Unlike most of Singer's stories, this has a woman as its main character and New York and Paris as its setting. Bela is a lonely child who lies to her parents and the teachers of her Lower East Side public school. She makes up a crudely racist story about a black man who wants to lure her into his car, and she causes her parents much distress by claiming that her mother has a lover. Suddenly, at the age of sixteen, she simply stops talking altogether and refuses to date or go anywhere except work. Having saved enough money to buy a one-way ticket to Europe, Bela begins once again to fabricate stories about her past and changes her name from Katz to the more exotic Saradatshi. Her travels reverse the movement of Jews from Europe to America, following instead the path taken by the bohemian and artistic community she enters in the Parisian Latin Quarter. Bela becomes a familiar part of the Quarter's landscape, posing for futurist painters who cannot pay her, rewriting the incomprehensible poetry of modernist poets who are never published, selling the paintings of poor but proud artists, nursing the sick, attending the funerals of the friendless. These activities are all of a piece: lost causes that cannot be redeemed.

Bela's creative powers, by contrast, suggest both vibrant energy and danger. Her stories take on a life of their own, blurring the distinction between truth and fantasy, and allowing no median ground between deceptive articulation and utter silence. Are her stories a sign of creativity or of madness? Are they imaginative or merely untrue? "Bela Saradatshi" asks its readers to confront the epistemological difference between a liar or madwoman and a storyteller. Bela lives as if she believes her own stories, spending money she has supposedly acquired from a wealthy husband, living with an imaginary lover, choosing to remain within the fiction of a successful marriage rather than return to her parents' home. Her real situation, by the end of the story, is quite different:

she is alone, poor, and celibate. Storytelling provides neither solace nor succor; in this story it is simply a delusion.

With the character of Bela, Singer adds another dimension to his depiction of ineffectual individuals. Passive individuals are at the center of each of the stories in *Friling*, the collection that ends with "Bela Saradatshi." Although she is the most energetic and creative of these characters, even these qualities fail to differentiate her fate from theirs. Bela is a parody of the artist. Singer protects that role only by creating this character as a woman and a fantasist; she is thus rendered powerless and eccentric.

II

Nowhere do the possibilities and limitations of art emerge more clearly than in "Stantsye Bakhmatsh," the only story whose protagonist is unquestionably a writer. It is also one of the few first-person narratives Singer wrote and one of the few to contain a subtitle: *an epizod fun der rusisher revolutsye* [An episode from the Russian Revolution]. "Stantsye Bakhmatsh" offers an extraordinary view of the function of art and of the strategies Singer developed in order to turn attention away from his narrative's critique of the artist's effete status. The subtitle underscores Singer's insistence on the representational nature of his stories: they are literary creations self-consciously contextualized by being deliberately grounded in a particular time and place. This emphasis is especially significant in a story told by and about a writer. It is one element in the series of questions about literature that Singer raises more provocatively here than elsewhere. How are the connections among truth, history, and fiction perceived? What motivates the act of writing? How do social realities affect it? What is the role and status of the writer in revolutionary times? How does Yiddish function as a literary language?

"Stantsye Bakhmatsh" is literally Singer's final word on these questions. It is the last story to appear in the *Forverts* before his sudden death, and it thus retrospectively invites interpretation as a summing-up of what had come before. The story does indeed recapitulate earlier themes and structures. Published in late 1943, it is set in the period from which Singer's writing never escaped: the barely seven years that included the beginning of World War I, the Russian Revolution, and the end of the Polish-Soviet war. The narrator and his family flee Kiev when the Soviets are driven from the city, unwilling to withstand yet again the pogroms Jews suffer at the hands of each invading army. Separated from his family by the "chaos of revolution and war" (*Dertseylungen*, p. 324), the narrator finds them again in a small, remote Ukrainian village that none of them can leave. In this unnamed town, all the familiar signs of order are subverted. Even time is defamiliarized when the Soviets advance the clock by four hours because of a shortage of heating and lighting materials. Church icons are used by an army officer as fuel; the head of the hospital is a "Christianized (*fargoyisht*) Jew" (p. 327); when he wants to obtain pen and paper in order to write, the anonymous narrator is told by an official that he must write a request using the very materials he lacks. Time, identity, institutions of government lose all meaning in the extraordinary upheaval of these days. Distracted only by the frequent funerals in the town, the narrator says: "fun groys langvaylikeyt hob ikh dertrakht zikh tsum gedank tsu prubirn epes oyfshraybn" [Out of great boredom I hit upon the idea of trying to write up something] (p. 327). What he intends to write remains unclear, but writing is encoded as an idle pastime motivated by, but incapable of affecting, historical events. Instead of learning the contents of anything the narrator writes, the reader encounters a tale about the narrator rather than by him, a tale that concerns the process of writing.

Singer creates an allegory of the Yiddish author who writes in contexts that are always hostile. Not only must the narrator attempt the nearly impossible task of obtaining writing materials, but he is even told by a proud Ukrainian officer that he must request them in the language of the land. "Although I couldn't write a single word of Ukrainian," the narrator muses, "I agreed to the bewhiskered official's order, assuring myself of the advice that Jews always gave themselves in such a case: write faulty Russian and it will come out good Ukrainian" (p. 327). The mildly amused tone of the narrator's solution to the language problem points quite seriously to the situation of Jews and of Yiddish writers. The politics of language acquisition is an important Jewish concern, connected at various times with the insularity of the Jewish community, with Enlightenment ideals favoring citizenship, with secular education and the use of non-Jewish European languages, and with language decorums that reserved Hebrew for written, sacred, or scholarly texts and Yiddish for the spoken language of common people. As Singer's own search for another literary language may indicate, writing Yiddish prose under these circumstances was by no means a natural or inevitable choice even for native speakers. It may be absurd to think that the narrator in "Stantsye Bakhmatsh" could write Ukrainian, but it is by no means clear that he will (as he does) write Yiddish. Like other Eastern European Jews, the narrator is a member of the multilingual community Max Weinreich has described as being typical of Jews.[5] Yiddish, the *lingua franca*, is only one of the languages available to such a community that also uses Hebrew as the sacred tongue and the coterritorial languages, which may change as national borders and military actions dictate. Singer's invocation of the language problem must be understood in this context. The writer, in a culture where language choice and proficiency are so problematic, can never take the most elemental materials of his art for granted.

Singer's narrator finally acquires paper with which to begin writing. A neighbor brings him a package of court proceedings written during czarist times. The image of Singer's narratives as courtroom procedure, pitting various views against one another until a single verdict is reached, is here made quite literal. The contents and effect of these pages on the writer are a remarkable statement about Yiddish and the authorial stance.

These were old, yellowed records about a court case involving a murderer by the name of Mikoliuk, who killed an entire village family because of his jealous lust for a young peasant girl whom he wanted to marry but whose family would not allow it. This same romantic murderer Mikoliuk constantly stood before my eyes and disturbed me in my writing. I pictured him to myself, along with the peasant girl he loved, her parents, brothers and sisters who would not give her to him. I saw each of them, their appearance and clothes and shape, as clearly as if I had known them intimately. I also heard their voices, their complaints and quarrels with the young Mikoliuk, whom they did not want to have in their family. They became so deeply embedded in my bones, all these people from a remote Russian village who had already been in the next world for several decades, perhaps along with their murderer Mikoliuk, that I could under no circumstances collect my thoughts and write the story that I wanted to write. As a result, I kept erasing and blotting in the attempt to inscribe my densely written Yiddish words between the lines of the calligraphed Russian records. (p. 328)

The Yiddish writer confronts two insurmountable problems: overpowering social realities and Yiddish itself. Singer's narrator juxtaposes ornate Russian and unwieldy Yiddish. The Russian story interferes with the one the narrator would write, constantly reminding him that the sensational aspects of this case are more interesting and more compellingly representational than anything he can create. The court case has the authority of historical documentation and is allowed precedence over the fiction the narrator tries to compose. Finally, Mikoliuk's tale will not yield to the imagination that, in "Stantsye Bakhmatsh," finds no voice and can compose no words.

Singer thus points to the limitations of Yiddish and the abiding interest of the real. But there is another more subtle critique suggested by the interpolated tale. Mikoliuk's story is lurid in its details and its presentation. The stylized writing, the ostentatious calligraphy, and the story of romance, revenge, and murder are all equally inappropriate for the Yiddish writer. There is, as Singer acknowledges here, interest in such tales among a Jewish audience. Yiddish writers could not ignore the extraordinarily popular *shund* literature commonly published in the same periodicals and on the very same pages as their own texts. In describing how difficult it is to fit a story into the interstices left by sensational tales, Singer continues the campaign against *shund* (and against many of his own detractors) launched more than fifty years earlier by Sholem Aleichem in *Shomers mishpet* [The trial of Shomer].[6] As we have seen, the distinctions between low and high culture, like the distinctions between *shund* and belles lettres, were a source of considerable tension in Yiddish culture. Singer makes the distinctions more complex by deliberately combining fact and fiction, Russian and Yiddish. The court case the narrator reads may be true, authenticated by a legal document, but it is also an ignoble tale that excites prurient interest. Yiddish literature—in this case, the narrator's own

Yiddish story—cannot emerge from such contexts. Like Mikoliuk and the family he murders, the narrator is in a remote village, but his situation bears no other resemblance to theirs. Their tale, it should be emphasized, does not inspire his own, but rather overwhelms it. The narrator is a Jew living in dangerous revolutionary times, and the tale he reads serves as no more than a diversion. If, as the story suggests, referentiality is compelling, then the narrator will have to turn not to such stories, which are irrelevant to his situation, but rather to the kind of story Singer goes on to write.

"Stantsye Bakhmatsh" returns to the narrator's writing only once. Caught in another political web, he tries to leave the town, but is accused of spying at the height of the Polish-Soviet war. Asked for his profession, he identifies himself as a *shrayber*, a writer. An official asks: "In which Soviet administrative office do you write?" When the narrator explains that he is not that kind of writer (i.e., clerk), but rather a *mekhaber*, an author who writes books and stories, the official asks, "Why do you write all that? . . . Who needs it?" The narrator cannot answer. "I myself didn't know why I write. Still less did I know who needed it. No one needed my primitive attempts, certainly not in these times" (p. 331). When his manuscript is discovered, the strange Yiddish letters are believed to be a secret code. Suspected of espionage, the narrator is saved only by the converted doctor. The doctor, with some difficulty, translates the Yiddish passages and proceeds to lecture about the usefulness of literature according to the best (and, for Singer, highly suspect) principles of socialist realism. The official drops his charges but not his contempt for the narrator's profession. "I understand if a person is a peasant, a doctor, a writer in an office," he says, "but I've never heard of this kind of writer, and I don't see why you need to go and ruin paper doing it" (pp. 333–34). He composes a poorly constructed, messy release, and that is the last sign of writing that the story offers.

As we have often seen elsewhere, the story's focus shifts, losing sight of the narrator's family, of the court proceedings, and even of the tale embedded between its lines. Finally given permission to leave, the narrator takes a train that is supposed to bring him to Kiev. En route, like the narrative itself, the train is often delayed and sidetracked. The Bakhmatsh station, one of its unexpected and unfamiliar stops, becomes significant to the narrator because of a scene he witnesses there. The train is full of smugglers, war casualties, soldiers and deserters of various armies, and the anti-Semitic jokes and songs they share. All passengers are asked to disembark in Bakhmatsh in order to be checked for contraband. The passengers of one car refuse, claiming immunity as Soviet sailors. These sailors have been the envy of everyone on the train who has heard the music and merriment coming from their car. The commander of the troops who search the train is a Jew—"a cursed Jew," as one sailor calls him (p. 346). A standoff between a Soviet sailor and the Jewish commander, both wearing Red Army uniforms, ensues. The sailor is larger than life, a physical giant who stands his ground firmly. But the Jew, a good-natured, confident man who is very good at his job and nonplussed by the sailor's show of strength and firearms, emerges as the victor. The scene, de-scribed at considerable length, is an entirely transparent attempt to create a Jewish hero. The commander is reminiscent of Pinkhas Fradkin in "Baym shvartsn yam," the story Singer had published a year earlier. As we have seen, Singer used Fradkin, the Zionist-turned-Red-Army-hero, to examine the possibilities and implications of power. Both Fradkin and this commander exercise authority in an army that is ultimately not theirs, and they are repeatedly reminded of their otherness. Acceptance and normalcy will always elude these men. But while this suggests a Zionist, or at least political, alternative (however equivocal) in "Baym shvartsn yam," that hope has already been discarded a year later in "Stantsye Bakhmatsh." Similarly, both Fradkin and the commander have power, but it appears enviable only in contrast to the powerlessness of the narrator, who resorts to writing ineffectual stories.

"Stantsye Bakhmatsh" expresses a distinctive relationship to place. Places are named, but not people, and there is a pseudoepic goal as the narrator tries to return home to Kiev. The quest becomes a mock epic, deflated even as it is invoked and replaced by the topoi of Jewish wandering and suffering under all regimes. There can be, then, no meaningful concept of Jewish leadership or of Jewish homecoming—not a surprising conclusion for a story written in the middle of World War II.

The connections between the tale of the Jewish soldier (itself a painfully poignant symbol at this historical moment) and the rest of "Stantsye Bakhmatsh" are difficult to discern. There are important differences between him and the writer who narrates the story. Both are secular Jews, but they share nothing else. The writer works with borrowed, used materials and produces a text that is repressed in the story. The results of the commander's actions are evident; he continues to have real power even if that power can be exercised only in a limited area over dissolute characters. In the series of episodes that comprise "Stantsye Bakhmatsh," this account of the scene at the Bakhmatsh station seems to fit into the space left by the narrator's missing text. It is certainly the kind of narrative that the story suggests he should have written: dramatic, based on observed realities that are compelling, relevant to his situation as an Eastern European Jew.

III

Singer was consistent in maintaining the belief that social reality was the primary constraint on artistic creativity and also its primary subject. In several critical essays he sought to explicate the function of literature by examining this paradox. There is a striking series of contrasts between the ideas he professed and the literary texts he produced. He criticized the close connection in Yiddish letters between journalistic and creative writing,[7] yet he continued to write both. His earliest theoretical essay, "Di proze in undzer tsayt" [Prose in our time, 1922], pursued an argument proposed by Dovid Bergelson in an influential essay written three years earlier and published, like Singer's essay, in *Bikher-velt*. Bergelson argued that poetry [*dikhtung*] and society [*gezelshaftlekhkeyt*] went in separate ways during "times of *sturm und drang*," poetry necessarily relying on old forms and the new society necessarily rejecting them.[8] Singer, too, argued that prose could not adequately confront "times of *sturm und drang*."[9] Yet, in stories and novels he wrote about precisely such times. Viewing Yiddish literature as a whole, he defended it as worthy of comparison with Polish and other modern literatures,[10] and pointed to the literary sophistication of modern Yiddish writers exposed not only to the Yiddish literary tradition but familiar, as well, with European literatures.[11] He urged better translations into and from Yiddish,[12] argued that Yiddish orthography should be standard-ized[13] and that Yiddish must be protected against the contemporary practice of incorporating regionally used foreign (Polish, Russian, English) words that could not be understood by all Yiddish speakers.[14] Nonetheless, his own texts show the influence of what he himself considered linguistic impurities. He posited the equivalent of canon formation as a significant part of the Yiddish literary agenda, and lamented the distance and disputes among Yiddish writers of different nations.[15] Yet he acknowledged no literary antecedents and could claim no heirs. He argued that just as class concepts functioned differently in Jewish culture than in the broader European culture, so did literary divisions; "just as aristocratic and crude elements mingle in our streets, so do refinement and simplicity [mingle in our literature]," he noted, observing that this differentiated Yiddish from the literatures surrounding it,[16] the literatures to whose ranks he often aspired.

The limitations of prose and of Yiddish culture plagued Singer. He maintained that prose writers (unlike poets) could not react immediately to the apocalyptic historical events in which they were enmeshed, and he insisted that only when these events were seen from a distance, in retrospect, could they become the material of imaginative re-creation.[17] In practice, such events were not actually recollected in tranquillity by Singer himself. His texts about World War I, the Russian Revolution, Polish invasions, and the rise of the Nazis were written, figuratively and often quite literally, before the smoke had cleared. Underlying the theory, however, was the lament that served as a refrain in his literary essays: writers are expected to take political positions in response to contemporary events. The corrupting influence of politics always seemed more acute to Singer within Yiddish culture because the Jews were always living *in extremis*, forced to respond to uniquely cataclysmic upheavals.[18]

Singer's insistence that literature and politics should be separated was somewhat disingenuous. His disavowal of party politics, his criticism of Communists, Bundists, and Zionists, even the act of writing for the *Forverts*, were in themselves a political stance. As we have seen in his renunciation of Yiddish literature, Singer wanted to be free of the political quarrels in which each journal and newspaper was mired. But he could never escape them. On the contrary, he entered the fray with considerable vigor. He responded to attacks directed at him and, just as frequently, he took the offensive, castigating other writers, journals, and institutions.[19] He attacked the reading public with equal vigor. Suggesting, early in his career, that artists could choose one of two paths—"either to be the lord of the masses or to be a slave to the masses"—he regretted the extent to which writers were censoring themselves, simplifying their art in order to give the public what it seemed to want.[20] For many years, he criticized both the Yiddish theater in Poland for producing *shund* and the public for demanding it.[21] When he refrained from *ad hominem* attacks, his literary essays seemed designed to heighten the tone of contemporary debates, to elevate his objections by casting them not merely as ammunition in the battle of the journals then under way, but rather as cultural criticism.

By the 1940s, World War II had rendered these quarrels insignificant. The war did not force him to reevaluate his views of literature and culture; it seemed instead to confirm what he had always believed. Political and social ideas were, in his view, as inimical to literature now as they had appeared to be when *Steel and Iron* was first reviewed, or when Singer accused critics of preferring social commentary to literary creativity.[22] Periodically, in letters to his most faithful correspondent, Melekh Ravitch, Singer echoed the comments he had made when he had renounced Yiddish literature in 1928. Writing, and particularly writing Yiddish literature, was an entirely specious enterprise in the face of contemporary events. He had said this, too, in 1926 in the midst of his travels in Poland. In correspondence with Opatoshu, he had pointed to the suffering he saw within every Jewish community he visited and wondered "what worth do all our aspirations and conflicts have in comparison with what our Jews are now enduring?"[23] And yet, then as during World War II, he continued to write, claiming that although he knew it was meaningless, he could not escape it.[24] Neither could his colleagues.

In 1943, in the middle of the war, the literary journal *Svive* [Surroundings] conducted a symposium on the goals of literature in general and Yiddish in particular. Singer's response may appear startling when compared to either the letters he was writing at much the same time or his stories and novels. "Literatur," he declared in the title of his essay, "darf farshafn genus" [Literature should yield enjoyment]. He asserted that writers should embrace ideas that readers have always known: that people read for pleasure, for amusement and entertainment, seeking comprehensible plots concerning interesting individuals. Writers must build "love plots," he wrote; their main theme should be "a he and a she."[25]

Sh. Niger argued against this naive position, insisting that even Singer must realize that an ideational focus was no less an integral part of a story's content than its characters or plot.[26] Fiction, Niger reminded his readers, should entertain *and* educate. This position, however, was not as antithetical to Singer's longstanding beliefs as Niger suggested. In the first edition of *Literarishe bleter*, Singer, too, had insisted that sophisticated "thought" [*gedank*] was a sign of the best literature.[27] The differences between Singer and Niger in 1943 are much less significant than the historical context in which they were voiced. Niger began his essay by asking: "Is this a time to enter into speculations about theories of literature and art?" In retrospect, Singer's statement about literature and enjoyment must be seen as a terribly poignant comment at this moment. More uncertain about the function of literature than he had ever been, painfully aware that it was essentially irreleveant to every remaining Jew in Eastern Europe, no longer able to valorize the concept of literary merit, he was left not quite silent, but in retreat to a position that bears little relationship to any plot or theme he had ever developed.

Still, even here, he struck a consistent chord: *goles* [exile], he wrote, overwhelms the writer, making it impossible to create *genus* [enjoyment], compelling him to analyze and comment rather than to entertain. Literary criticism and explication were the derivative products of exile; the greatest works of Jewish literature (he cites the Book of Ruth and the Song of Songs) were written when the Jews lived "a normal life in their own land."[28]

Modern Jews, according to Singer, had never enjoyed such normalcy in any land. Given these circumstances, the writer could only continue to write almost against his will and certainly in defiance of his contemporary situation. The plight of the artist, as "Stantsye Bakhmatsh" revealed most clearly, was to undertake the task of creative production despite the extraordinary material and psychic obstacles he faced, in full knowledge that his work might put him at personal risk and that it could not alter the external forces against which it struggled. The creative imagination, in short, arises out of opposition and rejection. It seeks to negate a reality it can never excape.

SIX

The Autobiographical Imagination

In der fargangenhayt bin ikh ale mol fargangen.
Vi a vunder fargangen.
Un in itster bin ikh geven a kheyder-yingl,
Vos hot gelebt mit gemore-gezangen,
Vi a kheyder-yingl darf lebn,
Mit a tsugeshporter zun,
In an oysgetrakhtn palats
Fun yidishe tsores.

> Glatshteyn, "Mayn kinds-kinds fargangenhayt"

In the past I always passed away.
I passed like a wonder.
And in the now, I lived
As a heder-boy should live,
With *Gemore*-melodies,
With a sun saved up for me,
In an invented palace
Of Jewish grief.

> Jacob Glatshteyn, "My Children's-Children's
> Past" [translated by Benjamin and Barbara
> Harshav]

One significant context of Singer's fiction has thus far been relatively muted in this study. The family to which Singer attributed his own earliest artistic inspiration offers another view of the themes we have encountered in his fiction. It is appropriate, having considered the artist as character, to turn to the autobiographical construction of the writer as artist. Singer could not have known that when he made a similar transition, he would write his last work. *Fun a velt vos iz nishto mer [Of A World That Is No More]*[1] is an autobiographical memoir, a fitting conclusion to his career and his life. But it need not stand alone as a retrospective view of the family, the community, or the self. Singer's memoir is most revealing when read along with the autobiographical texts written by his siblings, Esther Singer Kreitman (1891–1954) and Isaac Bashevis Singer (born 1904). Taken as a group, Kreitman's *Der sheydim-tants* [The demons' dance], (1936), Singer's *Of a World That Is No More* and Bashevis's *Mayn tatns bezdn-shtub* [My father's rabbinical courtroom] (1955)[2] offer a unique perspective on the single story that each family constructs about itself and the different narratives that its individual members can create out of that story. They present an unusual opportunity to examine the dynamics of autobiography and the crafted nature of Singer's memoirs.[3]

The three Singers portray the same family and cultural environment, yet reveal strikingly different views of their surroundings and of one another. It is by no means surprising that siblings have contrasting perceptions of the influences they have shared, but rarely are they all authors, and rarely do all three inscribe their differences in their writing. (One is reminded of Alice, William, and Henry James.) The limitations of either historicist or modernist readings of Singer's texts are made all the more apparent by these narratives. In reading *Of a World That Is No More*, as in autobiography generally, readers encounter an articulation of a problem that had always plagued Singer: the tension between fictive and representational constructions of the self and society.

Singer's memoirs provide a portrait of the artist as a child and young adolescent. Examining the relationship between memory and history, he places himself at the center of two stories, one that concerns the development of the individual and the other that depicts a society about to disappear. *Of a World That Is No More* also articulates its own hermeneutics. The first sentence is an encomium on memory: "How marvelous and incomprehensible is the human mind in the way it receives pictures, often unimportant ones, which it hoards forever and in the way it discards pictures, often very important ones, which it does not want to keep" (p. 15). Singer justifies the structure of his narrative by telling his readers that memory is selective, discontinuous, and defies interpretation by keeping its motivations hidden. The memoir is episodic, framed by a loose chronological progression, but with chapters that remain independent of one another.

Singer begins his memoir with what he claims as his first memory, a celebration of Nicholas II's coronation (little more than a year after Singer's birth). He thus locates himself in a specific temporal frame that has personal and national significance. But, as in much of his fiction, it is the Jewish world that his family inhabits and not the gentile world beyond it that forms the primary public locus of his stories here. He tells of the lasting impressions made by all that he witnessed in his father's and especially his grandfather's *bezdn-shtub* [rabbinic courtroom] and in their homes. Commenting on his early artistic sensibilities, Singer discloses his childhood preference for stark realism (p. 17), his urge to draw pictures, and (like Yolek of "Leymgrubn") to fashion figures out of clay (p. 230). Curious character types and the lives of common people were a source of fascination for him. He acknowledges his family's piety, but he deems it increasingly unsatisfying and meaningless to him. Knowing that he is expected to follow in the footsteps of the men of the family and become a rabbi, he expresses a longing to be free of the prescribed life of religious study, lamenting that "no matter what one did, it was considered a sin" (p. 38). Yet Singer is securely rooted in the world he rejects. It even exposes him to the broader social environment for which he yearns. A wide range of problems enter his father's *bezdn-shtub* as Jews come to his father so that he may serve as arbiter of their woes. "Dos lebn hot zikh arayngerisn tsu mayn foter in bezdn-shtub, vu ikh hob gedarft lernen toyre" [Life tore its way into my father's rabbinic courtroom, where I was supposed to be studying Torah], Singer writes (p. 205). Life, by which Singer usually means the forbidden world of secular books, politics, love, and sexuality, tempts him to move beyond the home into which it has forced its way.

This early exposure is to be understood as the inspiration for his writing, lending it not only fascinating scenes and characters but also authenticity and significance. Published serially and posthumously in the *Forverts*, the memoir was entitled "Emese pasirungen" [True events], validating these recollections of a world that once existed. We encounter scenes and characters that appear in Singer's fiction, as if he were here providing information that would encourage us, retrospectively, to view his earlier novels and short stories as accurate representations. He recounts the fascinating story of Yoshe Kalb told by his father, who is reported to have known the man (p. 203). He introduces Briton, a dog whose name appears in other stories, as well as the real-life models of the beggars, peddlers, teachers, hasidic charlatans, pious Jews, and bastards, in addition to the scandals and customs that abound in his fiction. With the exception of *Yoshe Kalb*, he does not mention any of his stories or novels by name, even when he invokes the figures whom he claims as their sources. In the act of writing such a text, he not only historicizes the fictional universe he has created, but also in effect becomes the final arbiter of this world that is no more.

In two essays written in 1924, Singer offered a number of observations that he may well have had in mind when he wrote his own memoirs twenty years later. In a review of Z. Segalovitch's autobiographical *Zeligs yorn* [Zelig's years], he suggested that in turning to autobiography, writers might focus on themselves in so exclusive a way as to lose sight of the broader dimensions of their work and of all sense of proportion and organization. The best autobiographical memoirs, Singer suggested, were those "through which a world emerged." Description for the sake of autobiography was, in his view, insignificant; descriptions of characters and scenes must provide a view of a wider context if they were to be considered artistically worthy of notice.[4] In an essay about Sholem Aleichem's autobiography, *Funem yarid* [From the fair], Singer modified this suggestion, offering a view that located the writer firmly within the autobiographical text. He wrote that *Funem yarid* could be understood as "not only [as] the key to Sholem Aleichem's protagonists . . . to the entire fair of his characters, their lives, goals, histories, and adventures, but also [as] the key to Sholem Aleichem himself, to Sholem Aleichem's genius."[5] Singer undoubtedly hoped *Of a World That Is No More* would be understood in similar terms, as a key to his own art and also to the world from which it emerged.

In telling the story of his own early life and the life of Eastern European Jews at this historical moment, Singer suggests that his life is exemplary and that he can therefore lay claim to a public function. His life is presented as a model for a view of the challenges faced by his generation, caught between traditional familial expectations and the beckoning outside world. At the same time, as a writer, he can also claim an interesting perspective on the typical life he has lived.

In certain respects, Singer, Bashevis, and Kreitman appear as one another's chorus, echoing each other's perceptions of their family and, more rarely, of the construction of the self within that family. Each of the Singers presents a similar anatomy of the family. The father portrayed in the three narratives is oppressively religious, a gentle, naive man, and a simpleton in worldly matters. The siblings also write the same story of the dynamics between their parents, no doubt reflecting the vocabulary and constructs encountered in their home. All three repeatedly use the same word to describe their father: he is a *batlen* [impractical, inefficient, innocent], but warmer and more loving than his wife. Each of the siblings describes their mother as the more aloof parent, an intelligent, learned woman "with a masculine head," as Singer writes (p. 33). The parents, each the youngest and most indulged of their respective families, seem ill-matched and utterly incapable of providing a *heymish* [homey] environment. All three writers characterize the differences between their parents as a series of tensions between the father's adherence to hasidic enthusiasm and the mother's *misnagdic* upbringing. These tensions express themselves as a conflict between passion and reason in which traditional male and female roles are reversed. "My parents would have been a well-matched pair," claims Singer, "if my mother had been my father and my father, my mother" (p. 33). Bashevis sees these tensions repeated in his siblings, who now restore gender roles to their traditional order. He writes that he and his brother took after their unsentimental mother, while their sister took after their emotional father (p. 158).

Each of the Singers claims a rebellious spirit and a desire to move beyond a restrictive, all-encompassing religious environment. Their texts proclaim their own status as revelations of the self. Autobiography, the subject of much critical discussion in recent years, links the self (*autos*) etymologically and symbolically to the authorial, the authoritative, and the authentic.[6] But if the interrogation of the self is a staple of autobiographical writing, it is, as we have seen, an especially problematic one in Yiddish literature. The reading of Yiddish texts as period pieces capturing destroyed historical moments rich in ethnographic interest is at odds with the autobiographical and modernist interest in the self. There is a tension between the focus on community, traditionally understood to be the primary Jewish concern, and the focus on the individual and the self.[7] In the three Singer narratives, the self must declare its separation or difference from the community and its norms. Reading these autobiographies, or Singer's texts in general, as representative of the social life of the community would deflect attention away from the individuals who are their subjects. It would also obscure the perception that society, like the self, is carefully and deliberately constructed in these texts: although firmly grounded in a particular time and place, none can escape interpretation as narrative creation.

The attempt to constitute the self as separate from the community is especially acute when a strong myth of community has arisen—as it has in Jewish culture—to offset the individual powerlessness that hinders self-definition and articulation. This problem of claiming a place for the self in the act of writing is different from the problem—which has become virtually a cliché of contemporary criticism—of the indeterminacy of the self. The story of individual lives, psychoanalysis tells us, can be examined and rewritten by being reinterpreted. A Freudian model points to the reconstruction of the past in autobiography, rather than to the accuracy of specific occurrences. A Lacanian model focuses on the narrative created by the subject and on the extent to which the self is alienated by the very language it uses.[8] The preliminary need to assume a subjectivity traditionally denied them as Jews, that is, to view the subject as an integrated self with a sense of agency, is ultimately a more important consideration in reading the Singers' texts than the poststructuralist claim that no such entity exists.

The distinction we have examined in Singer's fiction between the social construction of the individual and the psychological construction of the self becomes more pronounced in the narrative he writes about himself. The notion of self-writing is problematic not only because the concept of the self is problematic, but also, as Paul Eakin reminds us, because "the self that is the center of all autobiographical narrative is necessarily a fictive structure,"[9] a character placed in a text. In autobiography, the distance between author, narrator, and subject diminishes, but textuality as a construction remains. Autobiography, claiming to be self-reflexive and revelatory, suggests a pattern to a life whose significance is rendered in the telling and reading of it. Unlike diaries or journals, autobiographies posit a reader whose view of the subject will be shaped by the text and will in turn shape it through interpretation. "It is the ear of the other that signs," Derrida writes. "The ear of the other says me to me" and thus identifies the self.[10] Autobiography, in other words, is as much a function of reading and interpretation as it is of writing and creation.[11] The interpretive power inherent in the ordering of events, the shifting temporal perspectives necessitated by writing about one's past self in the present and leaving the story of one's own life open-ended underscore the crafted nature of autobiographies and the problems we have reading them.

Singer's autobiographical memoir encourages the naive belief in referentiality that generally accompanies the reading of autobiographical texts. In addition, his remembrance of things past leads to a view of his present status as an author, supporting the view that autobiographies disclose more about the self at the moment of writing than about the past self who is the ostensible subject of the writing.[12] *Of a World That Is No More* illustrates what Avrom Fleishman calls "the interplay of I-past and I-present,"[13] the writer's presentation of self at the time of writing and at the time figured in the narrative.

There are differences among the ways in which autobiography, autobiographical memoir, and autobiographical novels are read, differences that the Singer narratives illuminate. Autobiography is generally identified by the chronological ordering of verifiable details telling the story of the writer's own life, the presumption of truth distinguishing our reading of it from the way in which other narratives are approached. Autobiographical memoir carries a similar presumption of truth, but is structured thematically or idiosyncratically. Karl Weintraub offers another distinction, suggesting as well a check on the modernist urge to elide all traces of the representational. "In memoir external fact . . . is translated into conscious experience," he writes, "but the eye of the writer is focused less on the inner experience than on the external realm of fact. The interest of the memoirist is on the world of events."[14] Autobiographical fiction is more removed from the details of the subject's life, using that life as a model, but not necessarily a strictly representational one.[15] The Singer brothers write their autobiographies as memoir; their sister writes hers as a novel with a third-person narrator. The choices are telling, pointing to Kreitman's urge to contain the representational, to distance herself from the limitations imposed on her own life. The use of the memoir form allows Singer and Bashevis to point more directly to the social world around them and their own place within it.

The gender differences are significant, illuminating other important distinctions among the three narratives. Kreitman shares little of her brothers' interest in the true past. Her novel may also invite us to question conventional beliefs about women's writing which suggest that when women turn to autobiography, they are likely to turn to diaries, journals, and memoirs rather than fiction.[16] Obviating even the illusion of an imposed chronological or thematic structure, such genres are generally considered more fitting for the fragmentary view of women's lives. They make no claim to public significance or even to having a public. Bashevis's rare acknowledgment of his sister's literary talent presents her as the writer of smart, humorous letters—as if to buttress a belief in the epistolary mode as being appropriate to women.[17] But the evidence of Kreitman's autobiographical novel as well as her other fiction (which also contains unmistakable autobiographical elements) points in other directions.[18] By choosing fiction rather than a genre that proclaims its own referentiality, she frees herself of some of the constraints her brothers seem to welcome. They had already established a certain authority as writers before turning to the details of their own lives and could thus presume that readers would be interested in them as public figures; Kreitman had no such status. Memoirs provided Singer and Bashevis with a different kind of authority as representatives of a culture that had since been destroyed. Their texts are more conventional than hers, structured on a set of personal reminiscences and social analyses with which Yiddish readers were familiar.[19] In writing her first novel, *Der sheydim-tants*, Kreitman could hope to claim for herself the authorial role her brothers had achieved in fiction. She could also assert an imaginative independence from some of the repressive details of her own life.

Comparisons of *Der sheydim-tants, Fun a velt vos iz nishto mer*, and *Mayn tatns bezdn-shtub* offer a more intriguing view of Kreitman than of Singer or Bashevis. This is partly due to how little is known about her, apart from her own writing and an occasional comment by Bashevis. The oldest, and the only surviving girl in a family of four children, she has been regarded as the family fantasist, a hysteric subject to nervous breakdowns, perhaps—as Bashevis claims—an epileptic, or, alternately, one possessed by a dybbuk,[20] an unstable, difficult daughter who was finally shipped off to be married to a diamond cutter in Belgium. Singer, writing during her lifetime, referred to Kreitman only to acknowledge the tension between them, attributing it to her understandable jealousy at being ignored in favor of the boys in the family. The closest he comes to depicting his sister may be in "Bela Saradatshi," wherein the protagonist's situation bears a resemblance to Kreitman's image in the family. Living a life of fantasy as a way of avoiding reality, alone in a foreign country, unable to surrender their own artistic pretensions, and eccentric, Bela and Kreitman are encoded as similar types of the difficult female.

Bashevis devotes a chapter of his memoir to his sister, and in the very act of doing so he effectively sets her apart from the rest of the family, framing her as a separate being not woven into the fabric of their lives; she is, rather, an "issue" to be addressed. Singer, on the other hand, reappears throughout *Mayn tatns bezdn-shtub*. Few autobiographers write about their siblings, Estelle Jelinek reminds us; this is particularly true of the oldest child because "the self of the oldest child is rarely threatened or influenced by younger siblings."[21] In the case of the Singers, however, gender clearly supersedes birth order. Singer rarely writes about his siblings, but both Kreitman and Bashevis must confront the eldest son. And both view him as leading the way toward enlightenment and the secular world.

Kreitman's *Der sheydim-tants*, written before her younger brothers' memoirs, is never mentioned by either Singer or Bashevis, and one can only speculate on the extent to which it may have inspired their own reminiscences.[22] Bashevis, the youngest of the three siblings, was following more closely in the literary footsteps of his brother. By 1955, when Bashevis published his memoir, both of his siblings had died, Israel Joshua eleven years earlier and Esther (or Hinde, as she was called in the family) just one year earlier. Her death left him as the only survivor of the family, the one who would write the final family romance in a memoir that could no longer be disputed. Bashevis, actually writing after the death of every member of his family—some at the hands of the Nazis —generally writes more fondly than either of his siblings about their parents and the social environment. More emphatically than Singer's book, Bashevis's memoir must be understood as a memorial to his family and their culture.

Each of the siblings refers to the same historical periods, but each of their texts has a distinct primary chronological and geographic focus. Kreitman, born in 1891, was two years older than Singer, thirteen years older than Bashevis. Her novel takes the family through thinly disguised replications of Kreitman's own movements from Leontchin to the Radziminer hasidic court, to Bylgoray, to Warsaw, and on to Belgium. It ends, like Bashevis's memoir, in the shadow of World War I. Singer's memoirs describe the move to Leontchin when he was three years old and end when he is approximately fourteen, as his family leaves for the Radziminer court (1907). There is some speculation that Singer projected a memoir of three volumes that were to have begun with childhood and brought him to his life in America; if so, his sudden death in 1944 put an abrupt end to this project.[23] Bashevis's earliest memories begin where Singer's end, as if he were continuing the same narrative. He describes the move to Radzimin and then focuses on the family's life in Warsaw. Bashevis wrote his memoirs at the age of fifty, the age at which his brother had died. Most striking is the similarity in the age span of the brothers' reminiscences. Like Singer, Bashevis begins his memoirs in his third year and ends them when he is about fourteen, an age they both equate with early sexual awareness and confusion. (Only later would Bashevis turn to subsequent years, and much of that work remains in serialized form in the *Forverts*, neither translated nor published as a book in Yiddish,[24] a sign of how differently the author views these works from his first autobiographical writing.) Nowhere, I believe, is Bashevis's dependence on his brother more telling than in this unacknowledged echo of the autobiography Singer had managed to complete. It is certainly more revealing than either the largely reverential tones with which Bashevis refers to his brother or the literary rivalry about which some have speculated. That echo of an eleven-year span (from the age of three to fourteen) is, itself, hauntingly repeated in the eleven-year span that separated the brothers in age, and the eleven years that separated the death of Singer and the publication of Bashevis's memoirs.

Kreitman's novel focuses on much the same historical period as Bashevis's memoirs, but with a significantly different personal focus. We meet her protagonist when she is fourteen, the age at which her brothers' memoirs stop. The young woman's need to formulate and articulate her own separation becomes the subject of her novel. For Singer and Bashevis, dawning sexuality marks the end of an era, the end of the family life that is at the center of their memoirs, and thus the end of a distinct period in the stories they construct about themselves. Kreitman's protagonist, Deborah, barely recalls her childhood, viewing it as only a preparation for adolescence and maturity, which, however unhappy, are the focus of her narrative and of her attempt to free herself from the past. She depicts a tortured desire for education and, primarily, for love, a desire to share in the world, even the limited world of a home that relegates its daughter to the status of household drudge. Memory haunts her, forcing her only to relive unhappiness.

In contrast, Bashevis constructs memory in the way his brother does. The themes, language, and structure of *Mayn tatns bezdn-shtub* recall the episodic organization and reminiscing tone of Singer's text. Several of the chapters begin with "di tir hot zikh geefnt" [the door opened]. Like Singer's "dos lebn hot zikh arayngerisn" [life forced its way in], the reflexive verb construction (the door opened itself; life forced itself in) signals the writer's own innocence in witnessing the outside world and the inevitability of exposure to it. The focus on the *bezdn-shtub* testifies to an important connection between domestic and religious life. The *shtub* is part of the household; it is the father's study, where the community came with ritual questions and where the brothers received much of their religious education. Because it appears at first as a domestic setting, we might expect to find it in Kreitman's novel where, instead, it assumes only a minor role. Deborah remains entirely excluded from the *shtub*, privy to neither its legal arguments nor its educational function. Everyone, including the reader, has knowledge that is denied her. She enters the *bezdn-shtub* only to perform domestic chores. No knowledge will thrust its way into her view; knowledge is deliberately withheld from her, forcing her to seek it elsewhere and on her own. Bashevis and Singer are first-person witnesses to the discussions that take place in the *shtub*. For them, it is the site of belonging, providing a place for the imagination, a firm grounding in a particular world.

His presence in the *bezdn-shtub* allows Bashevis to make the same claim to an exemplary life that Singer had made. It is a claim that many male, but virtually no female, autobiographers can voice.[25] It is not exemplary in the sense of being more worthy or more commendable than others, but rather typical. The brothers' lives, then, are significant because they reflect aspects of other lives as well and are therefore worthy of public notice. In the act of writing a novelistic account of her life, Kreitman acknowledges that she can have neither such a public, exemplary status nor a clear locus for her imagination.

Kreitman's desire to break free of the life her brothers imaginatively reclaimed is evident in the structure of her autobiographical text. She chooses a form that allows a multiplicity of perspectives and foci and is more richly textured than the memoirs her brothers wrote. Deborah remains the central protagonist and most sympathetic character, but other voices are clearly heard. There is no omniscient or privileged perspective, certainly not that of the individual commenting on the self. Nowhere is the contrast between Kreitman and her brothers more noteworthy. Singer and Bashevis tell their own stories as well as everyone else's and remain the unifying center of consciousness. Despite their loss of religious faith and their rebellion against the traditional Jewish world, they remain static characters. Deborah's views of herself often change, as do her views of the surrounding world. And frequently she is ignorant of the insights of other characters, which, in turn, makes those characters independent of her in a way that Singer and Bashevis never allow. *Der sheydim-tants* describes her escape from the claustrophobic atmosphere of her life, a necessary step beyond the home, beyond Poland, and finally beyond the strictures of an autobiographical verisimilitude that was never as confining to her brothers.

The evidence of these three autobiographical texts does more than add a certain piquancy to the usual questions raised by self-representation. Certainly, the opportunity to examine the work of siblings yields fascinating psychological material. But, more significantly, it raises an additional set of questions. These three texts point to the need to challenge simple referential readings of Singer's fiction. A narrow view of referentiality suggests a set of irreconcilable if not irrelevant tensions. Singer and Bashevis do not raise questions about the place of women in Jewish culture; for Kreitman, these are a primary concern. Reading Singer and Kreitman, one must recognize the extraordinary limitations they see in religious life; reading Bashevis, one is exposed to a milder view of it as a cohesive moral force. Singer and Bashevis attempt to re-create the past; Kreitman seeks to escape it. Yet each of these texts is written and read as a representation of a particular and common time, place, and experience. They highlight the crafted nature of the text constructed by Singer, who presumably shared with his siblings a similar story of genetic and social environments, but formed a very different narrative out of that material.

With himself as subject, Singer restrained his own most tragic vision. Shlomo Bikl maintained that in *Of a World That Is No More* Singer lost his stance as an objective third party to events, but instead became a principal in the action and therefore showed more "heart and pity" here than anywhere else.[26] Singer never possessed the objective voice with which Bikl credits and criticizes him, though he did indeed present a less critical view of Polish Jewry here than elsewhere. The world he had so fiercely sought to transcend in his own life was now perceived not only as the source of his own creativity, but also of a keen sensitivity to certain character types and social concerns and to a vanishing life that could be neither rejected nor embraced.

Afterword

In the end, the question of audience remains. The issue is obviously acute in the case of Yiddish literature, since we cannot avoid the terrible recognition that its texts have fared better than most of its reading public. Resurrection, we learn from the history of Yiddish, is a literary conceit, texts and words being able to survive in ways denied to communities and individuals. Singer believed in no social or religious resurrection and urged his readers to renounce all messianic ideas. He might have found it more difficult to reject the contemporary evidence for a particular form of literary resurrection with the same certainty.

At every stage, I have had to confront the fact that this book's language and idiom are foreign to the cultural landscape that is its subject, and that my subject's language is foreign to most of my readers. This study of Singer's fiction encourages modes of interpretation that his original audience would not have brought to the pages of the *Forverts*. Uncovering what Frank Kermode calls the "secrets" of the text is an act that only academics are afforded the time to do. But, Kermode reminds us, most writers enter into a "de facto contract or gentlemen's agreement" not with "*l'école*" but with "*la cour et la ville*." The positive reception of most fiction, in other words, depends in large measure upon its accessibility. The success of popular fiction, like that of ordinary acts of communication, depends on the novelist's ability to provide "the satisfactions of closure and the receipt of a message" that need not be didactic or ideological.[1]

The distance between *la ville* and *l'école* or, to return to the context before us, *dos folk* and *di hoykhe fentster*, shrinks in Yiddish culture, but it does not completely disappear. Popular culture is not low culture. The latter, associated in Yiddish with *shund*, existed in the columns of European and American publications side by side with works claiming an innovative, modern literary voice. And the two voices vied for the same diminishing public. Singer's ambivalence about this split expressed itself in various ways, the most striking of which was his choice of a woman's name as his pseudonym. Singer was accused of writing *shund* under the name G. Kuper. That he chose a woman's name and then suppressed that fact behind the initial letter (G. rather than Genya Kuper, his wife's full name) is surely noteworthy. In discussions of modernism there is a "Great Divide" that separates high art from mass culture, and Andreas Huyssen notes that "mass culture is somehow associated with woman while real, authentic culture remains the prerogative of men."[2]

A study of the relationship between popular culture and modernism in Yiddish literature remains an important item on the scholarly agenda. The modern Yiddish writers to whom I have referred confronted certain historical and cultural challenges in their writing. A study of Yiddish modernism would necessitate a careful reconstruction of the central role of the Yiddish periodical press, of migration, wars, and revolutionary movements, and of the diversity of responses to them. It could entail a related analysis of the popular appeal of hasidism in Jewish life and the criticism it received in Yiddish letters. The status of Yiddish as a literary language in the first decades of this century would also have to be considered. Here, however, I can only echo Mendele Moykher Sforim's famous refrain, used to underscore a comment even as he seemed to dismiss it as a digression: *"nisht dos ober bin ikh oysn"* [that's not my main point].

Singer suggested, somewhat disingenuously, that his desire was simply to tell stories. In none of his many fictions does he offer resolutions to the tensions in which his characters are mired. The stories tell of a modern reality in which Jews can ground themselves neither in any territory, nor in the dynamics of world history, nor even in the self. The imagination does not so much provide respite as it offers a means of articulating these perceptions for others to face. Singer's stories do not leave us wondering about the fate of their characters or their surroundings. Perhaps the only future he could have envisioned for the world he knew was textual. In the end, then, resurrection takes the form of one more audience.

Notes

1. Introduction to a World That Is No More

1. When the Jewish literary journal *Prooftexts* began publication in 1981, it marked the coming of age of such an approach, providing a scholarly forum for its expression.

2. Introductions to two recent anthologies of Yiddish poetry offer an excellent place to begin in this pursuit: *American Yiddish Poetry*, trans. and ed. Benjamin and Barbara Harshav, and *The Penguin Book of Modern Yiddish Verse*, ed. Irving Howe, Ruth Wisse, and Khone Shmeruk.

3. Ruth Wisse's compelling view of these links in the case of the New York *yunge* [young] is relevant to the Eastern European context, too. See *A Little Love in Big Manhattan*, especially Chapter 5.

4. See especially Robert von Hallberg, ed., *Canons*.

5. Dan Miron's study of the rise of modern Yiddish fiction, *A Traveler Disguised* (especially Chapter 1), offers the most convincing analysis of this process.

6. Y. Y. Trunk, *Idealizm un naturalizm in der yidisher proze*.

7. According to Singer's own chronology, his earliest story was "Leymgrubn" [Clay pits]. The story is dated 1916 in the collection *Perl* [Pearls]. *Leksikon fun der nayer yidisher literatur* [Biographical dictionary of modern Yiddish literature] cites an earlier story (and other stories following it) published in *Dos yidishe vort* [The Yiddish (or Jewish) word]; the journal is not available in Israel or America. This story, whose title is not given but which is described as being about an old maid, is identified as Singer's literary debut.

8. "Perl," signed with the date and place of composition, "Kiev, 1920," appeared first in the short-lived journals *Ringen* (Warsaw, 1921) and in *Sambatyon* (Riga, 1922). In the latter, Singer added a dedication to the New York poets known as *di yunge* [the young], whom he had not yet met. "Perl" was reprinted in the *Forverts* (Jan. 7 –16, 1923).

In correspondence with Cahan (Apr. 28, 1928) and in the pages of the *Forverts* years later, Singer claimed that small-minded political conflicts in the U.S.S.R. had prevented the story's publication there. In the article "A briv fun Amerike" [A letter from America, June 7, 1942], he described the difficulty he had encountered and the aid he had received from Cahan. A portion of the article was reprinted Feb. 20, 1944, after Singer's death (an introductory note inaccurately claims it was first published in the newspaper on June 20, 1942).

9. See, for example, the letter written to Ravitch from New York, dated Oct. 2, 1932.

10. Recent reissues of Singer's novels in translation include *Yoshe Kalb* (New York: Schocken, 1988), *The Family Carnovsky* (New York: Schocken, 1988), *The Brothers Ashkenazi* (New York: Atheneum, 1980, and New York: Carroll & Graf, 1985), *Of a World That Is No More* (New York: Faber & Faber, 1987), *Yoshe egel* (Tel Aviv: Dvir, 1988), *Ha-achim Ashkenazi* (Tel Aviv: Zmora-Bitan, 1987), and *Beit Karnovsky* (Tel Aviv: Am Oved, 1987).

11. Markish, "Di yidishe literatur in Poyln" [Yiddish literature in Poland], *Shtern*, Minsk, 3 (March 1927): 27.

12. Fuks, "Khoyzek oder akhrayes?" [Ridicule or responsibility?], *Literarishe bleter*, no. 10 (March 11, 1927): 193–94.

13. Georg Lukács, *Realism in Our Time*, Chapter 1.

14. Sh. Bikl, *Shrayber fun mayn dor* [Writers of my generation], 326. All translations from Yiddish are my own.

15. Y. Y. Trunk, *Di yidishe proze in Poyln in der tkufe tsvishn beyde velt-milkhomes* [Yiddish prose in Poland between the two world wars], 108, 122.

16. M. Taykhman, "Di epopee fun yidishn Lodz" [The epopee of Jewish Lodz], *Literarishe bleter*, no. 20 (May 15, 1936): 313.

17. Sh. Niger, "Perl," *Bikher-velt*, no. 1–2 (1923): 59. See also his review of *Di brider Ashkenazi*, *Di tsukunft* 41 (December 1936): 806–13.

18. Ravitch, "Di mishpokhe Karnovski," *Di tsukunft* 49 (March 1944): 157.

19. Abraham Bezanker, *Nation* (June 23, 1969): 800–802; Phoebe Adams, *Atlantic Monthly* (February 1969): 133.

20. Richard Elman, *New York Times Book Review* (July 25, 1971): 17–18.

21. Howe, introduction to *The Brothers Ashkenazi*, xiii. See also Sinclair, *The Brothers Singer*.

22. Brody, "A Chassidic Chronicle (Review of *The Sinner*)," *Nation* (May 10, 1933): 533.

23. Rapaport, "Y. Y. Zingers dertseylungen" [I. J. Singer's stories], *Di tsukunft* 54 (March 1949): 158. The article carries a by-line indicating actual date and place of composition. Reprinted in Rapaport, *Oysgerisene bleter* [Random leaves], 246–59.

24. Bashevis repeated this view in an interview I conducted with him (April 30, 1979).

25. Singer, "A briv fun Amerike" [A letter from America].

26. For another view of this group's significance, see my article "Consider Warsaw."

27. Zeitlin, "Y. Y. Zinger, der mentsh un der kinstler" [I. J. Singer, the man and the artist (introduction to *Fun a velt vos iz nishto mer*)], 7.

28. In a retrospective look at Singer's connection with the Yiddish stage, the writer, director, and actor Maurice Schwartz (who was involved with the production of each play except *Khaver Nakhmen*) claimed that Singer planned two more dramatic pieces: a historical drama about Bar Kochba and, in collaboration with Schwartz and Bashevis, a musical comedy based on Bashevis's stories. See Schwartz, "Y. Y. Zinger—der dramaturg" [I. J. Singer—the dramatist].

In its news report about Singer's funeral, the *Forverts* (Feb. 12, 1944) also claimed that, hoping to improve the current state of the Yiddish theater, Singer had decided to write an epic drama about Bar Kochba.

In 1957, a copy of a dramatic comedy by Singer was reported to have been found in the archives of the *Forverts*. The comedy, "In goldenem land" [In the golden land], was described as a play in three acts, the first and last located in America, the second in Poland. *Forverts* (Nov. 15, 1957; Nov. 22, 1957).

Melekh Ravitch wrote that Singer had been contemplating several major novels before his death, including one to be called *175 East Broadway* (the address of the *Forverts*). The work, designed on "a larger scale even than *The Brothers Ashkenazi* . . . was to depict the mighty, dynamic, dramatic upsurge and efflorescence of American Jewry in the course of four or five decades." (The article can be found in a Yiddish manuscript copy in the Ravitch collection of the YIVO Archives and also in English translation: Ravitch, "I. J. Singer: On the Twenty-fifth Anniversary of His Death.")

II. The Wandering Jew

1. Schwartz wrote that Singer came to America with fragments of his own dramatization of the novel, but that he accepted Schwartz's version. Schwartz, "Y. Y. Zinger —der dramaturg" [I. J. Singer—the dramatist], *Forverts* (Mar. 4, 1944).

2. Niger, "On a tsenter" [Without a center], *Di tsukunft* 29 (May 1924): 325–29.

3. Singer, "Vegn di Varshever shriftn" [About the *Warsaw Writings*], *Literarishe bleter*, no. 5 (Feb. 4, 1927): 83–84. He offered praise for very few of the entries in this collection; one exception he made was for a story written by his younger brother, Isaac Bashevis, called "Eyniklekh" [Grandchildren].

4. Mayzl, "Der veg fun der yidisher literatur far di letste fuftsn yor" [The path of Yiddish literature in the last fifteen years], *Haynt yubiley bukh, 1908–1928* [*Haynt Anniversary Book*], (Warsaw: Haynt, 1928), 30–32.

5. The Czernowitz Conference of 1908 brought together individuals from various countries and political leanings. It considered the role of Yiddish, concluding that it had to be recognized as a national language of the Jewish people.

The YIVO (*Yidisher visnshaftlikher institut*) [Institute for Jewish Research], was founded in Vilna in 1925. It became the major repository for information on Yiddish-speaking Jewry, training scholars and developing a wide network of *zamlers* [collectors] who gathered materials about history, linguistics, literature, and folk culture within their communities.

6. "A derklerung fun shriftshteler Y. Y. Zinger" [An explanation by the writer I. J. Singer], *Folkstsaytung* (Warsaw, Apr. 20, 1928).

7. In correspondence with Cahan (Aug. 9, 1928), he referred, in particular, to the attacks on his writing found in the *Frayhayt* and *Tog*.

8. Sh. Niger, "Y. Y. Zinger, *Shtol un Ayzn*," *Bikher-velt*, no. 2 (1928): 43–48.

9. *Bikher-velt*: Kh. Sh. Kazdan, "Der kinstler in geyeg nokh frayhayt" [The artist in pursuit of freedom], no. 3 (1928): 1–7; M. Z[ilberfarb], "Mayse Zinger" [The Singer affair], no. 3 (1928): 61–63; Kazdan, "Dos knekhtishe lid funem frayen Zinger" [The slavish song of the free Singer], no. 4 (1928): 69–72.

10. A. Hamer, "Zinger iz do" [Singer is here], *Frayhayt* (July 11, 1928). See also *Frayhayt* (Oct. 25, 1927; Mar. 28, 1928; July 25, 1928; Dec. 26, 1928). The word *tsitsilistishn* [orthodox-socialist] is a combination of the word for the ritual fringes worn by Orthodox Jews, *tsitses*, and the adjective for socialist, *sotsialistish*.

Singer claimed that the *Frayhayt* was angry with him because he had not agreed to their request that he serve as their correspondent (*Forverts*, Mar. 23, 1928). The *Frayhayt* informed its readers (Mar. 28, 1928) that it was Singer himself who had earlier approached the newspaper seeking to leave the *Forverts*. Singer categorically denied this (in a letter to Cahan dated Apr. 28, 1928). He had, however, written to his friend and colleague, Joseph Opatoshu (Jan. 3, 1927), asking him to make an arrangement with the *Frayhayt* or even the *Tog* for the publication of *Steel and Iron* and his USSR travelogue, because he believed the *Forverts* was no longer publishing his work as quickly as it might. (Opatoshu, a coeditor of the *Literarishe bleter*, was in New York, working with the *Tog*.) Singer complained that Cahan had not relied exclusively on him to report from the Soviet Union, sending the writer H. D. Nomberg as well, and that the *Forverts* was publishing Nomberg's reports rather than his own. Singer told Opatoshu that he had been approached by the *Frayhayt* earlier and was now prepared to accept their offer. Opatoshu urged him to let the matter drop, and in the end, Singer took his advice.

The letter to Opatoshu is located in the Opatoshu collection at the YIVO Archives and is reproduced in *Zamlbikher* 7 (1948), edited by Opatoshu and H. Leivick.

11. Singer wrote Cahan (Apr. 28, 1928) that he wanted to learn another European language (not Polish) and would be happiest if he could come to America and learn English.

In his introduction to the 1965 English edition of *Yoshe Kalb*, Isaac Bashevis referred to his brother's desire to learn Hebrew, German, or French.

See also Bashevis, "Vi azoy *Yoshe Kalb* iz geshafn gevorn" [How *Yoshe Kalb* was created], *Forverts* (Apr. 18, 1965).

12. Part of the following discussion of the novel appeared as an afterword to the Hebrew translation of *Yoshe Kalb*: "Lo gibor, lo metoraf, lo hote" [Neither saint, nor madman, nor sinner] (Tel Aviv: Dvir, 1988).

13. Cahan himself assumed credit for Singer's return to literature in an article he wrote for the *Forverts* announcing forthcoming publication of *Yoshe Kalb*: "A nayer glentsindiker roman fun Y. Y. Zinger" [A magnificent new novel by I. J. Singer], *Forverts* (May 21, 1932).

Nakhman Mayzl, however, claimed that he, his family, and Bashevis knew that Singer was already engaged in writing *Yoshe Kalb* even before Singer met with Cahan in Berlin.

Nakhman Mayzl, "Y. Y. Zinger—der mentsh un kinstler" [The man and artist], *Yidishe kultur*, no. 6 (March 1944): 24.

14. Sh. Niger, "*Yoshe Kalb*—A historisher roman" [A historical novel], *Di tsukunft* 38 (February 1933): 116–22.

15. Sadan urged that the play be erased from Ohel's repertoire (1944), referring to it as "that bacchanalia of abominations." Sadan, *Orhot u'shvilim* [*Ways and paths*], 31.

16. Mukdoyni lamented the absence of pathos and humor in the novel and play, criticizing both its eroticism and its lovelessness. Mukdoyni, "Yoshe Kalb in teater," *Morgn-zhurnal* (Nov. 11, 1932).

17. Y. Y. Trunk, "Y. Y. Zinger." *Di tsukunft* 49 (March 1944): 149–54. See also *Di yidishe proze in Poyln in der tkufe tsvishn beyde velt-milkhomes* [Yiddish prose in Poland between the two world wars], Chapter 18.

18. Nakhman Mayzl, "Arum Y. Y. Zingers *Yoshe Kalb*" [Concerning I. J. Singer's *Yoshe Kalb*], *Literarishe bleter* 41 (October 1935): 653–54.

19. Leslie Fiedler later noted that in the thirty years separating the novel's first and second English editions, American popular tastes had changed dramatically. The first English edition (1933) had been a success; the second (1965) was largely unnoticed because the intervening years had brought its audience to "a moment uncongenial to I. J. Singer's icy and uncompromising rationalism, his impatience with the world of *yiddishkeit* . . . and especially with chasidim." Fiedler, "Marx and Momma," *Collected Essays*, vol. 2, 130.

20. Aaron Zeitlin, "Vegn Y. Y. Zinger un zayn nayem roman" [About I. J. Singer and his new novel], *Globus*, no. 6 (December 1932): 72–79.

21. Page numbers refer to the 1956 edition published by Matones. Translations are my own.

22. The end of Book One underwent significant revisions before book publication. In the pages of the *Forverts*, serialization ends on July 9 with a note stating that revisions from Singer's own hand were received after the relevant installments had been printed. These installments, published July 11–19, comprise Book One, chapters 8–12 in the novel. The revisions do not represent a major change in the plot. In both versions the love between Nahum and Malkele is clear, as are his tortured sense of sin, her frustrated sexuality, the fire she causes in the Nyesheve court, and the physical consummation of their love. But the new version slows the action, making five chapters out of the original one, lengthening the time sequence, and, most significantly, elaborating on the concern with sensuality and sin.

Y. Rapaport accused Cahan of duping the public with these supposedly newly discovered revisions; he claimed they simply pandered to those readers who complained that the scenes between the lovers were too short. (*Vokhnshrift far literatur* [Literary weekly], no. 32 [Aug. 4, 1932]: 2.)

23. In the first *Forverts* text, the connection to Nahum is more explicit. Here, Malkele is taken with labor pains exactly nine months after the Nyesheve fire. The revision erases this detail.

24. Basing his analysis on the writings of Sh. Ansky, the noted folklorist and author of "The Dybbuk", David Roskies traces the penetration of Christian imagery into Yiddish fiction in the early years of the twentieth century. See Roskies, *Against the Apocalypse*, Chapter 10. Irving Howe also examines the image of Christ as it appeared in Yiddish belles lettres (*World of Our Fathers*, 449–51).

25. For a comprehensive study of these themes in Jewish thought, see Arnold Eisen, *Galut: Modern Jewish Reflection on Homelessness and Homecoming*.

26. R. Edelmann, "Ahasuerus, the Wandering Jew," in *The Wandering Jew: Essays in the Interpretation of a Christian Legend*.

27. For a further discussion of these themes, see Yosef Yerushalmi, *Zakhor: Jewish History and Jewish Memory*, and Gershom Sholem, *The Messianic Idea in Judaism and Other Essays in Jewish Spirituality*.

28. Michael Seidel, *Exile and the Narrative Imagination*, 8.

29. Ibid., 197–98.

30. Bashevis, Introduction to *Yoshe Kalb*. Also in Yiddish: Bashevis, "Vi azoy *Yoshe Kalb* is geshafn gevorn" [How *Yoshe Kalb* was created].

31. Mordkhe Shtrigler, "Yoshe Kalb der ershter" [Yoshe Kalb, the first], *Di tsukunft* 57 (April 1952): 181–86. The article is dated Warsaw, 1939. It also appears as the introduction of Shtrigler's *Georemt mitn vint* [Arm in arm with the wind], a novel based on the same figure and often reminiscent of Singer's text.

32. M. A. Ger, "Ver iz geven Yoshe Kalb? Mayne bagegenishn mit im" [Who was Yoshe Kalb? My meetings with him], *Haynt*, Warsaw, Aug. 3, 1932.

Earlier, an announcement for the novel proclaimed that it was "nisht keyn oysgetrakhter nomen" [not a made-up name] but rather based on a real figure who had caused a major sensation in the Jewish world (*Haynt*, July 1, 1932).

33. "A tsvey-toyznt-yoriker toes," 602.

34. Letter in the Ravitch archive, dated Aug. 11, 1942.

35. Letter in the Ravitch archive, dated Sept. 8, 1943.

36. Both died during the war, although Singer himself died without learning their fate. His father had died earlier. His brother, Isaac Bashevis, was safe in New York; his sister, Esther Kreitman, was in London during the war.

37. In *The Brothers Singer*, one of the few English-language studies to consider Singer's fiction (albeit without reference to the Yiddish originals), Clive Sinclair points out that Leontshin, his birthplace, was also literally built on sand and that "this topographical detail assumes metaphorical status as the fate of Polish Jewry unfolds" (p. 11).

III. The Past As Present

1. Part of the following discussion of the novels is based on my article "Hahoveh ke-avar b'romanim shel Y. Y. Zinger" [The present as past in the novels of I. J. Singer].

2. The earliest population statistics for Lodz begin in 1793, when there were eleven Jews in a total population of less than one thousand. Philip Friedman, "Tsu der geshikhte fun yidn in Lodzsh" [Toward the history of Jews in Lodz].

The growth of the Jewish and non-Jewish populations of Lodz are reflected in the following statistics:

Year	Total population	Jewish population (% of total)
1808	434	58 (13.4)
1827	2,837	397 (14.0)
1857	24,655	2,886 (11.7)
1897	309,853	98,386 (31.8)
1921	451,974	156,155 (34.5)

Bohdan Wasiutynski, *Ludnosc zydowska w Polsce w wiekach XIX i XX: Studium statystyczne* [Jewish population in Poland in the 19th and 20th centuries: Statistical studies], 28. I am grateful to Lucjan Dobroszycki of the YIVO Institute for his generous help in providing these figures.

Although *Di brider Ashkenazi* ends before the period of the Nazi invasion of Poland, it should be noted that in 1939 there were 233,000 Jews in Lodz, about one third of its total population. When the city was liberated in 1945, 870 Jews were left. (*Encyclopedia Judaica*).

3. Page numbers refer to the 1951 Yiddish edition published by Matones. Translations are my own.

4. Georg Lukács, *The Historical Novel*, 28.

5. Rivkin, *Undzere prozayiker* [Our prose writers] (New York: YKUF, 1951), 272. Reprinted from "Y. Y. Zingers letst verk" [I. J. Singer's last work], *Epokhe* (May 1944): 314–22.

6. This detail, inexplicably, is missing from Joseph Singer's translation of the novel. It appears in Samuel's earlier translation (p. 603).

7. M. Taykhman, "Di epopee fun yidishn Lodz" [The epopee of Jewish Lodz], *Literarishe bleter*, no. 20 (May 15, 1936): 313.

8. Sh. Niger, "Di brider Ashkenazi," *Di tsukunft* 41 (December 1936): 813.

9. Here Singer borrowed the title of the story he had published in the *Varshever almanakh* (1923). "*Shpinvebs*" appeared (with minor differences) in *Di tsukunft* in December 1923 under the title "Altshtot" [Old town] and was then collected, translated, and critiqued under this title.

10. Tolstoy has been discussed in similar terms. Such diverse critics as Percy Lubbock (*The Craft of Fiction*, 1921) and Victor Shklovsky (*Lev Tolstoy*, 1963), to name only two, refer repeatedly to parallel constructions in *War and Peace*. Shklovsky views history as the moving force in *War and Peace*, and Lubbock argues that the focus of the novel shifts between a historical moment and a more universal sense of individual development. It is by no means coincidental that similar arguments can be made for Singer's novel, since Tolstoy served as a primary model for many Yiddish writers.

11. These individuals are erased in Maurice Samuel's translation (1938), but are restored in the more recent translation by Singer's son, Joseph Singer (1980). Both translations omit a chapter (Book III, Chapter 14) devoted to the unnamed "leader of the New Russia," no doubt because the translators deemed its detailed attention to Lenin to be peripheral or even inaccessible to an English-American audience.

12. Fleishman, *The English Historical Novel*, 10, 123.

13. See Eagleton, *Marxism and Literary Criticism*, especially Chapter 3; Lukács, *Realism in Our Time*; and George Steiner's introductory essay to the latter.

14. Taykhman, "Di epopee fun yidishn Lodz."

15. Howe, Introduction to *The Brothers Ashkenazi* (1980), viii.
See also Sander L. Gilman, "Madness and Racial Theory in I. J. Singer's *The Family Carnovsky*"; Max F. Schulz, "The Family Chronicle as Paradigm of History: *The Brothers Ashkenazi* and *The Family Moskat*."

16. A. A. Mendilow, *Time and the Novel*.

17. Malka Magentsa-Shaked argues that there is a causal connection between the Holocaust and the creation of family sagas in Hebrew and Yiddish and that in Jewish literature the historical background plays a more significant role than in European family sagas. She considers Singer a representative Jewish writer in this regard. Magentsa-Shaked, "Singer and the Family Saga Novel in Jewish Literature," 28–29.

18. See Susan A. Slotnick, "Concepts of Space and Society: Melnits, Berlin and New York in I. J. Singer's Novel *Di mishpokhe Karnovski*."

19. Page numbers refer to the 1943 Yiddish edition published by Matones. Translations are my own.

20. In the letter to Ravitch in which he described his revisions of *The Family Karnovski*, he wrote: "You can imagine that all literary issues . . . have no significance for me given the present situation" (Dec. 24, 1940).

21. Paul Ricoeur, "Narrative Time," 186.

IV. Fictions of the Self

1. Trunk, "Y. Y. Zinger," *Di tsukunft* 49 (March 1944): 153; reprinted in *Di yidishe proze in Poyln in der tkufe tsvishn beyde velt-milkhomes* [Yiddish prose in Poland between the two world wars] (Buenos Aires: Tsentral-farband fun poylishe yidn in Argentiene, 1949), 125. Noakh Gris echoes this view of the novel in his article "Y. Y. Zinger," *Di tsukunft* 90 (January 1984): 24.

2. Page numbers refer to the 1959 Yiddish edition published by Matones. Translations are my own.

3. Avrom Fleishman, *The English Historical Novel*, 149.

4. Niger, "Di brider Ashkenazi fun Y. Y. Zinger," *Di tsukunft* 41 (December 1936): 806, 810.

In an earlier review of *Perl*, he had offered a similar analysis, arguing that Singer is less interested in the wholeness of characters than in their peculiarities. *Bikher-velt*, no. 1–2 (1923): 57–62.

5. The story first appeared in Warsaw as "Shpinvebs," [Spiderwebs] (*Varshever almanakh*, 1923) and as "*Altshtot*" in New York (*Di tsukunft*, December 1923) with only minor lexical and orthographic changes appropriate to the norms of each place of publication. In *Af fremder erd* (1925); English: "Old City," in Samuel (1938).

6. Maurice Samuel's English translation insists on this reading. A faithful translation of Singer's first sentence in this section is: "The next day, early in the morning, Fabian took Baltazar on a leash and went to the other side of the Vistula to drown him." Samuel renders this as: "It is the second morning after the death of Yellowbeak, and Fabian is leading Balthazaar by a leash to drown him in the Vistula." Samuel thus points more emphatically to the motivations that Singer does not articulate. Samuel restores the continuity that Singer had interrupted by interpolating the scenes with the young man and the priest between those of the death of Yellowbeak and the drowning of Baltazar. *Af fremder erd*, 57; Samuel, 132.

V. Creativity and the Artist

1. Maurice Beebe, *Ivory Tower and Sacred Fount: The Artist as Hero in Fiction from Goethe to Joyce*.

2. Mikhail Bakhtin, *Problems of Dostoevsky's Poetics*.

3. Sh. Niger wrote that Singer wanted "to be true to each character and situation without imposing his own sympathies and antipathies," but even Niger's reading of

Singer does not imply a multiplicity of narrative points of view. Niger, "Di brider Ashkenazi," *Di tsukunft* 41 (December 1936): 813. Niger is referring not only to *The Brothers Ashkenazi*, but to Singer's narrative method in general.

4. See especially Frank Kermode, *Romantic Image*, and Mario Praz, *The Romantic Agony*.

5. Max Weinreich, *History of the Yiddish Language*, especially 163–69 and Chapter 4.

6. Shomer (N. M. Shaykevitsh) was the most famous and prolific writer of *shund*, and he rivaled Sholem Aleichem himself in popularity.

7. Singer, "Frayhayt fun kinstler oder shklafn fun frayhayt" [Freedom of artists or slaves of freedom], *Di yidishe velt*, no. 1 (April 1928): 81–97.

8. Bergelson, "Dikhtung un gezelshaftlekhkeyt" [Poetics and society], *Bikher-velt*, no. 4–5 (1919): 5–16.

9. Singer, "Di proze in undzer tsayt," *Bikher-velt*, no. 2 (1922): 143–46. (Singer recast Bergelson's argument, but without referring to it directly.)

10. "A frage vos es loynt vegn ir a shmues ton: moderne ma-yofis" [A question worth discussing: modern cringers], *Literarishe bleter*, no. 84 (Dec. 11, 1925): 303–4.

11. "Di proze in undzer tsayt," 146.

12. "A frage vos es loynt vegn ir a shmues ton: moderne ma-yofis." See also "Kegn hefkeyres un ameratses: vegn iberzetsungen" [Against arbitrariness and ignorance: about translations], *Literarishe bleter*, no. 88 (Jan. 8, 1926): 26–27.

13. "A vikhtike frage" [An important question], *Literarishe bleter*, no. 103 (Apr. 23, 1926): 260–61.

14. "Farzeyenishn" [Freaks], *Literarishe bleter*, no. 25–26 (Oct. 31, 1924): 3.

15. "Yidishe shrayber fun ale lender fareynikt aykh" [Yiddish writers of the world, unite], *Literarishe bleter*, no. 43 (Oct. 28, 1927): 829–30. See discussion in Chapter 2 above.

16. "Yone Rozenfeld," *Literarishe bleter*, no. 39 (Jan. 30, 1925): 2.

17. "Di proze in undzer tsayt," and "Frayhayt fun kinstler oder shklafn fun frayhayt."

18. "Di proze in undzer tsayt," 146.

19. Many of these attacks appeared in the pages of *Literarishe bleter*. He accused Nomberg and Weissenberg of hypocrisy and opportunism after they criticized writers affiliated with *Literarishe bleter* of being in the employ of the well-established *Kultur-lige* ("Es muz gezogt vern" [It must be said], no. 10 (July 11, 1924): 5). He mocked Uri Zvi Greenberg for turning to the Yiddish press despite his rejection of his native tongue in favor of Hebrew ("Der dikhter on'em 'eyen' un di 'shprakh fun di Nalevkes'" [The poet without the letter "ě" and the "language of Nalevkes" (a Jewish area in Warsaw)], no. 51 (Apr. 24, 1925): 7). He criticized *Moment* for ignoring the cultural needs of Warsaw's Jews ("Di klyatshes fun 'pogotovye'-ketshl, oder di 'gikhe-hilf' fun *Moment* farn poylishn yidntum" [The mares of the emergency aid coach, or the *Moment*'s 'first aid' for Polish Jewry], no. 50 (Dec. 16, 1927): 992.

20. "'Eybik aynzam'" [Forever lonely: review of Z. Sagalovitch's *Zeliks yorn* (Zelik's years)], *Literarishe bleter*, no. 18 (Sept. 5, 1924): 2.

21. "A bild fun undzer teater-khurbn" [A view of the destruction of our theater], *Literarishe bleter*, no. 58 (June 12, 1925): 1. See also *Forverts* (May 13, 1923; Apr. 20, 1928; Apr. 26, 1929; Jan. 24, 1930; May 18, 1931); "Nokh amol 'vegn di tsvey dibukim'" [Once again 'about the two dybbuks'"], *Literarishe bleter*, no. 40 (Feb. 6, 1925): 6.

22. See "A fardinte premye" [A well-earned prize (on the naming of Wladislaw Reymont as Nobel Laureate)], *Literarishe bleter*, no. 29 (Nov. 21, 1924): 2.

23. The letter to Opatoshu (dated Feb. 4, 1926) is located in the Opatoshu collection

at the YIVO Archives and is reproduced in *Zamlbikher* 7 (1948), edited by Opatoshu and H. Leivick.

24. Letters to Ravitch dated Dec. 24, 1940; *erev Pesakh*, 1941; Feb. 8, 1943; July 28, 1943.

25. Singer, "Literatur darf farshafn genus," [Literature should create pleasure], *Svive*, no. 1 (January–February 1943): 70.

26. Sh. Niger, "Kunst-teoryes un kinstlerishe praktik" [Art theories and artistic practice], *Di yidishe tsaytung* (Apr. 5, 1943).

27. "Anatol Frans" [Anatole France], *Literarishe bleter*, no. 1 (Apr. 9, 1924): 1.

28. "Literatur darf farshafn gcnus," 72.

VI. The Autobiographical Imagination

1. The work appeared posthumously as "Emese pasirungen" [True events] in the *Forverts* (Apr. 15–Oct. 7, 1944); *Fun a velt vos iz nishto mer* (New York: Matones, 1946); English: *Of a World That Is No More*, trans. Joseph Singer (New York: Vanguard, 1970 and Faber & Faber, 1987). Page numbers refer to the Yiddish edition published by Matones. Translations are my own.

2. *Der sheydim-tants* (Warsaw: Bzoza, 1936); English: *Deborah*, trans. Maurice Carr (1946; London: Virago, 1983; New York: St. Martin's, 1984). Page numbers refer to the Yiddish edition.

Mayn tatns bezdn-shtub, Forverts (Feb. 19–Sept. 30, 1955). Partially translated into English: *In My Father's Court* (New York: Fawcett, 1962). Page numbers refer to the Yiddish edition (Tel Aviv: Peretz farlag, 1979).

3. This discussion of autobiography and the three Singer narratives is based on my article "The Family Singer and the Autobiographical Imagination." For a fuller consideration of Bashevis and Kreitman, see the article.

4. Singer, "'Eybik aynzam'" [Forever lonely], *Literarishe bleter*, no. 18 (Sept. 5, 1924): 3.

5. Singer, "Sholem Aleichems 'Funem yarid,'" *Literarishe bleter*, no. 23 (Oct. 10, 1924): 1.

6. The critical literature is vast, including several journal issues: *Genre* (March 1973), *New Literary History (Autumn 1977), Modern Language Notes* (May 1978); and collections of essays: James Olney, ed., *Autobiography: Essays Theoretical and Critical*; Estelle Jelinek, ed., *Women's Autobiography: Essays in Criticism*; Domna Stanton, ed., *The Female Autograph*; Shari Benstock, ed., *The Private Self: Theory and Practice of Women's Autobiographical Writings*; Bella Brodzki and Celeste Schenck, eds., *Life/Lines: Theorizing Women's Autobiography*.

7. David Roskies argues that the notion of Jewish autobiography is oxymoronic since a focus on individual choices and the idea of the unique self are alien to Jewish culture ("The Forms of Jewish Autobiography," unpub. manuscript). Yael Feldman examines a similar problem in modern Hebrew ("Gender In/Difference in Contemporary Hebrew Fictional Autobiographies"). See also Alvin Rosenfeld, "Inventing the Jew." Alan Mintz's study of Hebrew autobiography, *"Banished from Their Father's Table,"* offers a more thorough analysis of the modern tension between community and self in Jewish (specifically, Hebrew) culture.

8. For discussions of autobiography and psychoanalytic models, see Bruce Mazlish, "Autobiography and Psychoanalysis: Between Truth and Self-Deception"; Susan Friedman, "Women's Autobiographical Selves," in Benstock, ed., *The Private Self*, 34–62; Jeffrey Mehlman, *A Structural Study of Autobiography*, 35–39; Paul Jay, *Being in the Text*, 25–28; John Sturrock, "The New Model Autobiographer."

9. Paul John Eakin, *Fictions in Autobiography*, 3.

10. Jacques Derrida, *The Ear of the Other: Otobiography, Transference, Translation*, 51.

11. Philippe Lejeune's influential *L'Autobiographie en France* argued for such a perspective on autobiography.

12. Despite their different approaches, Elizabeth Bruss (*Autobiographical Acts*), Paul John Eakin, Avrom Fleishman (*Figures of Autobiography*), James Olney (*Metaphors of Self*), Roy Pascal (*Design and Truth in Autobiography*), and Karl Weinbtraub ("Autobiography and Historical Consciousness") agree about this temporal focus in autobiography.

13. Fleishman, 192.

14. Weintraub, 823.

15. These distinctions are not intended to suggest that autobiography is a separate genre as Pascal and William Spengemann (*The Forms of Autobiography*) have argued. Rather, they point to the difficulty in offering generic distinctions between autobiographical writing and other forms of imaginative narrative. Olney, Jay, Sidonie Smith (*A Poetics of Women's Autobiography*), and, most emphatically, Paul De Man ("Autobiography as Defacement") challenge the view of autobiography as a genre.

16. See the essays in Jelinek, especially her introduction and Patricia Meyer Spacks, "Selves in Hiding," 112–32.

17. In *Fun der alter un der nayer heym* [*Of the old and the new home*] he offers what must be read as a grudging acknowledgment of her literary work. Recalling that she returned to Warsaw with no luggage other than a bag of manuscripts, Bashevis writes, "Zi iz geven a gants feyike shrayberin un hot ongeshribn etlekhe gornisht keyn shlekhte bikher" [She was quite a talented authoress and wrote several books that were not at all bad]. *Forverts* (June 6, 1964). In addition to *Der sheydim-tants*, Kreitman wrote *Briliantn* [Diamonds; 1944] and a collection of short stories, *Yikhes* [Lineage/ancestral merit; 1949]. She also translated Dickens's *A Christmas Carol* and George Bernard Shaw's *The Intelligent Woman's Guide to Socialism and Capitalism* into Yiddish.

18. A number of critics have challenged the simple distinction between male autobiographies as linear and coherent and female autobiographies as discontinuous and fragmented. See especially Domna Stanton, "Autogynography: Is the Subject Different?" *The Female Autograph*, 3–20; Catherine R. Stimpson, "The Female Sociograph: The Theater of Virginia Woolf's Letters," *The Female Autograph*, 168–79; Celeste Schenck, "All of a Piece," *Life/Lines*, 281–305; Sidonie Smith, 17–18.

19. Sholem Aleichem's autobiography is an obvious precursor, as are the autobiographies written by the other *klasikers* of Yiddish literature, Sh. Y. Abramovitsh and Y. L. Peretz.

20. Bashevis, *Mayn tatns bezdn-shtub*, Chapter 27; "Fun der alter un der nayer heym," *Forverts* (June 6, 1964).

21. Jelinek, "Introduction," *Women's Autobiography*, 11.

22. Another intriguing source of speculation is Clive Sinclair's claim that the mother, Batsheva Singer, once told her daughter that she had written an autobiography "which she subsequently considered profane and destroyed." Sinclair does not cite his source, and I can find no other proof either that Kreitman knew of this autobiography or that her mother had indeed written one. Sinclair, *The Brothers Singer*, 44.

23. Aaron Zeitlin's preface to the Yiddish text (New York: Matones, 1946) makes this claim. Y. Botoshanski echoes it in "Y. Y. Zingers shvanen-lid" [I. J. Singer's swan song], *Der veg* (June 21, 1947).

24. Khone Shmeruk refers to several texts that have met this fate, most notably the reminiscences *Fun der alter un der nayer heym* (*Forverts*, Sept. 21, 1963–Sept. 11, 1965) and three novels. See Shmeruk, "Bashevis Singer—In Search of His Autobiography."

There were also two sequels to *Mayn tatns bezdn-shtub*. The first, subtitled *Mayn zeydns bezdn-shtub* [My grandfather's courtroom], appeared in the *Forverts* Oct. 7–Dec. 16, 1955; the second, *Der Shrayberklub* [The writer's club], Jan. 13–Dec. 28, 1956.

Bashevis also published *Tipn un geshtaltn fun amol un haynt* [Types and figures of bygone days and today], Apr. 7, 1961–Jan. 12, 1963. Each of these works appeared under the pseudonym Varshavsky.

A number of autobiographical texts have appeared in English, including *A Day of Pleasure and Other Stories, A Little Boy in Search of God, A Young Man in Search of Love, Lost in America,* and a volume combining the last three and adding an introduction, *Love and Exile.*

25. See Smith, Chapter 1; see also Brodzki and Schenck, "Introduction," *Life/Lines,* 1–15, and Carolyn G. Heilbrun, "'Privileged' Women," 62–76.

26. Bikl, *Shrayber fun mayn dor* [*Writers of my generation*], 326.

Afterword

1. Frank Kermode, "Secrets and Narrative Sequence," 84.

2. Andreas Huyssen, *After the Great Divide: Modernism, Mass Culture, Postmodernism,* 47.

Bibliography

These pages include primary and secondary sources. *Leksikon fun der nayer yidisher literatur* [Biographical dictionary of modern Yiddish literature] contains the only prior attempt at such a bibliography, but it is by no means complete and cites none of the articles Singer published under the name G. Kuper. A major obstacle to research concerning most modern Yiddish writers is the dearth of reliable scholarly tools. Singer was one of the many writers who published widely in the periodical press of America and Eastern Europe. Very few of these journals or newspapers—including the daily *Forverts*, with which Singer had a long and prolific relationship—are indexed.

The bibliography is divided into the following sections:

I. Works by I. J. Singer

a. Books

The following books are listed in chronological order. Each entry includes serialization dates, first editions, and English translations. An index of short stories is included where appropriate.

Perl [Pearls]. Warsaw: Kultur-lige, 1922: "Perl," "In vald," "In der fintster," "Magda," "Geleymt," "Leymgrubn," "Zamd," "Davnen," "Klepik," "Blay," "Tshuve."

Af fremder erd [On Foreign Ground]. Warsaw: Kletskin, 1925: "Altshtot," "In veg," "Yidn," "Af der fray," "Af der fremd," "Profesor Arkadi Gritshendler," "In kheyder," "Mames," "In heyse teg," "Blut," "Liuk."

Shtol un Ayzn. Forverts, Mar. 13–Aug. 1, 1927, every Sunday; Vilna: Kletskin, 1927. English: *Blood Harvest*, translated by Morris Kreitman. London: S. Low, Marsten & Co., 1935. *Steel and Iron*, translated by Joseph Singer. New York: Funk & Wagnalls, 1969.

Nay Rusland [New Russia]. Vilna: Kletskin, 1928. More than half of this travelogue appeared in the *Forverts* (beginning March 1927) under different headings, and the articles are listed separately in Section I.d.

Yoshe Kalb. Forverts, June 4–July 19, 1932, daily. Warsaw: the author, 1932; New York: Matones, 1956. English: *The Sinner*, translated by Maurice Samuel. New York: Liveright, 1933. Reissued as *Yoshe Kalb*. New York: Harper & Row, 1965, and Schocken, 1988.

Di brider Ashkenazi. Forverts, Dec. 1, 1934–July 7, 1935, daily excluding Sunday.

Warsaw: Bzoza, 1936; New York: M. N. Mayzil, 1937 and Matones, 1951.
English: *The Brothers Ashkenazi*, translated by Maurice Samuel. New York:
Knopf, 1936. Also translated by Joseph Singer. New York: Atheneum, 1980;
New York: Carroll & Graf, 1985.

Friling [Spring]. Warsaw: Bzoza, 1937: "Vili," "Friling," "Af keyver oves," "Elnt,"
"Bela Saradatshi."

Khaver Nakhmen. Forverts, Nov. 27, 1937–Mar. 22, 1938, daily excluding Sunday.
New York: M. N. Mayzil, 1938 and Matones, 1959. English: *East of Eden*,
translated by Maurice Samuel. New York: Knopf, 1939.

Di mishpokhe Karnovski. Forverts, Oct. 24, 1940–May 13, 1941, daily excluding
Sunday. New York: Matones, 1943. English: *The Family Carnovsky*, translated
by Joseph Singer. New York: Vanguard, 1969 and Schocken, 1988.

Fun a velt vos iz nishto mer (first as "Emese pasirungen" [True events]. *Forverts*, Apr.
15–Oct. 7, 1944. New York: Matones, 1946. English: *Of a World That Is No
More*, translated by Joseph Singer. New York: Vanguard, 1970 and Faber &
Faber, 1987.

Dertseylungen. New York: Matones, 1949: "Baym shvartsn yam," "Doktor
Georgie," "A fremder," "Sender Prager," "Dorfsyidn," "In di berg," "A
basherte zakh," "Stantsye Bakhmatsh."

b. Short Stories and Plays

Singer's stories are listed in alphabetical order and have been transliterated according
to standard YIVO orthography. Entries include first date of publication (where these
have been determined), extant versions, the collection in which the story appears, and
available English translations. The latter are indicated by references to Samuel, the
only translator who has turned his attention to the stories (in Maurice Samuel, *The
River Breaks Up*. New York: Alfred A. Knopf, 1938 and Vanguard, 1976).

"A basherte zakh" [Something destined]. *Forverts*, Apr. 20–May 1, 1943.
Dertseylungen (1949).

"A fremder." *Forverts*, Apr. 25, 1937. *Dertseylungen* (1949). English: "A Stranger," in
Samuel.

"Af der fray" [At liberty]. *Di vog*, Warsaw, Sept. 1922. *Af fremder erd* (1925).

"Af der fremd." *Forverts*, Jan. 27, 1923. *Af fremder erd* (1925). English: "Alien
Earth," in Samuel.

"Af keyver oves" [Visiting the graveside of parents]. *Forverts*, Apr. 16, 23, 1933.
Literarishe bleter, July 14–Aug. 11, 1933. *Friling* (1937).

"Altshtot." First as "Shpinvebs" [Spiderwebs], *Varshever almanakh*, 1923. "Altshtot,"
Di tsukunft, Dec. 1923. *Af fremder erd* (1925). English: "Old City," in Samuel.

"Baym shvartsn yam" [Near the Black Sea]. *Forverts*, Apr. 2–16, 1942. *Dertseylungen*
(1949).

"Bela Saradatshi." *Forverts*, May 20, 27, 1934. *Friling* (1937).

"Blay" [Lead]. *Ringen*, Warsaw, 1922. *Perl* (1922).

"Blut." First as "Simkhe," *Forverts*, Sept. 10–Oct. 5, 1924. *Af fremder erd* (1925).
English: "Blood," in Samuel.

"Davnen" [Praying]. Signed 1918. *Perl* (1922).

"Doktor Georgie." *Forverts*, Nov. 7–14, 1936. *Dertseylungen* (1949). English: "Doctor
Georgie," in Samuel.

"Dorfsyidn" [Village Jews]. *Forverts*, Apr. 4–17, 1939. *Dertseylungen* (1949).

"Elnt" [Alone]. First as "Barg arop" [Downhill], *Forverts*, Aug. 12, 1933. *Friling* (1937).

Erdvey: drama in dray bilder [Earth pangs: a play in three scenes]. Warsaw:
Kultur-lige, 1922.

"Friling." *Friling* (1937). English: "Late Spring," in Samuel.

"Geleymt." First as "Af di gurkes" [On the hills]. *Der oyfgang*, Lodz, 1921. *Perl* (1922). English: "Paralysed," in Samuel.
"In der fintster" [In the dark]. Signed Kiev, 1919. *Khaliastre*, no. 1 (Warsaw, 1922): 21–29. *Perl* (1922).
"In di berg." *Forverts*, Sept. 26–Oct. 15, 1942. *Dertseylungen* (1949).
"In heyse teg" [During hot days]. *Forverts*, Oct. 19, 1924. *Af fremder erd* (1925).
"In kheyder" [In the heder]. *Af fremder erd* (1925).
"In vald" [In the forest]. *Baginen*, Kiev, 1919. *Perl* (1922).
"In veg" [En route]. *Af fremder erd* (1922). *Forverts*, Feb. 17, 1923.
"Klepik" [Contagious]. Signed Constantinograd, 1920. *Perl* (1922).
"Leymgrubn." Signed 1916. *Perl* (1922). English: "Clay Pits," in Samuel.
"Liuk." *Literarishe bleter*, Apr. 30–May 22, 1925; and *Forverts*, May 10 and 17, 1925. *Af fremder erd* (1925). English: "Luke," in Samuel.
"Magda" [Magda]. Signed 1917. *Oyfgang*, Kiev, 1919. *Perl* (1922).
"Mames" [Mothers]. *Forverts*, Mar. 17, 1923. *Af fremder erd* (1925).
"Perl." Signed Kiev, 1920. *Ringen* (Warsaw, 1921); *Sambatyen* (Riga, 1922); *Forverts*, Jan. 7–16, 1923; reprinted *Forverts*, Mar. 4–20, 1944. *Perl* (1922). English: "Pearls," in Samuel.
"Profesor Arkadi Gritshendler." *Forverts*, March 17, 1923. *Af fremder erd* (1925).
Savinkov: drame in 12 bilder [Savinkov: a play in 12 scenes]. *Globus*, no. 7 (Warsaw, January 1933): 1–69.
"Sender Prager." *Forverts*, Mar. 27–Apr. 1, 1937. *Dertseylungen* (1949). English: "Sender Praguer," in Samuel.
"Stantsye Bakhmatsh: an epizod fun der rusisher revolutsye" [Bakhmatsh Station: an episode from the Russian Revolution]. *Forverts*, Oct. 14–20, 1943. *Dertseylungen* (1949).
"Tshuve." *Perl* (1922). *Literarishe reviu*, Paris, 1926. English: "Repentance," in Samuel, and in Howe and Greenberg, *A Treasury of Yiddish Stories*. New York: Viking, 1953.
"Vili." *Forverts*, Apr. 7–25, 1936. *Friling* (1937). A version of "Vili" adapted for schoolchildren appeared after Singer's death, edited by Zalman Yefroykin (New York: Arbeter-ring mitelshul, 1948).
"Yidn" [Jews]. *Forverts*, Apr. 15, 1923; *Ilustrirte vokh*, no. 17 (Warsaw, Apr. 17, 1924). *Af fremder erd* (1925).
"Zamd." *Perl* (1922). *Forverts*, May 27 and June 3, 1923. English: "Sand," in Samuel, and in Howe and Greenberg, *A Treasury of Yiddish Stories* (New York: Viking, 1953).

c. Literary Essays, Articles, and Reviews

These essays are listed in alphabetical order. They have never been collected or translated. The essays Singer published in *Literarishe bleter* are included in this category.
"A bild fun undzer teater-khurbn" [A view of the destruction of our theater]. *Literarishe bleter*. no. 58 (June 12, 1925): 1.
"A briv fun Amerike" [A letter from America]. *Forverts*, June 7, 1942, reprinted Feb. 20, 1944.
"A derklerung fun shriftshteler Y. Y. Zinger" [An explanation by the writer I. J. Singer]. *Folkstsaytung*, (Warsaw), Apr. 20, 1928.
"A fardinte premye" [A well-earned prize (on the naming of Wladislaw Reymont as Nobel Laureate)]. *Literarishe bleter*, no. 29 (Nov. 21, 1924): 2.
"A frage vos es loynt vegn ir a shmues ton: moderne ma-yofis" [A question worth discussing: modern cringers]. *Literarishe bleter*, no. 84 (Dec. 11, 1925): 303–4.

"A perzenlekhe erklerung fun undzer mitarbeter Y. Y. Zinger" [A personal explanation by our colleague]. *Forverts*, Mar. 23, 1928.

"A tsvey toyznt yoriker toes'" [A two-thousand-year-old mistake]. *Di tsukunft*, 47 (Oct. 1942): 596–602.

"A vikhtike frage" [An important question]. *Literarishe bleter*, no. 103 (Apr. 23, 1926): 260–61.

"A.M. Fuks—'Afn bergl'" [A.M. Fuks—'On the hill']. *Bikher-velt*, no. 1–2 (1924): 24–25.

"An eygn vinkl" [Our own corner]. *Literarishe bleter*, no. 9 (Mar. 2, 1928): 163.

"Anatol Frans" [Anatole France]. *Literarishe bleter*, no. 1 (Apr. 9, 1924): 1.

"Der dikhter on'em 'eyen' un di 'shprakh fun di Nalevkes'" [The poet without the letter "ɛ" and the "language of Nalevkes" (a Jewish area in Warsaw)]. *Literarishe bleter*, no. 51 (Apr. 24, 1925): 7.

"Di klyatshes fun 'pogotovye'-ketshl, oder di 'gikhe-hilf' fun *Moment* farn poylishn yidntum" [The mares of the emergency aid coach, or the *Moment*'s 'first aid' for Polish Jewry]. *Literarishe bleter*, no. 50 (Dec. 16, 1927): 992.

"Di proze in undzer tsayt" [Prose in our time]. *Bikher-velt*, no. 2 (1922): 143–46.

"Dos fayer" [Review of Yiddish translation of Henri Barbusse's *The Fire*]. *Literarishe bleter*, no. 3 (May 23, 1924): 5.

"Dos land hot frayer opgeotemt" [The country breathed more freely]. *Literarishe bleter*, no. 99–100 (Mar. 26, 1926): 216.

"Es muz gezogt vern" [It must be said]. *Literarishe bleter*, no. 10 (July 11, 1924): 5.

"'Eybik aynzam'" [Forever lonely: review of Z. Segalovitch's *Zeliks yorn* (Zelik's years)]. *Literarishe bleter*, no. 18 (Sept. 5, 1924): 2–3.

"Farshvigene bikher" [Concealed books (about Y. Perle's "*Zind*" [Sins])]. *Literarishe bleter*, no. 6 (June 13, 1924): 3.

"Farzeyenishn" [Freaks]. *Literarishe bleter*, no. 25–26 (Oct. 31, 1924): 3.

"Frayhayt fun kinstler oder shklafn fun frayhayt" [Freedom of artists or slaves of freedom]. *Di yidishe velt*, no. 1 (Apr. 1928): 81–97.

"Kegn hefkeyres un ameratses: vegn iberzetsungen" [Against arbitrariness and ignorance: about translations]. *Literarishe bleter*, no. 88 (Jan. 8, 1926): 26–27.

"Kinstler oder kintsler" [Artist or artificer (Ilya Ehrenburg)]. *Literarishe bleter*, no. 23 (June 10, 1927): 429–30.

"Literatur darf farshafn genus" [Literature should create pleasure]. *Svive*, no. 1 (Jan.–Feb. 1943): 69–72.

"Mikoyekh khoyzek oder akhrayes (an entfer A.M. Fuks)" [Concerning ridicule or responsibility (a response to A.M. Fuks)]. *Literarishe bleter*, no. 10 (Mar. 11, 1927): 194.

"Mir un di galitsyaner" [We and the Galicians]. *Literarishe bleter*, no. 44 (Mar. 6, 1925): 2.

"Nokh amol 'vegn di tsvey dibukim'" [Once again 'about the two dybbuks']. *Literarishe bleter*, no. 40 (Feb. 6, 1925): 6.

"Peretz Markish." *Bikher-velt*, no. 5 (1923): 345–50.

"Sholem Aleichems 'Funem yarid'" [Sholem Aleichem's *From the Fair*]. *Literarishe bleter*, no. 23 (Oct. 10, 1924): 1.

"Vegn der literatur un kultur in Ratn-farband" [About the literature and culture of the Soviet Union]. *Literarishe bleter*, no. 1 (Jan. 7, 1927): 4–5.

"Vegn di Varshever shriftn" [About the *Warsaw Writings*]. *Literarishe bleter*, no. 5 (Feb. 4, 1927): 83–84.

"Vilne." *Literarishe bleter*, no. 94 (Feb. 19, 1926): 125.

"Vi s'vert gearbet in yidishn kunst-teater" [How things are done in the Yiddish Art Theater]. *Literarishe bleter*, no. 40–41 (Oct. 4, 1933): 647.

"Yidishe shrayber fun ale lender fareynikt aykh" [Yiddish writers of the world, unite]. *Literarishe bleter*, no. 43 (Oct. 28, 1927): 829–30.
"Yone Rozenfeld." *Literarishe bleter*, no. 39 (Jan. 30, 1925): 2.

d. Feature Articles in the *Forverts*

Singer served as a correspondent for the *Forverts* from 1923 until his death. The following is a chronological list of feature articles he published there under his own name. The influence of *Forverts* orthography is evident throughout, as are the Yiddish adaptations of English words that were a common practice of the newspaper.

May 13, 1923. "Der yidisher teater in Poyln lebt itst durkh a shvern krizis" [The Yiddish theater in Poland is now living through a difficult crisis].
Aug. 22, 1924. "Di yidishe shuln fun Poyln lebn itst iber a shreklekhe krizis" [The Jewish schools in Poland are now enduring a terrible crisis].
Sept. 1, 1925. "Bilder un stsenes in yidishe kvartaln in Pariz" [Pictures and scenes of the Jewish quarters in Paris].
Sept. 5, 1925. "Nokh halbe nakht in Pariz" [In the middle of the night in Paris].
Dec. 6, 1925. "Der amoliker kheyder" [The former heder].
Feb. 10, 1926. "Ershte briv vegn der shreklekher yidisher tragedie in Poyln" [First letters about the terrible Jewish tragedy in Poland].
Feb. 16, 1926. "Hungerbilder fun di yidishe shtet in Poyln" [Pictures of hunger from Jewish cities in Poland].
Feb. 20, 1926. "Der shreklekher yidisher hunger in Varshe vi er shpiglt zikh op in di shuln" [The horrible Jewish famine in Warsaw as reflected in the schools].
Feb. 23, 1926. "Undzer spetsieler korespondent Y. Y. Zinger shildert dos hunger-lebn in Vilne" [Our special correspondent I. J. Singer describes the famine in Vilna].
Feb. 25, 1926. "Bilder un stsenes fun der shreklekher noyt in Vilne." [Pictures and scenes of the terrible poverty in Vilna].
Feb. 27, 1926. "Di itstike lage fun di yidishe tsedoke-anshtaltn in Vilne" [The present situation of the Jewish charity institutions in Vilna].
Mar. 2, 1926. "Bilder fun der itstiker shreklekher noyt in di shuln fun Vilne un Bialistok" [Pictures of the current terrible poverty in the schools of Vilna and Bialystok].
Mar. 4, 1926. "Bialistok iz shoyn mer nit keyn shtot, nor a besalmen" [Bialystok is no longer a city, but rather a cemetery].
Mar. 6, 1926. "Di fartsveyfelte lage fun di yidishe arbeter in Lodzsh" [The desperate situation of the Jewish workers in Lodz].
Mar. 16, 1926. "Bilder fun noyt un elnt in di gasn un hayzer fun Lodzsh" [Pictures of poverty and loneliness in the streets and houses of Lodz].
Mar. 18, 1926. "Hungerbilder in a shtetl vos bashteyt durkhoys fun shnayder (Bzshezshin)" [Pictures of famine in a town consisting entirely of tailors].
Mar. 20, 1926. "Ven ale taykhn zoln zayn tint un ale mentshn shrayber volt men nisht gekent bashraybn dem groysn umglik fun di yidn in Poyln" [If all the rivers were full of ink and all people were writers, we would still be incapable of describing the great misfortunes of Jews in Poland].
Apr. 12, 1926. "Vi azoy lebn fort yidn in Poyln?" [How, indeed, do Jews live in Poland?]
    NOTE: Singer spent several months traveling in Russia, beginning in late 1926. His impressions of that trip were recorded in the pages of the *Forverts* and in *Nay Rusland*. With the exception of the entry dated May 19, versions of the following articles published in 1927 were included in *Nay Rusland*.
Mar. 4, 1927. "Af di gasn un di kafes, stors, hotels fun Moskve" [In the streets and the cafes, stores, hotels of Moscow].

Mar. 7, 1927. "Di tragedye fun tseshtertn familyen-lebn in Rusland" [The tragedy of unsettled family life in Russia].

Mar. 11, 1927. "A briv fun a yidisher kolonye in Vaysrusland" [A letter from a Jewish colony in White Russia].

NOTE: *Shtol un Ayzn* appeared in the *Forverts* every Sunday from March 13 until August 1, 1927. At the same time, articles by Singer and G. Kuper appeared.

Mar. 14, 1927. "A bazukh in Kharkov, Yekaterinoslav un Krivoy-rog" [A visit to Kharkov, Yekaterinoslav and Krivoy-rog (in the Ukraine)].

Mar. 18, 1927. "A briv fun di yidishe kolonyes in Soviet Rusland" [A letter from the Jewish colonies in Soviet Russia].

Mar. 25, 1927. "Vi azoy Odes zet itst oys" [What Odessa looks like now].

Mar. 28, 1927. "A bazukh in di yidishe derfer in Krim" [A visit to the Jewish villages in Crimea].

Apr. 1, 1927. "Tshikave bagegenishn, bilder, stsenes tsvishn yidishe kolonistn in Krim" [Curious encounters, pictures, scenes among Jewish colonists in Crimea].

Apr. 4, 1927. "Bilder funem lebn fun di yidishe farmers in Soviet Rusland" [Pictures of the lives of Jewish farmers in Soviet Russia].

Apr. 20, 1927. "Tshikave bagegenishn in Soviet Rusland" [Curious encounters in Soviet Russia].

Apr. 27, 1927. "Di farsheydene felker fun Soviet Rusland" [The varied peoples of Soviet Russia].

May 3, 1927. "Der pesimist: a bild fun itstikn Rusland" [The pessimist: A picture of present-day Russia].

May 14, 1927. "Vi halt es itst mit der rusisher un yidisher literatur in Soviet Rusland" [How are things with current Russian and Yiddish literature in Soviet Russia?].

May 19, 1927. "Tsvey briv vegn dem farshtorbenem sotsialistishn firer fun Poyln, der yid Dr. Feliks Perl" [Two letters about the deceased socialist leader of Poland, the Jew, Dr. Felix Perl].

June 4, 1927. "Vi azoy es zet itst oys Kiev" [What Kiev looks like now].

NOTE: Singer generally wrote feature articles under the name G. Kuper. He resumed such publication under his own name when he visited the United States in September 1932.

Sept. 15, 1932. "Y. Y. Zinger makht a shpatsir iber di gasn fun der ist sayd; er farglaykht zey mit di yidishe gasn in Varshe" [I. J. Singer takes a walk in the streets of the East Side; he compares them to the Jewish streets of Warsaw].

Sept. 17, 1932. "Di oremkeyt in Nyu York un di oremkeyt in di groyse shtet in Eyrope" [Poverty in New York and in the big cities of Europe].

Sept. 23, 1932. "Vos Y. Y. Zinger hot gezen in di neger kabareys in Harlem" [What I. J. Singer saw in the Negro cabarets of Harlem].

Sept. 27, 1932. "Me ken nit keyn land biz me zet es nit aleyn" [No one knows a country until one sees it for oneself].

Sept. 30, 1932. "Vos ikh glaykh yo un vos ikh glaykh nit in Amerike" [What I do and don't like in America].

Oct. 6, 1932. "Y. Y. Zinger dertseylt vos er hot gezen in Tchaynetaun" [I. J. Singer tells about what he saw in Chinatown].

Oct. 8, 1932. "Di kongregeyshens, khevres, parteyn, tsaytungen un literatn in Tchaynetaun" [The congregations, societies, newspapers and literati in Chinatown].

Oct. 13, 1932. "Frumkeyt iz a besere biznes in Nyu York vi in Varshe" [Piety is a better business in New York than in Warsaw].

Oct. 15, 1932. "Komishe erfarungen fun a grinem in Nyu York" [Comical experiences of a greenhorn in New York].

Oct. 29, 1932. "Ale gebn mir eytses" [Everyone gives me advice].

Nov. 2–3, 1932. "Tsu vayb un kinder" [To my wife and children].

Nov. 12, 1932. "B. Faygenboyms khaveyrim un talmidim in Varshe" [B. Faygenboym's friends and students in Warsaw].

Jan. 17, 1933. "Tsurik in Poyln: shildert zayn rayze aheym" [Back in Poland: Describing his journey home].

> NOTE: When Singer returned to Poland, he resumed publication under G. Kuper.

Mar. 29, 1933. "Y. Y. Zinger hot a geshprekh mit Urke Nakhalnik" [I. J. Singer has a conversation with Urke Nakhalnik].

> NOTE: Singer emigrated to the United States in March 1934. For several months, articles appeared in the *Forverts* under both by-lines: I. J. Singer and G. Kuper. The former were primarily about life in America.

Apr. 6, 1934. "Y. Y. Zinger bakukt di yidishe kvartaln fun Nyu York durkh zayne varshever briln" [I. J. Singer looks at the Jewish quarters of New York through his Warsaw lenses].

Apr. 10, 1934. "Rivington strit durkh varshever briln" [Rivington Street through Warsaw lenses].

Apr. 14, 1934. "Nyu yorker gasn durkh varshever briln" [New York streets through Warsaw lenses].

Apr. 18, 1934. "Dos lebn fun di yidishe arbeter in Nyu York gezen durkh varshever briln" [The life of Jewish workers in New York seen through Warsaw lenses].

Apr. 21, 1934. "Yidishe gesheftn in Nyu York gezen durkh varshever briln" [Jewish businesses in New York seen through Warsaw lenses].

May 18, 1934. "Y. Y. Zinger bashraybt dem natsi miting in Medison Skver Garden" [I. J. Singer describes the Nazi meeting in Madison Square Garden].

June 27, 1934. "Nyu yorker bilder" [New York pictures].

Aug. 27, 1934. "Y. Y. Zinger bazukht dem arbeter-ring sanatoryum" [I. J. Singer visits the Workman's Circle sanitorium].

Oct. 23, 1934. "Tsu gast baym 'shvartsn got' in Harlem" [On a visit to the 'black god' in Harlem].

Oct. 24, 1934. "Der shvartser got fun Harlem—ver er iz un vi azoy er hot zikh gemakht far a got" [The black god of Harlem—who he is and how he made himself into a god].

Oct. 25, 1934. "Der 'shvartser got' fun Harlem hot shoyn amol gekrogn a yor prizon" [The 'black god' of Harlem was once sentenced to a year's prison term].

Oct. 27, 1934. "Der shvartser 'novi' velkher firt milkhome kegn dem shvartsn got fun Harlem" [The black 'prophet' who is at war with the black god of Harlem].

> NOTE: No feature articles appeared under the names Singer or Kuper during the five-year period in which *Di brider Ashkenazi, Khaver Nakhman,* and *Friling* were published.

Sept. 9, 1939. "Der kharakter fun di shtet in Poyln velkhe gefinen zikh untern natsishn fayer" [The character of the Polish cities that find themselves under Nazi attack].

Sept. 13, 1939. "Varshe—grester yidisher tsenter in Eyrope" [Warsaw—the largest Jewish center in Europe].

Sept. 16, 1939. "Lodzsh—di greste yidishe industriele shtot in Poyln" [Lodz—the largest Jewish industrial city in Poland].

Sept. 21, 1939. "Lemberg—di vikhtikste yidishe shtot in Galitsye" [Lemberg—the most important Jewish city in Galicia].

Sept. 25, 1939. "Kroke—a denkmol fun der poylisher un yidisher geshikhte" [Cracow —a monument to Polish and Jewish history].

Sept. 28, 1939. "Vilne—Yerushalayem delite un ir badaytung in yidishn lebn" [Vilna —the Jerusalem of Lithuania and its significance in Jewish life].

Oct. 5, 1939. "Prage, der teyl fun Varshe vos iz itst khorev gevorn" [Prage, the part of Warsaw that has now been destroyed].

Oct. 14, 1939. "Frier hot Hitler getribn yidn, itst traybt er kristn" [First Hitler chased Jews out of their homes; now he is chasing Christians].

Oct. 21, 1939. "Der general un der rov (vegn gayst un shverd)" [The general and the rabbi (about the spirit and the sword)].

Nov. 18, 1939. "In 4tn 'raykh' baym Hodson" [In the Fourth Reich, near the Hudson].

Nov. 28, 1939. "Di groys-kapitalistn fun vilner yatke-gas" [The big capitalists in Vilna's Yatke (Butcher shop) Street].

Jan. 6, 1940. "Vinter in ketskil-berg" [Winter in the Catskill Mountains].

Jan. 13, 1940. "Tsvishn yidishe farmers in di berg" [Among Jewish farmers in the mountains].

July 15, 1940. "Y. Y. Zinger bashraybt zayn rayze fun Nyu York nokh Los Andzseles" [I. J. Singer describes his trip from New York to Los Angeles].

July 27, 1940. "Dos tsoyberland Kalifornia iz vi a fantastishe muvi" [The magical land of California is like a fantastic movie].

Aug. 3, 1940. "Vos men zet forndik baym breg funem pasifishn yam" [What one sees traveling the coast of the Pacific Ocean].

Aug. 10, 1940. "Inmitn zumer tuen zikh on mentshn in koldres un loyfn hern muzik" [In the middle of summer, people wear blankets and run to hear music].

Aug. 17, 1940. "A yidishe 'geto' ayngetunken in blumen, palmen, un orandzs-boymer (Los Andzseles)" [A Jewish 'ghetto' steeped in flowers, palm trees, and orange trees (Los Angeles)].

Aug. 24, 1940. "Vos me zet un me hert in di muvi-studyos fun Holivud" [What one sees and hears in the movie studios of Hollywood].

Sept. 21, 1940. "Tshikave yidn bagegnt men forndik iber Amerike" [One meets curious Jews traveling through America].

Sept. 28, 1940. "Tshikave mentshn in der muvi kolonye fun Holivud" [Curious people in the movie colony of Hollywood].

Oct. 5, 1940. "Der yarid fun 'heylike' mentshn in Kalifornye" [The spectacle of 'holy' people in California].

Oct. 19, 1940. "A galekhte mit a roytn tseylem afn buzem un mit gefarbte lipn" [A priest's wife with a red cross on her bosom and painted lips].

NOTE: *Di mishpokhe Karnovski* appeared daily, excluding Sunday, from October 24, 1940 through May 13, 1941.

June 12, 1941. "An oytomobil-rayze iber Amerike" [A car trip through America].

June 19, 1941. "Y. Y. Zinger shildert dem vundersheynem park, Sekvaye, in Kalifornye" [I. J. Singer describes the gorgeous park, Sequoia, in California].

June 26, 1941. "Der barimter khinezisher kvartal fun San Fransisko" [San Francisco's famous Chinatown].

July 3, 1941. "Bilder, stsenes un bagegenishn in di kleyne shtetlekh fun der vayter vest" [Pictures, scenes, and encounters in the small towns of the Far West].

July 10, 1941. "A rayze iber dem barimtn Yeloston park" [A trip through the famous Yellowstone Park].

July 17, 1941. "Di midel-vest, di raykhe kenigraykh fun veyts un korn" [The Midwest, the rich kingdom of wheat and corn].

July 24, 1941. "Shikago, di grenets shtot tsvishn ist un vest" [Chicago, the border city between East and West].

Aug. 12, 1941. "Tshikave yidishe tipn in di shtetlekh fun Amerike" [Curious Jewish types in the towns of America].

Aug. 21, 1941. "Mishigen—di melukhe fun oytomobiln" [Michigan—the automobile state].

May 3, 1942. "A geshprekh mit der barimter norveger shraybern Zigrid Undset vegn di natsis" [A conversation with the famous Norwegian writer Sigrid Undset about the Nazis].

June 26, 1943. "Tsum ondenk Dovid Druk, der bavuster yidisher shriftshteler vos iz itst geshtorbn" [In memory of Dovid Druk, the well-known Yiddish writer who has recently died].

II. Contributions to the *Forverts* by G. Kuper

The following articles, listed in chronological order, appeared in the *Forverts* under Singer's pseudonym; most carry a by-line identifying them as "fun undzer poylishn [or varshavn] korespondent, G. Kuper" [by our Polish (or Warsaw) correspondent, G. Kuper].

NOTE: *Shtol un ayzn* was serialized Mar. 13–Aug. 1, 1927.

March 26, 1927. "Vos s'hot zikh opgeton in Pshemishl mitn protses fun radzinimer rebn un der yidene fun Stanton Strit Nyu York" [What happened in Pshemishl with the trial of the rabbi of Radimin and the woman from Stanton Street, New York].

May 17, 1927. "Komishe un tragishe stsenes in varshever bezdn-shtibl" [Comic and tragic scenes in a Warsaw religious courtroom].

May 24, 1927. "Pasirungen in Varshe in velkhe es zaynen farmisht amerikaner" [Events in Warsaw in which Americans are implicated].

June 3, 1927. "A shoyderlekhe familien-drame in a yidisher familye fun Varshe un Amerike (A foter hayrat zayn eygene tokhter un hot mit ir a kind)" [A horrible family drama in a Jewish family from Warsaw and America (A father marries his own daughter and has a child with her)].

June 8, 1927. "'Rabonim' fun varshever untervelt mishpetn a khosid far a miese geshikhte" ["Rabbis" of the Warsaw underworld put a hasid on trial because of an ugly story].

June 19, 1927. "Berg mit yidishe berd valgern zikh in a forshtetl lebn Varshe" [Mountains of Jewish beards lying in a town near Warsaw].

June 22, 1927. "A geshikhte mit a batkhn vos flegt farfirn un farkoyfn khsidishe meydlekh" [A story about a man who entertains at weddings, who used to seduce and sell hasidic girls].

July 1, 1927. "Komishe bildlekh un stsenes fun yidishn lebn in Poyln" [Funny pictures and scenes of Jewish life in Poland].

July 20, 1927. "A yid mit bord un peyes a geferlekher shvindler un froyenfarfirer" [A Jew with beard and earlocks: A terrible swindler and seducer of women].

July 23, 1927. "Der groyser yontev in Poyln ven men hot fun Pariz gebrakht di beyner fun barimtn dikhter Yulius Slovatski" [The great holiday in Poland when the bones of the famous poet Julius Slovatski were brought from Paris].

July 27, 1927. "Sensatsionele un komishe geshikhte tsvishn 'gute yidn' khsidim un stam klekoydesh" [Sensational and comical story between hasidic rabbis and ordinary Jewish clergy].

July 28, 1927. "An amerikaner yid farshpart in Poyln zayn froy in a meshugoyem-hoyz" [An American Jew in Poland imprisons his wife in an insane asylum].

Aug. 10, 1927. "Dervust zikh, az er hot untergeshribn a papir, az zayn eygene mame iz an oysgelasene, nemt er zikh dos lebn" [Learning that he signed a paper saying that his own mother is a loose woman, he takes his life].

Aug. 12, 1927. "A kamf af toyt un lebn tsulib oylem-habe" [A life and death battle for the sake of the world to come].

Aug. 18, 1927. "Komishe un ernste bildlekh fun yidishn lebn in Poyln" [Comical and serious pictures of Jewish life in Poland].

Aug. 27, 1927. "Bilder fun yidishe hinter-geslekh un untervelt in Varshe" [Pictures of Jewish back alleys and the underworld in Warsaw].

Sept. 6, 1927. "In der shtot vu s'hot gelebt di yidishe kenign fun Poyln (Kazimir)" [In the town where the Jewish queen of Poland lived].

Sept. 8, 1927. "Dray minim yidn vos ale hobn zikh faynt" [Three sorts of Jews who hate one another].

Sept. 17, 1927. "An oysshtelung fun kalikes" [An exhibit of cripples].

Sept. 29, 1927. "Bilder fun yidishn lebn in Tshekoslovakay" [Pictures of Jewish life in Czechoslovakia].

Oct. 3, 1927. "Vi azoy es lebn itster di yidn fun Tshekoslovakay" [How the Jews of Czechoslovakia live now].

Oct. 13, 1927. "A vaybershe revolutsye in a rebishn hoyf in Poyln" [A women's revolution in a rabbi's courtyard in Poland].

Oct. 22, 1927. "Khsidim khapn tsu slikhes di rebetsin mitn gabe in rebns shlof-tsimer" [During penitential prayers, hasidim catch the rabbi's wife with his aide in the rabbi's bedroom].

Oct. 25, 1927. "Amerikaner yidisher yunger-man dervust zikh plutsling az er iz an umgezetslekh kind fun a tatn a krist" [American Jewish youth suddenly learns he is an illegitimate child of a Christian father].

Oct. 29, 1927. "Der 'sultan' Zalmen Kishke mit zayne zeks vayber" [The "sultan" Zalmen Kishke and his six wives].

Oct. 31, 1927. "Tsulib sode-vaser raysn zikh arum a gants shtetl yidn" [Because of soda water, an entire town of Jews quarrels].

Nov. 5, 1927. "A varshever rovs a zun, an ile, vil zikh shmadn um yom kiper" [Brilliant son of a Warsaw rabbi wants to convert on Yom Kippur].

Nov. 12, 1927. "Tsvey komishe pasirungen fun dem yidishn lebn in Varshe" [Two comical events in Jewish life in Warsaw].

Nov. 14, 1927. "Mentshn vos kumen betn modne toyves baym korespondent fun 'Forverts' in Varshe" [People who come to ask for strange favors of the *Forverts* correspondent in Warsaw]. (A similar feature essay, signed by Y. Y. Zinger, appeared in *Haynt yubiley-bukh, 1908–1928* [*Haynt* anniversary book], p. 28, under the title "Toyves" [Favors].)

Nov. 19, 1927. "Zayn onkl, a farbrenter khosid, hot im khasene gemakht mit a tsigaynerin" [His uncle, an ardent hasid, married him off to a gypsy].

Dec. 3, 1927. "Itshele vil nisht shlogn keyn heshaynes shlogt Shprintsele mit im kapores" [Itshele doesn't want to perform the Succoth ceremony, so Shprintsele attacks him].

Dec. 8, 1927. "A tcholent-skandal in Varshe" [A stew-scandal in Warsaw].

Dec. 10, 1927. "Komishe mayses fun lebn fun der yidisher untervelt in Poyln" [Funny stories of the life of the Jewish underworld in Poland].

Dec. 15, 1927. "Amerikaner yidisher yunger-man antloyft mitn tatns yunge froy keyn Varshe (un er lozt iber dem foter zayn eygn vayb mit tsvey kinder)" [American Jewish youth runs away to Warsaw with his father's young wife (and leaves his father with his own wife and two children)].

Dec. 17, 1927. "Bay der khupe dervisn zikh di mekhutonim az der khosn iz gor a krist" [At the wedding, the in-laws learn the groom is a Christian].

Dec. 18, 1927. "Tsulib a kapriz fun a yung rebetsin tsebunteven zikh di khsidim" [Because of the whim of a rabbi's young wife, hasidim rebel].

Dec. 19, 1927. "Undzer varshever korespondent bashraybt di levaye fun H. D. Nomberg" [Our Warsaw correspondent describes the funeral of H. D. Nomberg].

Dec. 21, 1927. "Yidishe ganovim in Varshe hobn zeyer eygenem gerikht tsu bashtrofn eygene mentshn" [Jewish thieves in Warsaw have their own trial to punish their own people].

Dec. 23, 1927. "A mayse vi fun toyznt un eyn nakht" [A story that could have come from *One Thousand and One (Arabian) Nights*].

Dec. 29, 1927. "Tokhter fun a raykhn khosid farlibt zikh in a daytshn ofitsir un samt zikh af ir muters keyver" [Daughter of a rich hasid falls in love with a German officer and takes poison at her mother's grave].

Jan. 2, 1928. "Vi gefelt aykh aza dintoyre? Frumer yid shrayt gevald, az er iz der foter fun dem kind vos zayn dinstmeydl hot geboyrn, ober zayn vayb gleybt im nit" [How do you like this kind of religious lawsuit? Religious Jew screams that he is the father of the child his maid bore, but his wife doesn't believe him].

Jan. 17, 1928. "Shoykhetke trogt a kurtse kleydl un hele zokn vert a 'revolutsye' in 3 shtetlekh in Poyln" [Ritual slaughterer's wife wears a short dress and light stockings: "Revolution" follows in 3 Polish towns].

Jan. 19, 1928. "Tragish geshikhte mit a Nyu yorker yidn velkhe iz gekumen tsu gast keyn Poyln" [Tragic story of a New York Jew visiting Poland].

Jan. 21, 1928. "A mieser koolisher skandal in Varshe" [An ugly communal scandal in Warsaw].

Jan. 24, 1928. "In Lune bay Grodno flakert a milkhome" [In Lune, near Grodno, a war is raging].

Jan. 28, 1928. "Varshever yidn hobn fun vos tsu lakhn" [Warsaw Jews have reason to laugh].

Feb. 1, 1928. "Zey zaynen hayntveltike vayblekh un viln az der beder zol oykh zayn a hayntveltike" [They are modern women and want the bath attendant to be modern, too].

Feb. 4, 1928. "A libes-skandal in a raykher khsidisher hoyz in Varshe" [A love scandal in a rich hasidic house in Warsaw].

Feb. 8, 1928. "Mazltov! Meshiekh iz geboyrn in Varshe" [Congratulations! Messiah is born in Warsaw].

Feb. 11, 1928. "Aza tshikave dintoyre hot nokh Varshe nit gezen" [Such a curious rabbinic trial has never been seen in Warsaw].

Feb. 15, 1928. "Tsulib zayn gelibte varft der foter avek zayn tokhter" [Because of his lover, a father discards his daughter].

Feb. 25, 1928. "Vos es hot zikh opgeton in Varshe ven di untervelt hot gepravet a sium haseyfer" [What happened in Warsaw when the underworld celebrated the conclusion of a scribe's writing of the Torah].

Feb. 28, 1928. "Komishe un tragishe pasirungen in di itstike shtet un shtetlekh in Poyln" [Comic and tragic events in contemporary Polish cities and towns].

Mar. 2, 1928. "Mir hobn di nemen fun der geshikhte nor mir kenen zey nit farefntlekhn" [We have the names involved in the story, but we can't publish them].

Mar. 17, 1928. "Tsvey shtetlekh firn milkhome tsulib shtot-meshugenem vos hot a raykhn tatn in Amerike" [Two towns at war over a town-madman who has a rich father in America].

Mar. 21, 1928. "Komishe pasirungen in yidishe shtet un shtetlekh in Poyln" [Comical events in Jewish towns and cities in Poland].

Mar. 26, 1928. "Bilder un stsenes in tog fun di valn in Varshe" [Pictures and scenes on election day in Warsaw].

Apr. 7, 1928. "Komishe pasirungen in yidishe shtet un shtetlekh in Poyln" [Comical events in Jewish towns and cities in Poland].

Apr. 17, 1928. "In Varshe kokht men zikh oykh mit fayts" [Warsaw also astir with fights].

Apr. 20, 1928. "Nayes fun der yidisher teater-velt in Poyln" [News from the Yiddish/Jewish theater world in Poland].

Apr. 30, 1928. "A 16 yorike meydl, an umgezetslekhe firshtin, ruft aroys a shrek in Varshe" [Sixteen-year-old-girl, illegitimate countess, frightens Warsaw].

May 5, 1928. "Tsulib a meydl vert R'Khaim Statsker oys 'gute-yid'" [Because of a girl, Reb Chaim Statsker is no longer a hasidic leader].

May 15, 1928. "Lustlike dintoyres in varsche" [Lively rabbinic trials in Warsaw.].

May 21, 1928. "Vos es hot zikh opgeton in Varshe ven der kenig fun Afganistan iz dortn geven tsu gast" [What happened in Warsaw when the king of Afghanistan visited].

May 26, 1928. "A farplonterter roman tsvishn an altn khosed fun Boston un a ksidishe yidene fun Poyln" [A complicated love story between an old hasid from Boston and a hasidic woman from Poland].

June 24, 1928. "Der balegole un di boyd punkt vi mit hundert yorn tsurik" [The coachman and the coach are just as they were one hundred years ago].

June 26, 1928. "A tragedye fun a yidisher froy velkhe hot nit gekent kumen tsu ir man keyn Amerike" [The tragedy of a Jewish woman who could not come to her husband in America].

July 1, 1928. "Bay di altvarg-hendler in Varshe" [At the old clothes dealers' in Warsaw].

July 17, 1928. "A 'rov' vos ligt nokh in di vikelekh konkurirt mit a rov shoyn in di yorn" [A "rabbi" still in diapers competes with an elderly rabbi].

July 19, 1928. "A sensatsionele lebns-geshikhte vi fun a roman aroysgenumen" [A life's story sensational enough to have been taken from a novel].

July 26, 1928. "A mayse mit a dibuk vos aktyorn hobn aroysgetribn fun a meydl in Tarnopol" [A story of dybbuk actors exorcised out of a girl in Tarnopol].

Aug. 4, 1928. "A freylekhe dintoyre bay varshever rabonim" [A lively rabbinic trial in Warsaw].

Aug. 14, 1928. "Bildlekh fun ganovim-gesl in Varshe" [Pictures of Thieves' Street in Warsaw].

Aug. 19, 1928. "Shtetlisher moser farmasert yidn nokhn toyt" [Town informant reports on Jews after death].

Aug. 28, 1928. "A komisher onfang un a troyriker sof" [A comical beginning and a sad end].

Sept. 9, 1928. "Muter un tokhter nemen zikh eyn yungn balibtn un ermordn dem man un foter fun der familye" [Mother and daughter take one young lover and kill the husband and father of the family].

Sept. 11, 1928. "Yunge tentser, doktoyrim un 'gute yidn' makhn gute gesheftn in poylishe varembeder" [Young dancers, doctors, and hasidic leaders do good business at Polish spas].

Sept. 21, 1928. "Komishe geshikhtes fun dem yidishn lebn in Poyln (A milkhome tsulib a nign)" [Comical stories of Jewish life in Poland (A war over a tune)].

Nov. 24, 1928. "Af a konferents fun frume yidn sotsialistn" [At a conference of devout Jews who are socialists].

Dec. 2, 1928. "A merkvirdikn gabe fun a ganovim besmedresh in Varshe" [A remarkable warden of a thieves' synagogue in Warsaw].

Dec. 16, 1928. "Tsvey interesante geshikhtes fun yidishn lebn in Poyln" [Two interesting stories of Jewish life in Poland].

Dec. 23, 1928. "Vi azoy R'Fayfke Shnayderl iz gevorn a barimter rebe" [How Mr. Fayfke Shnayderl became a famous rabbi].

Dec. 29, 1928. "Varshever untervelt 'heldn' shpiln yidish teater un tse'harg'enen zikh af der bine" [Warsaw underworld "heroes" perform in the Yiddish/Jewish theater and "kill" themselves on stage].

Jan. 2, 1929. "A tshikave dintoyre in dem varshever bezdn-shtub" [A curious trial in the Warsaw rabbinical courtroom].

Jan. 5, 1929. "Tsvey khasenes un a get bay eyn porl in der varshever 'untervelt'" [Two weddings and a divorce of one couple in the Warsaw "underworld"].

Jan. 19, 1929. "Vi azoy amerikaner yidn shtitsn zeyere kroyvim in Eyrope" [How American Jews support their relatives in Europe].

Jan. 26, 1929. "Tsvey komishe geshikhtes fun di yidishe shtetlekh in Poyln" [Two funny stories from the Jewish towns of Poland].

Feb. 2, 1929. "A geshikhte mit a 'mes' vos iz plutsling lebedik gevorn" [A story of a "corpse" that suddenly came to life].

Feb. 13, 1929. "80-yoriker shames fun Shnipishok iz zikh meyashev un vert an apikoyres" [80-year-old synagogue warden from Shnipishok reconsiders and becomes a heretic].

Feb. 16, 1929. "A tshikave geshikhte mit a lamed-vovnik in Poyln" [A curious story of one of the Thirty-six Just Men in Poland].

Feb. 23, 1929. "Shlekht az men folgt a vayb" [Obeying one's wife is bad].

Mar. 2, 1929. "Eyferzikhtike froy brent oys di oygn fun man un firt im itst arum vi a kind" [Jealous woman burns her husband's eyes out and now leads him around like a child].

Mar. 3, 1929. "Lublin hot zikh veynik vos tsu shemen kegn Nyu York mit ir nayer yeshive" [Lublin can now stand up to New York because of its new yeshiva].

Mar. 14, 1929. "Shoyderlekhe paynikungen fun kinder oyfgedekt in a poylishn oysbeserungs-anshtalt far yunge farbrekher" [Horrible child abuse revealed in a Polish reformatory for young offenders].

Mar. 16, 1929. "An onshikenish fun sheynhayts 'kenigins' af varshever yidn" [Beauty "queens" are a nuisance for Warsaw Jews].

Mar. 30, 1929. "Reb Shmerke der protsentnik" [Mr. Shmerke the moneylender].

Mar. 31, 1929. "Bloye tsitses tsi vayse tsitses? An interesanter kamf tsvishn khsidishe shtiblekh" [Blue ritual fringes or white ritual fringes? An interesting battle between hasidic prayerhouses].

Apr. 6, 1929. "Reb Yerakhmyel makht milyonen—es redt zikh azoy" [Mr. Yerakhmyel makes millions—or so it's said].

Apr. 17, 1929. "Bilder fun Berlin" [Pictures from Berlin].

Apr. 23, 1929. "Er iz geven der kargster yid in Varshe" [He was the stingiest Jew in Warsaw].

Apr. 26, 1929. "Vi halt es mitn yidishn teater in Poyln" [How are things in the Yiddish theater in Poland].

May 2, 1929. "A briv fun undzer varshever korespondent vegn komarover-rov-geshikhte" [A letter from our Warsaw correspondent about the Komorave rabbi's story].

May 15, 1929. "A sekte fun khsidishe bokherim in Poyln velkhe paynikn zikh" [A sect of young hasidic men in Poland who torture themselves].

May 29, 1929. "Nokh a briv vegn ershtn may yontev in Poyln" [Another letter about the May 1 holiday in Poland].

June 5, 1929. "A shoyderlekhe yidishe familyen-tragedye in Varshe" [A dreadful Jewish family tragedy in Warsaw].

June 12, 1929. "A tragish-komishe dintoyre in Varshever bezdn-shtibl" [A tragicomical trial in a Warsaw rabbinic courtroom].

June 19, 1929. "Vos a henger dertseylt vegn zayne karbones un vegn zayn 'arbet'" [What a hangman tells about his sacrifices and his "work"].

June 24, 1929. "Meydlekh vos tshepen zikh tsu fremde froyen un rufn zey 'mame' kedey oystsupresen fun zey gelt" [Girls who latch onto unknown women and call them "mother" in order to force money out of them].

June 26, 1929. "Poyln hot oykh a 'halivud' mit shoyshpiler un skandaln" [Poland has its own "Hollywood" with actors and scandals].

July 9, 1929. "A tragishe geshikhte mit a 'diuk' in Poyln" [A tragic story of a dy(bb)uk in Poland].

July 18, 1929. "Komishe geshikhtes fun kleyne yidishe shtetlekh in Poyln" [Comical stories of small Jewish towns in Poland].

Aug. 1, 1929. "Varshever un vilner ganovim makhn a por 'dzsabs' af an amerikaner polisman" [Warsaw and Vilna thieves "do a job" on an American policeman].

Aug. 11, 1929. "Azelkhe kinder zaynen a klole far tate-mamen" [Such children are a curse to their parents].

Aug. 16, 1929. "A sedre libes-mordn in Varshe" [A series of love-murders in Warsaw].

Aug. 18, 1929. "A komishe mayse in a yidisher shtetl in Poyln vos past far di alte fintstere tsaytn" [A comical story in a Jewish town in Poland that is appropriate to old, dark times].

Aug. 20, 1929. "Di groyse sensatsye mit dem amerikaner Moris Baskin vos hot gehayrat 62 froyen in Poyln" [The great excitement over the American Morris Baskin, who married 62 women in Poland].

Aug. 25, 1929. "A yidishe parnose in der alter heym vos geyt unter" [A Jewish means of livelihood in the old country that is passing away].

Sept. 7, 1929. "Der 'amerikaner konsul bendzsamin' shteyt oyf tkhies-hameysim" [The 'American Consul Benjamin' arises from the dead].

Sept. 15, 1929. "Yidishe bekers in der alter heym farlirn zeyer broyt" [Jewish bakers in the old country lose their livelihood].

Sept. 22, 1929. "Komishe geshikhtes fun kleyne yidishe shtetlekh in Poyln" [Comical stories of small Jewish towns in Poland].

Oct. 7, 1929. "A rov kemft kegn zayn shtetl mit a kapitl tilim" [A rabbi fights his town using Psalms].

Oct. 10, 1929. "Poylishe yidn, galitsianer un litvakes, mishn zikh itst oys in di poylishe shtet" [Polish Galician and Lithuanian Jews come together in Polish cities].

Oct. 26, 1929. "Rosh-hashone baym gerer rebn" [New Year's with the Gerer rabbi].

Nov. 5, 1929. "A rov in trobl tsulib dem amerikaner bokher vos hot in Poyln khasene gehat 60 mol" [A rabbi in trouble because of the American youth who got married 60 times in Poland].

Nov. 9, 1929. "Varshever frume un nit-frume untervelt mentshn hobn a dintoyre" [Devout and nondevout people from Warsaw underworld have a rabbinic trial].

Nov. 28, 1929. "Er nemt zikh on farn koved fun damen un derharget a mentshn" [He sticks up for the honor of women and kills someone].

Nov. 30, 1929. "A khinezerin, a komediantke, hengt zikh in Varshe nokh der forshtelung in tsirk" [A Chinese clown hangs herself in Warsaw after her circus performance].

Dec. 12, 1929. "Tsulib a mafter hot an amerikaner opgekoylet a shtetl in Poyln" [Because of the synagogue reading from the Prophets, an American destroys a town in Poland].

Dec. 20, 1929. "Vi azoy a kluge katsevte hot getsvungen a beyzn rov aroptsunemen a kheyrem" [How a clever ritual slaughterer's wife forced a mean rabbi to overturn a ban].

Jan. 6, 1930. "Luft parnoses tsu velkhe yidn khapn zikh itst in Poyln" ["Airy" livelihoods to which Jews now flock in Poland].

Jan. 9, 1930. "Di shmad-bavegung tsvishn poylishe yidn in di letste yorn" [The movement toward conversion among Polish Jews in recent years].

Jan. 21, 1930. "Er vil bentshn khanike-likht un zi shtelt a kristmas-boym, geyt men zikh getn" [He wants to light the Hannukah candles and she erects a Christmas tree, so they are going to divorce].

Jan. 23, 1930. "A blonde kind vos iz geboyrn gevorn bay brunete eltern" [A blonde child born to brunette parents].

Jan. 24, 1930. "Di shvere lage fun dem yidishn teater in Poyln" [The difficult plight of the Yiddish theater in Poland].

Jan. 26, 1930. "Vitsn-zoger, khoyzek-makher, kibetsers un leytsim bay yidn" [Jokers, ridiculers, kibitzers and clowns among Jews].

Feb. 8, 1930. "Di toyte shtot Pinsk" [The dead city of Pinsk].

Feb. 9, 1930. "Yidishe vitsler, kibitser, un leytsim un zeyer role in amolikn yidishn lebn" [Jewish jokers, kibitzers and clowns and their role in earlier Jewish life].

Feb. 22, 1930. "Bilder fun der shreklekher noyt in Lodzsh un arumike shtetlekh" [Pictures of the terrible poverty in Lodz and surrounding towns].

Feb. 27, 1930. "Vos fun der alter yidisher fabrikshtot Smorgon iz itst gevorn" [What has now become of the old Jewish factory-town, Smorgon].

Mar. 3, 1930. "Di groyse noyt bay di yidn in Grodno" [The great poverty of the Jews in Grodno].

Mar. 10, 1930. "Mezritsh, di yidishste shtot in Poyln" [Mezritsh, the most Jewish town in Poland].

Mar. 13, 1930. "A shtetl in Poyln vu es iz nokh geblibn a yidisher geto" [A town in Poland where there still remains a Jewish ghetto].

Mar. 19, 1930. "Vos Brisk iz geven amol un vos zi iz haynt" [What Brisk was once and what it is now].

Mar. 31, 1930. "Vi azoy es lebn itst di yidn inem gegnt vos Poyln hot tsugenumen bay Daytshland" [How Jews now live in the area Poland took from Germany].

Apr. 5, 1930. "Der eyn-togiker shtrayk fun di yidishe sokhrim un kremer in Poyln" [The one-day strike of Jewish businessmen and shopkeepers in Poland].

Apr. 7, 1930. "A brukliner alter yid vos iz geforn keyn Varshe shtarbn, valgert zikh dort arum un ken nisht kumen tsurik" [An old Jew from Brooklyn who went to Warsaw to die is roaming around there and can't come back].

Apr. 12, 1930. "Yidn in Poyln vos kokhn zikh iber raykhe yerushes fun oysgeshtarbte kroyvim." [Jews in Poland in an uproar over rich inheritances of dead relatives].

Apr. 28, 1930. "Varshever untervelt held dershosn in gerikht" [Warsaw underworld hero shot in court].

May 1, 1930. "A shatkhn vos iz gekumen monen bay a toytn shatkhonesgelt" [A matchmaker who came to demand his fee of a dead man].

May 7, 1930. "Ofitsirn tantsn mit yidishe meydlekh af a yidishn bal un in shtetl iz khoyshekh" [Officers dance with Jewish girls at a Jewish ball, and all hell breaks loose in town].

May 10, 1930. "A ganef makht shlekhte biznes tsulib dem krizis—vil di vayb a get" [A thief makes a poor living because of the crisis—so his wife wants a divorce].

May 11, 1930. "Tsulib an oks geyt a yidish shtetl af redlekh" [Because of an ox, a Jewish town is turned topsy-turvy].

May 13, 1930. "Di geshikhte mit der bombe vos men hot gefunen in der hoyz fun sovietishn ambasador in Varshe" [The story of the bomb found in the Soviet ambassador's house in Warsaw].

May 28, 1930. "Vi es iz gefayert gevorn der ershter may in Varshe un gants Poyln" [How the first of May was celebrated in Warsaw and throughout Poland].

June 2, 1930. "Mit a katar hot er avekge'har'get a mafter in shul un farloyren a raykhe kale" [With a cold he "did in" the synagogue reading of the Prophets and lost a rich bride].

June 4, 1930. "Vanderungen fun a yidishn emigrant fun Rusland vos klingen vi a mayse fun toyznt un eyn nakht" [Wanderings of a Jewish emigré from Russia that sound like a story out of *One Thousand and One (Arabian) Nights*].

June 9, 1930. "Tsores fun a grodner almone vemens bild iz gefeln gevorn a biznesman in Sout-afrike" [Troubles of a widow from Grodno whose picture pleased a South African businessman].

June 14, 1930. "Yunge muter ganvet aroys ir kind un antloyft mit im in an eroplan" [Young mother kidnaps her child and flees with him in an airplane].

July 18, 1930. "A komishe mayse mit a Nyu yorker yidn velkher iz gekumen keyn Poyln gebn khalitse zayn shveygerin" [A comical story of a New York Jew who came to Poland in order to release his sister-in-law from the obligation of levirate marriage].

July 20, 1930. "Vi azoy kristlekhe shrayber shildern yidn in zeyere verk" [How Christian writers portray Jews in their works].

July 30, 1930. "Amerikaner aktyorn in Poyln" [American actors in Poland].

Aug. 2, 1930. "Tsulib a tragishe libe hot er farlozn di bine un iz gevorn fanatish frum" [Because of a tragic love, he left the stage and became fanatically devout].

Aug. 9, 1930. "A shtetl in Poyln vu der rov lebt nor fun petsh" [A town in Poland where the rabbi lives only off of slaps].

Aug. 31, 1930. "Bildlekh fun di galitsyaner varembeder" [Pictures of Galician spas].

Sept. 20, 1930. "Vos der 'Hayas' hot geton far umgliklekhe emigrantn in Poyln in letstn yor" [What HIAS (Hebrew Immigrant Aid Society) did for unfortunate emigrants in Poland last year].

Sept. 21, 1930. "A rayze iber di varembeder, ven es shviblt un griblt mit yidn" [A trip around the spas when they are packed full of Jews].

Sept. 28, 1930. "Krinitse—di shtot vuhin s'forn akores fun Poyln geholfn tsu vern" [Krinitse—the town to which barren women in Poland go for help].

Sept. 29, 1930. "Der amerikaner krizis filt zikh zeyer shver bay di kroyvim in Poyln" [The American crisis is being strongly felt by relatives in Poland].

Oct. 5, 1930. "Tipn un bilder, vos men bagegnt in shtet un shtetlekh fun Poyln" [Types and pictures encountered in Polish towns and cities].

Oct. 18, 1930. "Freylekhe dintoyre tsvishn man un vayb in Varshe" [Lively rabbinic trial between husband and wife in Warsaw].

Oct. 19, 1930. "A merkverdike sekte in Poyln vos dint tsum tayvl" [A remarkable sect in Poland that worships the devil].

Oct. 26, 1930. "An interesante bukh fun poylish-yidishn dikhter Yulian Tuvim" [An interesting book by the Polish-Jewish poet Julian Tuvim].

Oct. 30, 1930. "Shvartser khazn fun Amerike makht on a tuml tsvishn poylishe yidn" [Black cantor from America creates a stir among Polish Jews].

Nov. 11, 1930. "A yidisher teater far kaptsonim in Varshe" [A Yiddish/Jewish theater for paupers in Warsaw].

Nov. 13, 1930. "Khsidim 'praven tish,' zingen un khapn a tentsl in a vagon fun a poylisher ban" [Hasidim celebrate, sing and dance in a car of a Polish train].

Nov. 17, 1930. "In Varshe iz itst opgehaltn gevorn an internatsyonaler kongres tsu bakemfn prostitutsye" [In Warsaw, an international congress to combat prostitution has just been held].

Dec. 5–6, 1930. "Bilder un stsenes in di yidishe kvartaln fun Varshe erev di valn" [Pictures and scenes from the Jewish quarters of Warsaw on the eve of the elections].

Dec. 28, 1930. "Der shtumer yidisher maler Minkovski: zayn merkvirdike lebns-geshikhte" [The mute Jewish painter Minkovsky: The amazing story of his life].

Jan. 2, 1931. "S'iz punkt 100 yor zint Poyln hot gemakht dem ershtn oyfshtand kegn Rusland" [It's exactly 100 years since Poland first revolted against Russia].

Jan. 13, 1931. "In Poyln zaynen faran a sakh mener agunes vayl zey kenen nit kumen tsu zeyere froyen in Amerike" [In Poland there are many deserted husbands because they cannot come to their wives in America].

Jan. 15, 1931. "A tshikave parnose in Poyln—men handlt mit gornit un men fardint" [A curious livelihood in Poland—people deal in nothing and earn a living].

Jan. 29, 1931. "Raysereyen tsvishn poylishe shriftshteler tsulib di gepaynikte deputatn in der brisker festung" [Quarrels among Polish writers because of the tortured deputies in the Brisk fortress].

Jan. 31, 1931. "Zaynvl Lapidus der psikholog" [Zainvel Lapidus the psychologist].

Feb. 8, 1931. "Di yidishe tsaytungen fun Eyrope shpayzn zikh mitn 'Forverts'" [The Yiddish newspapers in Europe live off of the *Forverts*].

Feb. 11, 1931. "Reb Leybele Shnayder mit zayn harem vayber in varshever bezdn-shtibl" [Mr. Laibele Schneider and his harem in a Warsaw rabbinic courtroom].

Feb. 14, 1931. "Sensatsyoneler protses in Varshe fun an ofitsir vos hot ermordet amolikn gelibtn fun zayn froy" [Sensational trial in Warsaw of an officer who murdered his wife's former lover].

Feb. 17, 1931. "Sensatsyoneler protses in Varshe fun 5 sotsialistn far veln kloymersht varfn a bombe af Pilsudskin" [Sensational trial in Warsaw of 5 socialists for ostensibly wanting to throw a bomb at Pilsudski].

Mar. 3, 1931. "Gevezene balebatim kumen keyn Varshe geyen iber di hayzer" [Former landlords come to Warsaw to beg from door-to-door].

Mar. 7, 1931. "A gantse vokh iz er in Varshe a 'soykher' un a melamed un donershtik un fraytik geyt er iber hayzer" [All week long he is a "businessman" and teacher in Warsaw, and on Thursday and Friday he goes begging from door-to-door].

Mar. 21, 1931. "10 yorike meydele di parnose-geberin fun ir familie" [10-year-old girl supports her family].

Mar. 25, 1931. "Vi azoy yidishe arbeter un sokhrim in Poyln vern bislekhvayz tremps un betler" [How Jewish workers and businessmen in Poland are gradually becoming tramps and beggars].

Apr. 8, 1931. "Poylishe rikhter muzn paskenen vi lang a rov darf shteyn shimenesre" [Polish judge must decide how long a rabbi should take to recite the Eighteen Benedictions].

Apr. 14, 1931. "A komisher protses in Varshe tsvishn a grafin un ir gelibtn, a yid mit a langer kapote" [A comical trial in Warsaw between a countess and her lover, a Jew with a long gaberdine (traditionally worn by observant Jews)].

Apr. 23, 1931. "Yidn in poylishe shtetlekh raysn zikh arum tsulib meysim" [Jews in Polish towns quarrel because of corpses].

May 5, 1931. "Yidishe misyonern makhn itst zeyer gute biznes in Poyln" [Jewish missionaries now do brisk business in Poland].

May 9, 1931. "Interesante tipn un bilder fun emigrantn-hotel in Varshe" [Interesting types and pictures of emigrant-hotels in Warsaw].

May 10, 1931. "Der shpanender protses ibern man vos hot untergeleygt [a] bombe in sovietisher ambasade in Varshe" [The exciting trial of the man who threw a bomb at the Soviet embassy in Warsaw].

May 15, 1931. "Di fayerungen fun ershtn may in Varshe un in gants Poyln" [The May 1 celebration in Warsaw and all of Poland].

May 18, 1931. "Di itstike lage fun dem yidishn teater in Poyln" [The present situation of the Yiddish theater in Poland].

May 24, 1931. "Frume vayber fun 200 shtet in Poyln haltn op a tsuzamenfor" [Religious women from 200 Polish cities hold a convention].

June 2, 1931. "A varshever shvindler farkoyft zayne karbones shtotishe parks, kars un ayznban treks" [Warsaw swindler sells his victims city parks, cars, and railroad tracks].

June 13, 1931. "Vos es tut zikh op in Poylishe shtetlekh bay valn tsu di kehiles" [What happens in Polish towns during communal elections].

June 14, 1931. "Der krizis in der yidisher prese in Poyln" [The crisis in the Yiddish/ Jewish press in Poland].

June 23, 1931. "Naye eyntslheytn fun pogrom in Zlotshev lebn Kelts" [New incidents of pogroms in Zlochev near Kielce].

June 27, 1931. "Vi azoy men ekzaminirt yidishe aktyorn in varshever artistn fareyn" [How Yiddish/Jewish actors are examined in Warsaw artist's union].

July 4, 1931. "'Forverts' korespondent hot a geshprekh mit a hoykhn poylishn baamtn vegn der lage fun di yidn" [*Forverts* correspondent has a conversation with a highly placed Polish official about the situation of the Jews].

July 5, 1931. "A yid vos heyst Avremele un firt zikh loyt Aynshteyns teorye" [A Jew called Avremele who behaves according to Einstein's theory].

July 7, 1931. "Vos ken men ton tsu farlaykhtern di yidishe lage in Poyln" [What can be done to ease the Jewish problem in Poland].

July 9, 1931. "Frume yidn in poylishe shtetlekh firn a milkhome kegn nakete vaybershe hent" [Religious Jews in Polish towns wage a war against women's naked hands].

July 19, 1931. "Khaver Morits der royter" [Comrade Morris, the red].

July 29, 1931. "Komishe stsenes un bilder bay di letste valn tsu der varshever kehile" [Comical scenes and pictures of the recent elections to the Warsaw Jewish community council]..

July 31, 1931. "Poylishe gegnten vu es zaynen nito keyn yidn" [Polish regions where there are no Jews].

Aug. 1, 1931. "Poylishe yidn kenen rateven a sakh parnoses vos geyen unter" [Polish Jews can save many means of livelihood that are going under].

Aug. 24, 1931. "Tipn vos me bagegnt zumer in kurerter" [Types met in summer health spas].

Aug. 27, 1931. "A naye boykot-hetse kegn yidn in Poyln" [A new boycott threat against the Jews in Poland].

Sept. 4, 1931. "100 toyznt yidishe kinder in Poyln veln hayyor blaybn on skuls" [100,000 Jewish children in Poland will remain without schools this year].

Sept. 6, 1931. "Groyser yontev fun der internatsyonaler shprakh esperanto in Kroke un Varshe" [Great celebration of the international language Esperanto in Cracow and Warsaw].

Sept. 15, 1931. "Der Poylisher deputat Halyavko vemen ukrayner teroristn hobn ermordet." [The Polish deputy Halyafko who was murdered by Ukrainian terrorists].

Oct. 13, 1931. "Rayserayen tsvishn di yidishe aktyorn in Poyln" [Squabbles among Jewish/Yiddish actors in Poland].

Oct. 18, 1931. "A koledzs vu es vern oysgebildet hint tsu firn blinde" [A college where dogs are trained to lead the blind].

Oct. 21, 1931. "Volt es bay aykh in Amerike geven meglekh?" [Would it be possible for you in America?]

Nov. 11, 1931. "Frume yidn in Poyln hobn groyse tsores fun naye politseyshe parondkes" [Observant Jews in Poland have great troubles with the new police ordinances].

Nov. 18, 1931. Vos s'hot zikh opgeton in Varshe ven khuliganishe studentn hobn ongehoybn pogroms in yidishe gasn" [What happened in Warsaw when student hooligans began pogroms in Jewish streets].

Nov. 19, 1931. "Undzer korespondent shildert dem sensatsionel-politishn protses in Varshe" [Our correspondent describes the sensational political trial in Warsaw].

Nov. 27, 1931. "'Forverts' korespondent shildert dem pogrom in Vilne" [*Forverts* correspondent describes the pogrom in Vilna].

Nov. 28, 1931. "Vos s'hot zikh opgeton in Vilne dem 'shvartsn dinstog' [What happened in Vilna on "Black Tuesday"].

Dec. 7, 1931. "Di ershte teg nokh dem pogrom in Vilne" [The first days after the pogrom in Vilna].

Dec. 30, 1931. "Poylisher profesor tret aroys mit an artikl kegn di pogromtshikes" [Polish professor comes forth with an article against the pogromists].

Jan. 10, 1932. "Poyln redt itst fil vegn a merkverdike geshikhte vos hot pasirt mit 25 yor tsurik" [Poland now discussing a remarkable story that happened 25 years ago].

Jan. 17, 1932. "Zayn tate flegt zitsn bay der gemore un zayn mame flegt makhn a lebn" [His father used to sit over the Gemara, and his mother used to make a living].

Jan. 19, 1932. "Der toyt fun dem barimtn Poylishn historiker der meshumed Krauzhar" [The death of the famous Polish historian, the apostate Kraushar].

Jan. 30, 1932. "Di amolike yidishe teritorialistishe organizatsye iz vider oyfgelebt gevorn" [The former Jewish Territorialist Organization has once again arisen].

Feb. 1, 1932. "Af a tsuzamenfor fun rabonim in Varshe" [At a gathering of rabbis in Warsaw].

Feb. 3, 1932. "Vos es hot zikh opgeton in Poyln ven der gerer rebbe iz opgeforn keyn erets-yisroel" [What happened in Poland when the Hasidic leader, the Gerer rabbi, left for the land of Israel].

Feb. 8, 1932. "'Forverts' korespondent hot a geshprekh mit dem barimtn firer fun der poylisher sotsialistisher partey, Dr. Liberman, vegn itstiker lage in Poyln" [*Forverts* correspondent has a conversation with the famous leader of the Polish socialist party, Dr. Liberman, about the present situation in Poland].

Feb. 12, 1932. "Vu iz beser tsu zayn an oreman, in Poyln tsi in Amerike?" [Where is it better to be poor, in Poland or in America?].

Feb. 13, 1932. "Interesante protsesn fun untervelt-heldn in Varshe" [Interesting trials of underworld heroes in Warsaw].

Feb. 14, 1932. "Keyn tsores nito, ober trern un shpas zaynen faran a sakh" [No sorrows, but lots of tears and jokes].

Feb. 21, 1932. "Vi azoy yidn in Poyln narn op dem antisemitizm un dem krizis" [How Jews in Poland confound anti-Semitism and the crisis].

Feb. 29, 1932. "A komishe geshikhte funem lebn fun yidishe shtetlekh in Poyln" [A funny story of the life of Jewish towns in Poland].

Mar. 3, 1932. "Vi azoy men shtarbt nit itst fun hunger in Varshe" [How one does not starve to death now in Warsaw].

Mar. 6, 1932. "Fun vos yidn in Poyln makhn itst a lebn" [How Jews in Poland make a living now].

Mar. 9, 1932. "Khsidisher yungerman fartribn fun shtetl far zogn az gerer rebbe iz geforn keyn Yisroel zikh kurirn" [Hasidic youth driven out of town for saying that the Gerer rabbi went to Israel to heal himself].

Mar. 23, 1932. "Khsidishe kestkinder firn a blutike milkhome mit zeyere shvers" [Hasidic children boarding with their in-laws engage in a bloody war with their fathers-in-law].

Mar. 28, 1932. "Men bayt oys kunst un poezye af eyer un tsibeles" [Art and poetry are exchanged for eggs and onions].

Apr. 3, 1932. "Tsvey yidishe tiranen vos hobn mit etlekhe hundert yor tsurik gehersht in galitsien" [Two Jewish tyrants who ruled in Galicia several hundred years ago].

Apr. 7, 1932. "Varshever alderman iz geven der firer fun a bande reketirs un merder" [Warsaw alderman was the leader of a band of racketeers and murderers].

Apr. 9, 1932. "Di 13 pianistn velkhe hobn gevunen prayzn bay dem veltkontest in Varshe" [The 13 pianists who won prizes at the worldwide contest in Warsaw].

Apr. 21, 1932. "Tsulib amerikaner aktyorn redn poylishe yidn english" [Because of American actors, Polish Jews speak English].

Apr. 28, 1932. "Vi azoy yidn in Poyln hobn zikh gegreyt tsu peysakh" [How Jews in Poland prepared themselves for Passover].

May 3, 1932. "Di mapole fun di vilner antisemitn af dem pogrom-protses fun di dray yidn" [The defeat of the Vilna anti-Semites in the pogrom-trial of the three Jews].

May 7, 1932. "A geshmadte yidishe meydl fun Amerike ermordert in a misionern-hoyz in Varshe" [A Jewish girl from America, converted to Christianity, murdered in a missionary house in Warsaw].

May 13, 1932. "Aktyorn un tentserins shpiln tragedye in varshever gerikht" [Actors and dancers perform a tragedy in a Warsaw court].

May 19, 1932. "Vi men hot gefayert dem ershtn may in Varshe un andere poylishe shtet" [How May 1 was celebrated in Warsaw and other Polish cities].

June 2, 1932. "Di amerikaner yidishe aktyorn vos shpiln itst in Poyln" [The American Yiddish actors now performing in Poland].
   NOTE: *Yoshe Kalb* was serialized daily, June 4 through July 19, 1932.

June 6, 1932. "A geshprekh mit Tsili Adler, velkhe shpilt itst in Poyln" [A conversation with Celia Adler, who is now performing in Poland].

June 8, 1932. "400 'mener agunes' in Poyln endlekh opgeforn tsu zeyere froyen in Amerike" [400 "deserted husbands" in Poland finally leave to join their wives in America].

June 20, 1932. "Tragedyes un komedyes vos shpiln zikh op tsvishn amerikaner mener un zeyere froyen in Poyln" [Tragedies and comedies taking place between American men and their wives in Poland].

June 28, 1932. "A tragedye fun libe un mord in di 'hoykhe fentster' fun Varshe" [A tragedy of love and murder in Warsaw high society].

July 7, 1932. "A geshprekh mit Moris Shvartz af zayn bazukh in Varshe" [A conversation with Maurice Schwartz during his visit to Warsaw].

July 16, 1932. "Tshikave pasirungen in yidishe shtetlekh fun Poyln" [Curious occurrences in Jewish towns in Poland].

July 21, 1932. "Vos forshteyer fun yidishe shtetlekh dertseyln vegn lebn fun yidn in Poyln" [What representatives of Jewish towns tell about Jewish life in Poland].

Aug. 9, 1932. "Rayserayen tsvishn poylishe yidn baym farteyln di 1000 surtifikets tsu forn keyn Palestine" [Fights between Polish Jews when 1000 certificates to Palestine are given out].

Aug. 13, 1932. "Bakanter yidisher aktyor gefunen a dershtiktn. Gasnfroy arestirt" [Familiar Jewish/Yiddish actor found strangled. Streetwalker arrested].

Aug. 21, 1932. "Vilder vald in Poyln vu tsar Nikolay flegt geyn af yagd" [Wild forest in Poland where Czar Nicholas used to go hunting].

Sept. 6, 1932. "G. Kuper dertseylt vegn zayn rayze ibern yam af an amerikaner shif" [G. Kuper tells of his trip over the sea on an American ship].

Sept. 9, 1932. "Der farfaser fun *Yoshe Kalb*' baklogt zikh az im iz shver tsu farshteyn di amerikaner" [The author of *Yoshe Kalb* complains that it is difficult for him to understand Americans]. (This first article written on American soil is signed "G. Kuper [I. J. Singer].")

Sept. 10, 1932. "Iz der poylisher dikhter Adam Mitskevitsh far'sam't gevorn fun antisemitishe polyakn?" [Was the Polish poet Adam Mickiewicz "poisoned" by anti-Semitic Poles?].

Note: Singer's articles concerning his first trip to America (September 1932) were published under his own name and are listed in I.d. above. He resumed publishing under the name Kuper when he returned to Warsaw in January 1933.

Jan. 21, 1933. "Yidn in Poyln gefinen zikh oys modne naye biznes" [Jews in Poland find strange new businesses for themselves].

Jan. 22, 1933. "Di yidishe kehile fun Varshe git aroys a merkverdik interesantn bukh" [The Jewish community of Warsaw publishes a remarkably interesting book].

Jan. 29, 1933. "Yidn in Poyln shtarbn a sakh veyniker eyder polyakn" [In Poland fewer Jews die than Poles].

Jan. 30, 1933. "Vi azoy poylishe inteligentn fun farsheydene parteyen viln leyzn di yidn-frage in Poyln" [How Polish intelligentsia of different parties want to solve the Jewish question in Poland].

Jan. 31, 1933. "Di nakht far zeyer toyt af der tliye" [The night before their death on the gallows].

Feb. 11, 1933. "Vos men darf visn baym shikn gelt tsu kroyvim in Rusland" [What one needs to know to send money to relatives in Russia].

Mar. 1, 1933. "Tsen toyznt yidn zaynen gekumen bavundern yidishn sport" [Ten thousand Jews came to marvel at Jewish sports].

Mar. 5, 1933. "In der poylisher literatur kokht itst mit a bukh fun a yidishn ganef" [Polish literature now astir because of book by Jewish thief].

Mar. 18, 1933. "Komishe geshikhtes un bildlekh fun yidishn lebn in kleyne shtetlekh fun Poyln" [Comical stories and pictures of Jewish life in small Polish towns].

Mar. 19, 1933. "Fartsveyflung—dos vort iz tsu shvakh fortsushteln di lage fun di yidn in Poyln" [Desperation—the word is too weak to describe the situation of Jews in Poland].

Apr. 1, 1933. "Tsulib dem tuml mit geshlosene bankn in Amerike vern tseshtert shidukhim in Poyln" [Because of the uproar over closed banks in America, betrothals are unsettled in Poland].

Apr. 4, 1933. "Vos antlofene daytshe yidn dertseyln vegn di shrekn in Berlin un in andere daytshe shtet" [What Jews who have fled Germany tell of the fears in Berlin and other German cities].

Apr. 12, 1933. "Rizike protestn fun poylishe yidn kegn di retsikhes in Daytshland" [Huge protests of Polish Jews against the violence in Germany].

Apr. 15, 1933. "Baym grenets vu yidn loyfn fun Daytshland in Poyln" [At the border where Jews flee Germany for Poland].

May 1, 1933. "In Poyln zaynen forikn sezon nit geven keyn arbetsloze yidishe aktyorn" [In the last season in Poland there were no unemployed Yiddish/Jewish actors].

May 4, 1933. "Der riziker protest-tsuzamenfor in Varshe kegn Hitlers yidnfarfolgung" [The huge protest rally in Warsaw against Hitler's persecution of Jews].

May 16, 1933. "Ayndruksfule fayerung fun ershtn may in Varshe un andere shtet" [Impressive May 1 celebrations in Warsaw and other cities].

May 22, 1933. "Yidishe yungelayt in hitleristishe broyne hemdlekh arbetn maysim in Varshe un andere poylishe shtet" [Jewish youth in Hitleristic brown shirts do all sorts of things in Warsaw and other Polish cities].

June 1, 1933. "Di rizike levaye fun dem fritsaytik-farshtorbenem bundishn firer M. Likhtenshteyn in Lodzsh" [The huge funeral in Lodz of the Bundist leader M. Likhtenshteyn, who died at an early age].

June 8, 1933. "In kleyne shtetlekh in Poyln tumlt zikh mit meysim vos kumen aynmonen khoyves" [In small towns in Poland there is an uproar about corpses who come to collect debts].

June 11, 1933. "Fun vos yidn in Poyln makhn a lebn hayntike tsaytn" [How Jews in Poland make a living nowadays].

June 28, 1933. "Yidn in Poyln vos makhn itst biznes tsulib hitlerizm in Daytshland" [Jews in Poland who do business because of Hitlerism in Germany].

July 4, 1933. "Libe, eyferzikht, laydn un freydn bay yunge kinder" [Love, jealousy, trials, and tribulations of young children].

July 10, 1933. "Me ervartet umruen in Daytshland dem vinter" [Unrest expected in Germany this winter].

July 13, 1933. "Mister Ruzvelt, git op di etlekhe dolar" [Mr. Roosevelt: return the few dollars].

July 21, 1933. "Tsvishn tsyonistn un revizionistn in Poyln kumen itst for milkhomes arum dem mord fun D'r Arlozorov" [Battles between zionists and revisionists in Poland over the murder of Dr. Arlozorov].

July 27, 1933. "A 'heyliker' hot getsapt blut fun poyertes in poylishe derfer" [A "holyman" bled peasant women in Polish villages].

Aug. 10, 1933. "Komishe geshikhtes fun yidishn lebn in poylishe shtet un shtetlekh" [Comical stories of Jewish life in Polish towns and cities].

Aug. 19, 1933. "Oreme yidn in Poyln vern krank un oysgerisn yogndik zikh nokh a bisl gezunt" [Poor Jews in Poland become sick and suffer in the pursuit of a bit of health].

Sept. 16, 1933. "Aza sensatsioneler mord hot shoyn Pariz lang nit gehat (fun Pariz)" [Paris has not had such a sensational murder in a long time (from Paris)].

Sept. 28, 1933. "Rirnde bilder un stsenes tsvishn daytshe yidn in Pariz" [Moving pictures and scenes among German Jews in Paris].

Oct. 6, 1933. "Heymloze daytshe un poylishe yidn in Pariz" [Homeless German and Polish Jews in Paris].

Oct. 8, 1933. "Vos der parizer komitet tut tsu helfn di daytshe yidn vos antloyfn fun Hitlern" [What the Paris committee is doing to help the German Jews who are fleeing Hitler].

Oct. 18, 1933. "Er molt a lebedike bild fun der itstiker Daytshland" [He paints a vivid picture of present-day Germany].

Oct. 25, 1933. "A shtetl in Poyln hot baleydikt a toytn yungen-man un ken zikh fun im nit oyskoyfn" [A town in Poland insulted a dead youth and can't ransom itself].

Oct. 28, 1933. "Tsvishn di elnte yidishe emigrantn in Pariz" [Among the lonely Jewish emigrés in Paris].

Nov. 7, 1933. "A vayser hon mit a roytn kam makht on a milkhome in a shtetl in Poyln in same yonkiper" [A white rooster with a red cockscomb creates a war in a town in Poland on the very day of Yom Kippur].

Nov. 19, 1933. "Di antisemitishe 'endek' partey fun Poyln un der kamf kegn ir" [The anti-Semitic "Endeks" party in Poland and the battle against it].

Nov. 23, 1933. "File yidn mit berd tuen zikh on militerish un klaybn zikh ayntsunemen Palestine" [Lots of bearded Jews put on military outfits and intend to conquer Palestine].

Jan. 10, 1934. "Der hunger shtrayk fun 300 alte layt in vershever moyshev-zkeynim" [The hunger strike of 300 elderly in a Warsaw old-age home].

Jan. 11, 1934. "Shvindler in Poyln farshteln zikh shoyn nit far amerikaner" [Swindlers in Poland no longer masquerade as Americans].

Jan. 18, 1934. "Interesante faktn un tsifern vegn boykot af daytshe skhoyres in Poyln" [Interesting facts and numbers about the boycott of German goods in Poland].

Jan. 25, 1934. "Vos an oyslender zet itst durkhforndik Daytshland" [What a foreigner now sees when traveling through Germany].

Jan. 27, 1934. "Pariz un Berlin, a farglaykh tsvishn di tsvey veltshtet" [Paris and Berlin, a comparison of these two world-cities].

Feb. 17, 1934. "Interesante yidishe gasn un yidishe tipn in Pariz" [Interesting Jewish streets and Jewish types in Paris].

Mar. 11, 1934. "Tipn un interesante figurn in dem parizer kinstler-kvartal" [Types and interesting figures in the Parisian artists' quarter].

Mar. 17, 1934. "In parizer kinstler-kvartal 'Monparnas' ken men laykht vern farlibt" [It's easy to fall in love in the Parisian artists' quarter, Montparnasse].
    Note: On March 23, 1934, an article on the first page of the *Forverts* announced the arrival of Singer and his family in New York.

Mar. 24, 1934. "Tsvishn di gebroykher fun batoybnde drogs in Parizer kafeen" [Among the users of addictive drugs in Parisian cafes].

Mar. 25, 1934. "Tshikave mentshn inem parizer kunst-kvartal Monparnas" [Curious people in the Parisian artists' quarter, Montparnasse].

Mar. 28, 1934. "Vos iz itst di lage fun di antlofene daytshe yidn in Frankraykh?" [What is the situation now of the German Jews who have fled to France?]

Mar. 31, 1934. "Shpasn un vitsn vos yidn hobn geshafn vegn peysekh" [Gags and jokes Jews have created about Passover].

Apr. 2, 1934. "Interesante tipn in dem parizer kunst kvartal Monparnas" [Interesting types in the Parisian artist quarter Montparnasse].
    Note: Articles in the *Forverts* began to appear regularly under both I. J. Singer and G. Kuper after Singer's arrival in New York; the latter were now categorized as *felyetonen*, or human-interest stories, and carried this description after most of the following titles.

Apr. 8, 1934. "Tipn un figurn fun kinstler un halbe-kinstler un binekinstler af eyn fus un kinstler vos khapn bloyz a kuk tsu dem kafe" [Types and figures of artists and semi-artists and would-be theatrical artists and artists who do no more than glance at a cafe].

Apr. 17, 1934. "A kluger aynfal" [A clever idea].

Apr. 19, 1934. "Nudistn, nudnikes un andere nudne zakhn" [Nudists, boring people, and other dull things].

Apr. 24, 1934. "An inteligenter lezer" [An intelligent reader].

May 3, 1934. "Dikhtung lekoved may" [Poetry in honor of May].

May 5, 1934. "Naronim vos vitslen zikh" [Fools who make jokes].

May 9, 1934. "Bravo Herr Gebels!" [Bravo, Herr Goebbels!].

May 13, 1934. "Yidn, kh'vil vern a 'prizoner'" [Jews, I want to become a "prisoner"].

May 16–21, 1934. "Zol brenen Eyrope" [May Europe burn].

June 1, 1934. "Heymishe yidn in Amerike" [Homey Jews in America].

June 15, 1934. "Der frayer kinstler" [The free artist].

June 22, 1934. "Der frayer gayst" [The free spirit].

July 5, 1934. "Bildlekh fun Kuni Ayland" [Pictures from Coney Island].

July 10, 1934. "Hitler halt vort" [Hitler keeps his word].

July 21, 1934. "Zuntik baym breg yam in Kuni Ayland" [Sunday at the beach in Coney Island].

July 25, 27, 31, 1934. "Afn shoys fun Kuni Ayland natur" [In the lap of nature at Coney Island].

Aug. 2, 4, 1934. "In di yidishe berg" [In the Jewish mountains].

Aug. 11, 1934. "Bilder fun di yidishe berg" [Pictures from the Jewish mountains].

Aug. 14, 1934. "Zinger un shpiler in di yidishe berg" [Singers and performers in the Jewish mountains].

Aug. 16, 1934. "Kibetser un vitsler in di yidishe berg" [Kibitzers and comedians in the Jewish mountains].

Sept. 6, 1934. "Er hot gemordet yunge froyen als 'nekome' far zayn muters laydn" [He murdered young women in "revenge" for his mother's suffering].

III. Critical Bibliography

Adams, Phoebe. "Short Review of *The Family Carnovsky*." *Atlantic Monthly* (February 1969): 133.

Almi, A. *In gerangl fun ideyen* [In the struggle of ideas]. Buenos Aires: Bukh gemeinshaft bei der yidisher ratzionalistisher gezelshaft, 1957.

Bakhtin, Mikhail. *Problems of Dostoevsky's Poetics* [1929]. Translated by R. W. Rotsel. Ann Arbor: Ardis, 1973.

Bashevis, Isaac. *A Day of Pleasure and Other Stories*. New York: Farrar, Straus, 1969.

———. *A Little Boy in Search of God*. New York: Doubleday, 1976.

———. "A por verter vegn zikh" [A few words about myself]. *Svive*, no. 6 (May 1962): 12–21.

———. *A Young Man in Search of Love*. New York: Doubleday, 1978.

———. *Der shrayberklub* [The writer's club]. *Forverts* (Jan. 13–Dec. 28, 1956).

———. *Fun der alter un der nayer heym* [From the old and the new home]. *Forverts* (Sept. 21, 1963–Sept. 11, 1965).

———. Introduction to *Yoshe Kalb*. New York: Harper & Row, 1965.

———. *Lost in America*. New York: Doubleday, 1981.

———. *Love and Exile*. New York: Doubleday, 1984.

———. *Mayn tatns bezdn-shtub*. *Forverts* (Feb. 19–Sept. 30, 1955). Tel Aviv: Peretz farlag, 1979. Partially translated into English: *In My Father's Court*. New York: Fawcett, 1962.

———. *Mayn zeydns bezdn-shtub* [My grandfather's courtroom]. *Forverts* (Oct. 7–Dec. 16, 1955).

———. *Tipn un geshtaltn fun amol un haynt* [Types and figures of bygone days and today]. *Forverts* (Apr. 7, 1961–Jan. 12, 1963).

———. "Vi azoy *Yoshe Kalb* iz geshafn gevorn" [How *Yoshe Kalb* was created]. *Forverts* (Apr. 18, 1965).

Beebe, Maurice. *Ivory Tower and Sacred Fount: The Artist as Hero in Fiction from Goethe to Joyce*. New York: New York University Press, 1964.

Benstock, Shari, ed. *The Private Self: Theory and Practice of Women's Autobiographical Writings*. Chapel Hill: University of North Carolina Press, 1988.

B[ergelson], D[ovid]. "Dray tsentern" [Three centers]. *In shpan*, no. 1 (April 1926): 84–96.

———. "Dikhtung un gezelshaftlekhkeyt" [Poetics and society]. *Bikher-velt*, no. 4–5 (1919): 5–16.

Bezanker, Abraham. "Three Generations (Review of *The Family Carnovsky*)." *Nation* (June 23, 1969): 800–802.

Bikl, Shlomo. *Shrayber fun mayn dor* [Writers of my generation]. New York: Matones, 1958.

Bloom, Harold, *The Anxiety of Influence*. New York: Oxford University Press, 1973.

Botoshanski, Y. *Portretn fun yidishe shrayber*. Warsaw: Literarishe bleter, 1933.

———. "Y. Y. Zingers shvanen-lid" [I. J. Singer's swan song]. *Der veg* (June 21, 1947).

Brody, Alter. "A Chassidic Chronicle (Review of *The Sinner*)," *Nation* (May 10, 1933): 533–34.

Brodzki, Bella, and Celeste Schenck, eds. *Life/Lines: Theorizing Women's Autobiography*. Ithaca: Cornell University Press, 1988.

Bruss, Elizabeth. *Autobiographical Acts*. Baltimore: Johns Hopkins University Press, 1976.

Buckley, Jerome. *Season of Youth*. Cambridge: Harvard University Press, 1974.

———. *The Turning Key*. Cambridge: Harvard University Press, 1984.

Cahan, Abraham. "A kritishe batrakhtung fun Zingers verk 'Khaver Nakhmen'" [A critical examination of Singer's *Khaver Nakhmen*]. *Forverts* (June 4, 1939).

———. "A kritishe batrakhtung: 'In di berg' fun Y. Y. Zinger" [A critical examination: I. J. Singer's "In the Mountains"]. *Forverts* (Oct. 25, Nov. 1, 1942).

———. "A nayer glentsindiker roman fun Y. Y. Zinger" [A magnificent new novel by I. J. Singer]. *Forverts* (May 21, 1932).

———. "A por verter vegn Zingers 'Emese pasirungen' [A few words about Singer's 'True Events']. *Forverts* (July 9, 1944).

———. "A nayer yidisher talant in Poyln" [A new Yiddish talent in Poland]. *Forverts* (Dec. 10, 1922).

———. "A bukh fun ertseylungen fun Y. Y. Zinger" [A book of stories by I. J. Singer]. *Forverts* (Jan. 7, 1923).

———. "Farvos iz '*Yoshe Kalb*' durkhgefaln af english?" [Why did *Yoshe Kalb* fail in English?]. *Forverts* (Jan. 6, 1934).

———. "Geshildert in Y. Y. Zingers roman *Di mishpokhe Karnovski*," [Portrayed in I. J. Singer's novel *The Family Karnovski*]. *Forverts* (Nov. 28, 1943).

———. "Entfern af vaytere fragn vegn '*Yoshe Kalb*' [Answers to further questions about *Yoshe Kalb*]. *Forverts* (Aug. 7, 1932). [Cahan was responding to a series of letters to the editor, "Meynungen un fragen vegn '*Yoshe Kalb*' [Opinions and questions about *Yoshe Kalb*], published in the *Forverts* July 23–Aug. 7, 1932.]

———. "Perzenlekhkaytn in yidishn teater" [Personalities of the Yiddish theater]. *Forverts* (Nov. 7, 1943).

———. "Vi azoy Y. Y. Zingers groyse kariere hot zikh ongefangen" [How I. J. Singer's great career began]. *Forverts* (Feb. 20, 1944).

———. "Vos far a verk iz Y. Y. Zingers roman 'Yoshe Kalb'? [What kind of work is I. J. Singer's novel *Yoshe Kalb*?]. *Forverts* (July 31, 1932).

———. "Y. Y. Zingers 'Brider Ashkenazi' in Shvartses teater" [I. J. Singer's *Di brider Ashkenazi* in Schwartz's theater]. *Forverts* (Sept. 23, 1937).

———. "Y. Y. Zingers 'Khaver Nakhmen' in nashonel teater" [I. J. Singer's *Khaver Nakhmen* in the National Theater]. *Forverts* (Oct. 7, 1939).

———. "Y. Y. Zingers kurtser roman 'A basherte zakh'" [I. J. Singer's novella 'Something Destined']. *Forverts* (May 23, 1943).

———. "Y. Y. Zingers talant als beletrist un als shafer far der bine" [I. J. Singer's talent as belletrist and as creator for the stage]. *Forverts* (Mar. 12, 1944).

———. "Y. Y. Zingers' 'Yoshe Kalb' af der bine fun Shvartses kunst-teater" [I. J. Singer's *Yoshe Kalb* on the stage of Schwartz's Arts Theater]. *Forverts* (Sept. 30, 1932).

De Man, Paul. "Autobiography as Defacement." *MLN* 94 (December 1979): 919–30.

Derrida, Jacques. *The Ear of the Other: Otobiography, Transference, Translation*. New York: Schocken, 1985.

Eagleton, Terry. *Marxism and Literary Criticism*. Berkeley: University of California Press, 1976.

Eakin, Paul John. *Fictions in Autobiography*. Princeton: Princeton University Press, 1985.

Edelmann, R. "Ahasuerus, the Wandering Jew." In *The Wandering Jew: Essays in the Interpretation of a Christian Legend*, edited by Galit Hasan-Rokem and Alan Dundes, 1–10. Bloomington: Indiana University Press, 1986.

Einhorn, David. "Y. Y. Zinger un di yidishe literatur fun zayn dor" [I. J. Singer and the Yiddish literature of his generation]. *Forverts* (Feb. 19, 1943).

Eisen, Arnold. *Galut: Modern Jewish Reflection on Homelessness and Homecoming*. Bloomington: Indiana University Press, 1986.

Elman, Richard. "Of a World That Is No More." *New York Times Book Review* (July 25, 1971): 17–18.

Entin, Yoel. "In yidishn teater: Y. Y. Zingers 'Yoshe Kalb,' in Moris Shvarts kunst-teater"

[In the Yiddish theater: Singer's *Yoshe Kalb* in Maurice Schwartz's Arts Theater]. *Di tsukunft* 37 (November 1932): 680–81.

Feldman, Yael. "Gender In/Difference in Contemporary Hebrew Fictional Autobiographies." *Biography* 11 (1988): 187–209.

Fiedler, Leslie. "Marx and Momma." In *Collected Essays*, vol. 2, 128–33. New York: Stein & Day, 1971.

Fleishman, Avrom. *The English Historical Novel*. Baltimore: Johns Hopkins University Press, 1971.

———. *Figures of Autobiography*. Berkeley: University of California Press, 1983.

Fried, Lewis. "Yoshe Kalb: I. J. Singer's Lonely Man of Faith." *Yiddish* 3 (Spring 1978): 40–47.

Friedman, Philip. "Tsu der geshikhte fun yidn in Lodzsh" [Toward the history of Jews in Lodz]. In *Lodzher almanakh* [Lodz almanac]. New York: Orion Press, 1934(?).

Frye, Northrop, ed. *Romanticism Reconsidered*. New York: Columbia University Press, 1963.

Fuks, A. M. "Khoyzek oder akhrayes?" [Ridicule or responsibility?]. *Literarishe bleter*, no. 10 (Mar. 11, 1927): 193–94.

———. "Y. Y. Zinger." *Literarishe bleter*, no. 79 (Nov. 6, 1925): 214–16.

Gaer, Joseph. *The Legend of the Wandering Jew*. New York: Mentor, 1961.

Ger, M. A. "Ver iz geven Yoshe Kalb? Mayne bagegenishn mit im" [Who was Yoshe Kalb? My meetings with him]. *Haynt* (Warsaw, August 3, 1932).

Gilman, Sander L. "Madness and Racial Theory in I. J. Singer's *The Family Carnovsky*." *Modern Judaism* 1 (1981): 90–100.

Girard, Rene. *Deceit, Desire, and the Novel*. Translated by Yvonne Freccero. Baltimore: Johns Hopkins University Press, 1965.

Gossman, Lionel. "History and Literature: Reproduction or Signification." In *The Writing of History*, edited by Robert H. Canary and Henry Kozicki, 3–39. Madison: University of Wisconsin Press, 1978.

Gris, Noakh. "Di publitsistik un literatur-kritik fun Y. Y. Zinger" [Publicist and literary critical writing by I. J. Singer]. *Di goldene keyt*, no. 113 (1984): 158–66.

———. "Y. Y. Zinger." *Di tsukunft* 90 (January 1984): 19–26.

Hamer, A. "Zinger iz do" [Singer is here]. *Frayhayt* (July 11, 1928). See also *Frayhayt* (Oct. 25, 1927, Mar. 28, 1928, July 25, 1928, Dec. 26, 1928).

Harshav, Benjamin and Barbara, trans. and eds. *American Yiddish Poetry*. Berkeley: University of California Press, 1986.

Hasan-Rokem, Galit, and Alan Dundes. *The Wandering Jew: Essays in the Interpretation of a Legend*. Bloomington: Indiana University Press, 1986.

Howe, Irving. "The Other Singer." *Commentary* 31, no. 3 (1966): 76–82.

———. Introduction to *The Brothers Ashkenazi*. New York: Atheneum, 1980.

———. *World of Our Fathers*. New York: Simon & Schuster, 1976.

Howe, Irving, Ruth Wisse, and Khone Shmeruk, eds. *The Penguin Book of Modern Yiddish Verse*. New York: Viking, 1987.

Huyssen, Andreas. *After the Great Divide: Modernism, Mass Culture, Postmodernism*. Bloomington: Indiana University Press, 1986.

Jay, Paul. *Being in the Text*. Ithaca: Cornell University Press, 1984.

Jelinek, Estelle, ed. *Women's Autobiography: Essays in Criticism*. Bloomington: Indiana University Press, 1980.

Kazdan, Kh. Sh. "Der kinstler in geyeg nokh frayhayt" [The artist in pursuit of freedom]. *Bikher-velt*, no. 3 (1928): 1–7.

———. "Dos knekhtishe lid funem frayen Zinger" [The slavish song of the free Singer]. *Bikher-velt*, no. 4 (1928): 69–72.

Kermode, Frank. *Romantic Image*. London: Routledge & Paul, 1957.

———. "Secrets and Narrative Sequence." In *On Narrative*, edited by W. J. T. Mitchell, 79–97. Chicago: University of Chicago Press, 1981.

———. *The Sense of an Ending: Studies in the Theory of Fiction*. New York: Oxford University Press, 1967.

Kochan, Lionel, ed. *The Jews in Soviet Russia since 1917*. Oxford: Oxford University Press, 1970.

Kreitman, Esther. *Briliantn* [Diamonds]. London: Poyels "Hebrew Dept.," 1944.

———. *Der sheydim-tants* Warsaw: Bzoza, 1936; English: *Deborah*. Translated by Maurice Carr, 1946; London: Virago, 1983; and New York: St. Martin's, 1984).

———. *Yikhes* [Lineage/ancestral merit]. London: Narod Press, 1949.

Leavis, F. R. *The Common Pursuit*. London: Chatto & Windus, 1952.

Lejeune, Philippe. *L'Autobiographie en France*. Paris: A. Colin, 1971.

Leksikon fun der nayer yidisher literatur [Biographical dictionary of modern Yiddish literature]. New York: Congress for Jewish Culture, 1960.

Lubbock, Percy. *The Craft of Fiction*. London: Jonathan Cape, 1921.

Lukács, Georg. *The Historical Novel*. Translated by Hannah and Stanley Mitchell. Boston: Beacon Press, 1962.

———. *Realism in Our Time* (1956). Translated by John and Necke Mander. New York: Harper & Row, 1964.

———. *The Theory of the Novel*. Translated by Anna Bostock. Cambridge: MIT Press, 1971.

Madison, Charles. *Yiddish Literature: Its Scope and Major Writers*. New York: Schocken, 1971.

Magentsa-Shaked, Malka. "Singer and the Family Saga Novel in Jewish Literature." *Prooftexts* 9 (January 1989): 27–42.

Markish, Peretz. "Di yidishe literatur in Poyln" [Yiddish literature in Poland]. *Shtern*, Minsk, 3 (March 1927): 20–28.

———. "Y. Y. Zinger—Erdvey" [I. J. Singer—Earth pangs]. *Bikher-velt*, no. 1 (1922): 41–42.

Mayzl, Nakhmen. "Arum Y. Y. Zingers Yoshe Kalb" [Concerning I. J. Singer's *Yoshe Kalb*]. *Literarishe bleter*, no. 41 (October 1935): 653–54.

———. "Der veg fun der yidisher literatur far di letste fuftsn yor" [The path of Yiddish literature in the last fifteen years]. In *Haynt yubiley bukh, 1908–1928* [*Haynt Anniversary Book*], 30–32. Warsaw: Haynt, 1928.

———. *Noente un vayte* [Near and far ones], vol. 2, 233–40. Vilna: Kletskin, 1926.

———. "Varshever almanakh." *Bikher-velt*, no. 1–2 (1924): 22–23.

———. "Y. Y. Zinger." *Literarishe bleter*, no. 131 (Nov. 5, 1926): 728–29.

———. "Y. Y. Zinger—der mentsh un kinstler" [The man and artist]. *Yidishe kultur*, no. 6 (March 1944): 18–26.

———. "Zingers roman 'Shtol un ayzn'" [Singer's novel *Shtol un ayzn*]. *Forverts* (Mar. 23, 1928).

Mazlish, Bruce. "Autobiography and Psychoanalysis: Between Truth and Self-Deception." *Encounter* 35 (October 1970): 28–37.

Mehlman, Jeffrey. *A Structural Study of Autobiography*. Ithaca: Cornell University Press, 1974.

Mendelsohn, Ezra. *The Jews of East Central Europe between the Two World Wars*. Bloomington: Indiana University Press, 1983.

Mendilow, A. A. *Time and the Novel*. London: Peter Nevill, 1952.

Meyerhoff, Hans. *Time in Literature*. Berkeley: University of California Press, 1968.

Miller, J. Hillis. *Fiction and Repetition*. Cambridge: Harvard University Press, 1982.

Mintz, Alan. *"Banished from Their Father's Table."* Bloomington: Indiana University Press, 1989.

Miron, Dan. *A Traveler Disguised*. New York: Schocken, 1973.

M[olodovsky], K[adia]. "Y. Y. Zinger." *Svive*, no. 7 (April–May 1944): 2–3.

Morodovsky, A. "Mikoyekh Y. Y. Zingers 'Savinkov'" [Concerning I. J. Singer's *Savinkov*]. *Literarishe bleter*, no. 44 (Nov. 3, 1933): 697–99.

Mukdoyni, A. "Yoshe Kalb in teater." *Morgn-zhurnal* (Nov. 11, 1932).

Niger, Shmuel. "Af fremder erd." *Di tsukunft* 30 (July 1925): 431–32.

———. "Di brider Ashkenazi fun Y. Y. Zinger." *Di tsukunft* 41 (December 1936): 806–13.

———. "Kunst-teoryes un kinstlerishe praktik" [Art theories and artistic practice]. *Di yidishe tsaytung* (Apr. 5, 1943).

———. "Mit a leydikn vogn: Savinkov" [With an empty wagon: "Savinkov"]. *Di tsukunft* 38 (December 1933): 733–37.

———. "On a tsenter" ["Without a center"]. *Di tsukunft* 29 (May 1924): 325–29.

———. "Perl." *Bikher-velt*, no. 1–2 (1923): 57–62.

———. "Yoshe Kalb—A historisher roman" [A historical novel]. *Di tsukunft* 38 (February 1933): 116–22.

———. "Y. Y. Zinger, *Shtol un Ayzn*." *Bikher-velt*, no. 2 (1928): 43–48.

Norich, Anita. "Consider Warsaw." *Spectrum* 1 (April–May 1983): 13–14.

———. "Hahoveh ke-avar b'romanim shel Y. Y. Zinger" [The present as past in the novels of I. J. Singer]. *HASIFRUT* (Summer 1986): 141–47.

———. "Lo gibor, lo metoraf, lo hote" [Neither hero, nor madman, nor sinner]. Afterword to Hebrew translation of *Yoshe Kalb*. Tel Aviv: Dvir, 1988.

———. "The Family Singer and the Autobiographical Imagination." *Prooftexts* 10 (January 1990): 91–107.

Olney, James, ed. *Autobiography: Essays Theoretical and Critical*. Princeton: Princeton University Press, 1980.

———. *Metaphors of Self*. Princeton: Princeton University Press, 1972.

Pascal, Roy. *Design and Truth in Autobiography*. London: Routledge & Paul, 1960.

Polonsky, Antony. *Politics in Independent Poland, 1921–1939*. Oxford: Clarendon Press, 1972.

Praz, Mario, *The Romantic Agony*. New York: Oxford University Press, 1951.

Rapaport, Y. *Literarishe bleter* [Literary leaves]. Warsaw: Flit, 1931.

———. *Oysgerisene bleter* [Random leaves]. Melbourne: Maller, 1957.

———. *Proletarishe literatur—pro un kontra* [Proletarian literature—pro and con]. Warsaw: Bzoza, 1936.

———. *Vokhnshrift far literatur* [Literary weekly], no. 32 (August 4, 1932): 2.

———. "Y. Y. Zingers dertseylungen" [I. J. Singer's stories]. *Di tsukunft* 54 (March 1949): 157–60.

Ravitch, Melekh. "Di mishpokhe Karnovski". *Di tsukunft* 49 (March 1944): 155–58.

———. "Der umbakanter zelner fun sotsializm" [The unknown soldier of socialism (Review of *Khaver Nakhmen*)]. *Di tsukunft* 45 (October 1939): 604–7.

———. "I. J. Singer: On the Twenty-fifth Anniversary of His Death." Translated by Sol Liptzin. *Jewish Book Annual* 26 (1968–69): 121–23.

———. *Mayn leksikon* [My lexicon]. Canada, 1945.

Reyzn, Zalmen. *Leksikon fun der yidisher literatur, prese un filologye* [Lexicon of Yiddish literature, press, and philology]. Vilna: Kletskin, 1928.

Ricoeur, Paul. "Narrative Time." In *On Narrative*, edited by W. J. T. Mitchell, 165–86. Chicago: University of Chicago Press, 1981.

———. *Time and Narrative*. Chicago: University of Chicago Press, 1984.

Rivkin, B. *Undzere prozayiker* [Our prose writers]. New York: YKUF, 1951.

———. "Y. Y. Zingers letst verk" [I. J. Singer's last work]. *Epokhe* (May 1944): 314–22.

Rogoff, Hillel. "'Di mishpokhe Karnovski' in yidishn kunst-teater" [The Family Karnovski in the Yiddish Arts Theater]. *Forverts* (Oct. 23, 1943).

Rosenfeld, Alvin. "Inventing the Jew." *Midstream* 21 (April 1975): 54–67.

Roskelenko, Harry. "Review of *Steel and Iron, The Family Carnovsky*." *New York Times Book Review* (Nov. 16, 1969): 72–73.

Roskies, David. *Against the Apocalypse*. Cambridge: Harvard University Press, 1984.

Sadan, Dov. *Orhot u'shvilim* [Ways and paths]. Tel Aviv: Am Oved, 1978.

Said, Edward. "On Repetition." In *The Literature of Fact*, edited by Angus Fletcher, 135–58. New York: Columbia University Press, 1976.

Schulz, Max F. "The Family Chronicle as Paradigm of History: *The Brothers Ashkenazi* and *The Family Moskat*." In *The Achievement of Isaac Bashevis Singer*, edited by Marcia Allentuck, 77–92. Carbondale: University of Southern Illinois Press, 1970.

Schwartz, Maurice. "Y. Y. Zinger—der dramaturg" [I. J. Singer—the dramatist]. *Forverts* (Mar. 8–11, 1944).

———. "Y. Y. Zingers 'Yoshe Kalb,'" *Literarishe bleter*, no. 46 (Nov. 11, 1932): 729–31.

Seidel, Michael. *Exile and the Narrative Imagination*. New Haven: Yale University Press, 1986.

Shklovsky, Victor. *Lev Tolstoy* (1963). English translation by Olga Shartse. Moscow: Progress, 1978.

Shmeruk, Khone. "Bashevis Singer—In Search of His Autobiography." *Jewish Quarterly* 29 (Winter 1981/82): 28–36.

———. "Jews and Poles in Yiddish Literature in Poland between the Two World Wars." *POLIN* 1 (1986): 176–95.

———. "Yiddish Literature in the USSR." In *The Jews in Soviet Russia since 1917*, edited by Lionel Kochan, 242–80. Oxford: Oxford University Press, 1970.

Sholem Aleichem. *Shomers mishpet* [The trial of Shomer]. Berditshev: Yakov Sheftil, 1888.

Sholem, Gershom. *The Messianic Idea of Judaism and Other Essays in Jewish Spirituality*. New York: Schocken, 1971.

Shoykhet, Z. "A geshprekh mit der froy fun dem emesn 'Yoshe Kalb' in Kroke in Galicia" [A conversation with the wife of the real Yoshe Kalb in Cracow in Galicia]. *Forverts* (Nov. 21, 1937).

Shtern, Yisroel. *Lider un eseyen* [Poems and essays]. New York: CYCO, 1955.

———. "Nisht farmitlung, nor kritik" [Not mediation, but criticism]. *Literarishe bleter* no. 7 (Feb. 18, 1927): 131.

Shtrigler, Mordkhe. *Georemt mitn vint* [Arm in arm with the wind]. Buenos Aires: Tsentral-farband fun poylishe yidn in Argentiene, 1955.

———. "Yoshe Kalb der ershter" [Yoshe Kalb, the first]. *Di tsukunft* 57 (April 1952): 181–86.

Sinclair, Clive. *The Brothers Singer*. London and New York: Allison & Busby, 1983.

Slotnick, Susan A. "Concepts of Space and Society: Melnits, Berlin and New York in I. J. Singer's Novel *Di mishpokhe Karnovski*." *German Quarterly* 54 (January 1981): 33–43.

Smith, Barbara Hernnstein. *On the Margins of Discourse*. Chicago: University of Chicago Press, 1978.

Smith, Sidonie. *A Poetics of Women's Autobiography*. Bloomington: Indiana University Press, 1987.

Spengemann, William. *The Forms of Autobiography*. New Haven: Yale University Press, 1980.

Stanton, Domna, ed. *The Female Autograph*. Chicago: Chicago University Press, 1984.

Steiner, George. Introduction to George Lukács, *Realism in Our Time*. New York: Harper & Row, 1964.

Sturrock, John. "The New Model Autobiographer." *New Literary History* (Autumn 1977): 51–63.

Taykhman, M. "Di epopee fun yidishn Lodz" [The epopee of Jewish Lodz]. *Literarishe bleter*, no. 20 (May 15, 1936): 312–14.

Taytelboym, A. "Der zin fun dem 'Brider Ashkenazi' derfolg" [The meaning of *The Brothers Ashkenazi*'s success]. *Literarishe bleter*, no. 21 (May 20, 1938): 349–50.

Trunk, Y. Y. *Di yidishe proze in Poyln in der tkufe tsvishn beyde velt-milkhomes* [Yiddish prose in Poland between the two world wars]. Buenos Aires: Tsentral-farband fun poylishe yidn in Argentiene, 1949.

———. *Idealizm un naturalizm in der yidisher proze* [Idealism and naturalism in Yiddish prose]. Warsaw: Kultur-lige, 1927.

———. "Y. Y. Zinger." *Di tsukunft* 49 (March 1944): 149–54.

Unger, Menashe. "Di geshikhte fun emesn Yoshe Kalb vi zi vert dertseylt in di alte shayles-tshuves sforim" [The history of the true Yoshe Kalb as told in the old religious responsa]. *Tog morgn-zhurnal* (June 3, 1953).

Veykhert, M. "Y. Y. Zinger—*Shtol un ayzn*," *Di yidishe velt* 2 (May 1928): 309–11.

von Hallberg, Robert, ed. *Canons*. Chicago: University of Chicago Press, 1984.

Wasiutynski, Bohdan. *Ludnosc zydowska w Polsce w wiekach XIX i XX: Studium statystyczne* [Jewish population in Poland in the 19th and 20th centuries: Statistical studies. Warsaw: Wyd. im. Mianowskiego, 1930.

Weinreich, Max. *History of the Yiddish Language* [1973]. Translated by Shlomo Noble. Chicago: University of Chicago Press, 1980.

Weintraub, Karl. "Autobiography and Historical Consciousness." *Critical Inquiry* 1 (June 1975): 821–48.

White, Hayden. *Metahistory: The Historical Imagination in Nineteenth-century Europe*. Baltimore: Johns Hopkins University Press, 1973.

———. "The Fictions of Factual Representation," In *The Literature of Fact*, edited by Angus Fletcher, 21–44. New York: Columbia University Press, 1976.

———. "The Value of Narrativity in the Representation of Reality." In *On Narrative*, edited by W. J. T. Mitchell, 1–23. Chicago: University of Chicago Press, 1981.

Wisse, Ruth. *A Little Love in Big Manhattan*. Cambridge: Harvard University Press, 1988.

Yerushalmi, Yosef. *Zakhor: Jewish History and Jewish Memory*. Seattle: University of Washington Press, 1982.

Zamlbikher 7 (1948): 453–59. (Letters from Singer to Joseph Opatoshu)

Z[ilberfarb], M. "Mayse Zinger" [The Singer affair]. *Bikher-velt*, no. 3 (1928): 61–63.

Zeitlin, Aaron. "Vegn Y. Y. Zinger un zayn nayem roman" [About I. J. Singer and his new novel]. *Globus*, no. 6 (December 1932): 72–79.

———. "Y. Y. Zinger, der mentsh un der kinstler" [I. J. Singer, the man and the artist (introduction to *Fun a velt vos iz nishto mer*)]. New York: Matones, 1946.

Index